Business

Business

David L. Kurtz
University of Arkansas, Emeritus

A WileyPLUS Learning Space Course

VICE PRESIDENT, EDUCATION	Tim Stookesbury
VICE PRESIDENT & DIRECTOR	George Hoffman
EDITORIAL DIRECTOR	Veronica Visentin
EXECUTIVE EDITOR	Lisé Johnson
SPONSORING EDITOR	Jennifer Manias
ASSISTANT DEVELOPMENT EDITOR	Emma Townsend-Merino
EXECUTIVE MARKETING MANAGER	Christopher DeJohn
DESIGN DIRECTOR	Harry Nolan
SENIOR CONTENT MANAGER	Dorothy Sinclair
SENIOR PRODUCTION EDITOR	Valerie Vargas
PRODUCT DESIGN MANAGER	Allison Morris
ASSOCIATE PRODUCT DESIGNER	Rebecca Costantini
SENIOR DESIGNER	Thomas Nery
COVER PHOTO	©ULTRA.F/Getty Images, Inc.

This book was typeset in 9.5/11.5 Source Sans Pro at Aptara®, Inc. and printed and bound by Strategic Content Imaging. The cover was printed by Strategic Content Imaging.

This book is printed on acid free paper. ∞

Founded in 1807, John Wiley & Sons, Inc. has been a valued source of knowledge and understanding for more than 200 years, helping people around the world meet their needs and fulfill their aspirations. Our company is built on a foundation of principles that include responsibility to the communities we serve and where we live and work. In 2008, we launched a Corporate Citizenship Initiative, a global effort to address the environmental, social, economic, and ethical challenges we face in our business. Among the issues we are addressing are carbon impact, paper specifications and procurement, ethical conduct within our business and among our vendors, and community and charitable support. For more information, please visit our website: www.wiley.com/go/citizenship.

Evaluation copies are provided to qualified academics and professionals for review purposes only, for use in their courses during the next academic year. These copies are licensed and may not be sold or transferred to a third party. Upon completion of the review period, please return the evaluation copy to Wiley. Return instructions and a free of charge return shipping label are available at www.wiley.com/go/returnlabel. If you have chosen to adopt this textbook for use in your course, please accept this book as your complimentary desk copy. Outside of the United States, please contact your local representative.

ISBN 13 978-1-119-11571-7

Printed in the United States of America.

TO THE STUDENT

Your *WileyPLUS Learning Space* course includes video lessons that bring the chapter concepts to life through high-interest stories and vivid, real-world examples. The individual video lectures, expert interviews, and interactive media are enhanced by additional engaging visual elements—such as graphics and definitions—to help activate your curiosity and deepen your understanding of the material.

The video lessons and the chapter reading content are coupled together to provide you with a more meaningful learning experience. In general, video lessons present an overview of the major concepts as well as real-world examples and applications. The accompanying etext provides greater detail and more in-depth coverage of the chapter concepts and may include media like videos and animations. For the best course experience and mastery of the concepts you will want to utilize the video and media materials alongside the etext and this printed course companion.

The video player allows you to experience the material at your own speed, stopping the video delivery to study graphics and media more closely, and then resuming the lesson when you're ready. The player also includes an editing tool that allows your instructor to customize your course, by adding additional questions, comments, and even more video.

How to Use this Print Companion

This Print Companion includes all of the text passages in the online course and will direct you on where to find more information in *WileyPLUS Learning Space*. This study tool, a secondary source for the reading, will reinforce your conceptual understanding and will help you make a deeper connection to the content. For ease of use, you'll find the following elements throughout:

- **Boldface type** is used to indicate figures, tables, and other elements.
- Marginal notes and small "thumbnail" images help you know where you can find art, figures, additional media, and Concept Check questions.
- Icons help direct you to all the resources in *WileyPLUS Learning Space*.

 View the large version of the figure.

 See the table or boxed feature.

 Play the video or animation.

 Answer the Concept Check questions.

TO THE INSTRUCTOR

Business, a *WileyPLUS Learning Space* course, couples comprehensive core content with a wealth of engaging digital assets to provide a dynamic teaching and learning environment for you and your students. The carefully crafted original video segments for each chapter's learning objectives use the power of personal storytelling via current examples to bring the chapter concepts to life for students. This model gives professors an excellent framework for flipping the class and providing a more interactive in-class experience. By assigning these videos, instructors will make the content personally relevant to their students and increase their motivation in the course.

Video segments feature academic and professional contributors who coach students through various topics using memorable examples and study tips. Each chapter also features a business professional who tells a story about a real business situation, showing students how the material relates to their future careers. In addition, the embedded video player includes an editing tool that allows you to customize your course, by adding your own questions, comments, and even more video.

Designed to engage today's student, *WileyPLUS Learning Space* will transform any course into a vibrant, collaborative, learning community.

WileyPLUS Learning Space is class tested and ready-to-go for instructors. It offers a flexible platform for quickly organizing learning activities, managing student collaboration, and customizing courses—including choice of content as well as the amount of interactivity between students. An instructor using *WileyPLUS Learning Space* is able to easily:

• Assign activities and add special materials
• Guide students through what's important by easily assigning specific content
• Set up and monitor group learning
• Assess student engagement
• Gain immediate insights to help inform teaching

WileyPLUS Learning Space now includes ORION, a personal, adaptive learning experience so that students can build their proficiency on learning objectives and use their study time more effectively especially before quizzes and exams. By tracking students' work, ORION provides instructors with insights into students' work without having to ask. Efficacy research shows that *WileyPLUS Learning Space* improves student outcomes by as much as one letter grade.

Boone & Kurtz *Business* also includes:

• Key Term Flashcards and Crossword Puzzles
• Video Cases
• Interactive Cases
• Learning Styles Survey
• Wiley Business Weekly Updates
• Student Study Guide
• Student Case Videos
• Business Hot Topics

CONTENTS

WileyPLUS Learning Space

Includes **ORION** Adaptive Practice

An easy way to help students learn, collaborate, and grow.

Designed to engage today's student, WileyPLUS Learning Space will transform any course into a vibrant, collaborative, learning community.

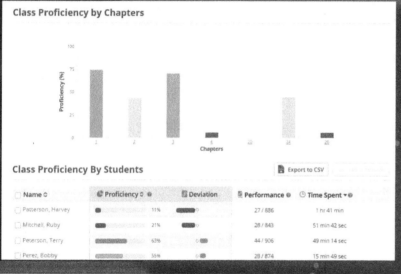

Identify which students are struggling early in the semester.

Educators assess the real-time engagement and performance of each student to inform teaching decisions. Students always know what they need to work on.

Facilitate student engagement both in and outside of class.

Educators can quickly organize learning activities, manage student collaboration, and customize their course.

Measure outcomes to promote continuous improvement.

With visual reports, it's easy for both students and educators to gauge problem areas and act on what's most important.

www.wileypluslearningspace.com

THE CHANGING FACE OF BUSINESS

> **WP LS** Go to your WileyPLUS Learning Space course for video episodes, examples, art, tables, Concept Checks, practice, and resources that will help you succeed in this course.

What Is Business?

What comes to mind when you hear the word *business?* Do you think of big corporations like General Electric or Boeing? Or does the local dry cleaners or convenience store pop into your mind? Maybe you recall your first summer job. The term *business* is a broad, all-inclusive term that can be applied to many kinds of enterprises. Businesses provide the bulk of employment opportunities, as well as the products that people enjoy.

For-Profit Organizations

Business consists of all profit-seeking activities and enterprises. Some businesses produce tangible goods, such as automobiles, breakfast cereals, and digital music players; others provide services such as insurance, hair styling, and entertainment, ranging from the Six Flags theme parks and NFL games to concerts.

Business drives the economic pulse of a nation. It provides the means through which its citizens' standard of living improves. At the heart of every business endeavor is an exchange between a buyer and a seller. A buyer recognizes a need for a good or service and trades money with a seller to obtain that product. The seller participates in the process in hopes of gaining profits—a main ingredient in accomplishing the goals necessary for continuous improvement in the standard of living.

Profits represent rewards earned by businesspeople who take the risks involved in blending people, technology, and information to create and market goods and services. We often think of profits as the difference between a firm's revenues and the expenses it incurs in generating these revenues. And while this is true, it is the *opportunity* for profits that serves as incentive for people to start companies, expand them, and provide high-quality goods and services.

The quest for profits is a central focus of business, but businesspeople also recognize their social and ethical responsibilities. To succeed in the long run, companies must deal responsibly with employees, customers, suppliers, competitors, government, and the general public.

Not-for-Profit Organizations

What do a local food pantry, the U.S. Postal Service, the American Red Cross, and your local library have in common? They are all classified as **not-for-profit organizations**, businesslike establishments that have primary objectives other than returning profits to their owners. These organizations play an important role in society. It is important to understand that these organizations need to make or raise money so that they can operate and achieve their social goals. Not-for-profit organizations operate in both the private and public sectors. Private sector not-for-profits include museums, libraries, trade associations, and charitable and religious organizations. Government agencies, political parties, and labor unions, all of which are part of the public sector, are also classified as not-for-profit organizations.

Not-for-profit organizations are a substantial part of the U.S. economy. Currently, more than 1.4 million nonprofit organizations are registered with the Internal Revenue Service in the United States, in categories ranging from arts and culture to science and technology. These organizations control more than $3 trillion in assets and employ more people than the federal government and all 50 state governments combined.[1] In addition, millions of volunteers work for them in unpaid positions. Not-for-profits secure funding from both private sources, including donations, and government sources. They are commonly exempt from federal, state, and local taxes.

Q Answer the **Concept Check** questions.

Factors of Production

From the earliest human settlements to the modern societies of today, all economic systems require certain inputs for successful operation. Economists use the term **factors of production** to refer to the four basic inputs: natural resources, capital, human resources, and entrepreneurship. **Table 1.1** identifies each of these inputs and the type of payment received by firms and individuals who supply them.

See **TABLE 1.1: What are the factors of production and their corresponding factor payments?**

Natural resources include all production inputs that are useful in their natural states, including agricultural land, building sites, forests, and mineral deposits. One of the world's largest wind farms, the Roscoe Wind Complex in Texas, generates enough power to support more than a quarter million homes. Natural resources are the basic inputs required in any economic system.

Capital, another key resource, includes technology, tools, information, and physical facilities. *Technology* is a broad term that refers to machinery and equipment such as computers and software, telecommunications, and inventions designed to improve production. Information, frequently improved by technological innovations, is another critical factor because both managers and operating employees require accurate, timely information for effective performance of their assigned tasks. Technology plays an important role in the success of many businesses. Sometimes technology results in a new product, such as hybrid autos that run on a combination of gasoline and electricity. Most of the major car companies have introduced hybrid models in recent years.

To remain competitive, a firm needs to continually acquire, maintain, and upgrade its capital, and businesses need money for that purpose. A company's funds may come from owner-investments, profits plowed back into the business, or loans extended by others. Money then goes to work building factories; purchasing raw materials and component parts; and hiring, training, and compensating workers. People and firms that supply capital receive factor payments in the form of interest.

Human resources represent another critical input in every economic system. Human resources include anyone who works, from the chief executive officer (CEO) of a global corporation to a self-employed writer or editor. This category encompasses both the physical labor and the intellectual inputs contributed by workers. Companies rely on their employees as a valued source of ideas and innovation as well as physical effort. Some companies solicit employee ideas through traditional means, such as an online "suggestion box" or in staff meetings. Others encourage creative thinking during company-sponsored hiking or rafting trips or during social gatherings. Effective, well-trained human resources provide a significant competitive edge because competitors cannot easily match another company's talented, motivated employees in the way they can buy the same computer system or purchase the same grade of natural resources.

Hiring and keeping the right people matter. Google employees feel they have a great place to work, partly because of the sense of mission—and the perks—the company provides.[2]

Entrepreneurship is the ability to see an opportunity and take the risks inherent in creating and operating a business. An entrepreneur is someone who sees a potentially profitable opportunity and then devises a plan to achieve success in the marketplace and earn those profits. By age 20, Jessica Mah was CEO of inDinero, a company that helps small businesses keep track of their money. Mah had "noticed that anything that touches money is much harder for entrepreneurs than it should be," so she took a risk and started a firm designed to help them.[3]

U.S. businesses operate within an economic system called the *private enterprise system*. The next section looks at the private enterprise system, including competition and private property.

Q Answer the **Concept Check** questions.

The Private Enterprise System

No business operates in a vacuum; rather, all operate within a larger economic system that determines how goods and services are produced, distributed, and consumed in a society. The type of economic system employed in a society also determines patterns of resource use. Some economic systems, such as communism, feature strict controls on business ownership, profits, and resources to accomplish government goals.

In the United States, businesses function within the **private enterprise system**, an economic system that rewards firms for their ability to identify and serve the needs and demands of customers. The private enterprise system minimizes government interference in economic activity. Businesses that are adept at satisfying customers gain access to necessary factors of production and earn profits.

Another name for the private enterprise system is **capitalism**. Adam Smith, often identified as the father of capitalism, first described the concept in his book, *The Wealth of Nations,* published in 1776. Smith believed that an economy is best regulated by the "invisible hand" of competition, the battle among businesses for consumer acceptance. Smith thought that competition among firms would lead to consumers' receiving the best possible products and prices because less efficient producers would gradually be driven from the marketplace.

The "invisible hand" concept is a basic premise of the private enterprise system. In the United States, competition regulates much of economic life. To compete successfully, each firm must find a basis for **competitive differentiation**, the unique combination of organizational abilities, products, and approaches that sets a company apart from competitors in the minds of customers. Businesses operating in a private enterprise system face a critical task of keeping up with changing marketplace conditions. Firms that fail to adjust to shifts in consumer preferences or ignore the actions of competitors leave themselves open to failure.

Throughout this book, the discussion focuses on the tools and methods that 21st century businesses use to compete and differentiate their goods and services. The text also discusses many of the ways in which market changes will affect business and the private enterprise system in the years ahead.

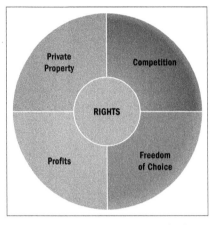

See **FIGURE 1.1 Basic Rights within a Private Enterprise System**

Basic Rights in the Private Enterprise System

For capitalism to operate effectively, people living in a private enterprise economy must have certain rights. As shown in ▤ **Figure 1.1**, these include the rights to private property, profits, freedom of choice, and competition.

The right to **private property** is the most basic freedom under the private enterprise system. Every participant has the right to own, use, buy, sell, and bequeath most forms of property, including land, buildings, machinery, and equipment, patents on inventions, individual possessions, and intangible properties.

The private enterprise system also guarantees business owners the right to all profits—after taxes—they earn through their activities. Although a business is not assured of earning a profit, its owner is legally and ethically entitled to any income it generates in excess of costs.

Freedom of choice means that a private enterprise system relies on the potential for citizens to choose their own employment, purchases, and investments. They can change jobs, negotiate wages, join labor unions, and choose among many different brands of goods and services. A private enterprise economy maximizes individual prosperity by providing alternatives. Other economic systems sometimes limit freedom of choice to accomplish government goals, such as increasing industrial production of certain items or military strength.

The private enterprise system also permits fair competition by allowing the public to set rules for competitive activity. For this reason, the U.S. government has passed laws to prohibit "cutthroat" competition—excessively aggressive competitive practices designed to eliminate competition. It also has established ground rules that outlaw price discrimination, fraud in financial markets, and deceptive advertising and packaging.[4]

Answer the **Concept Check** questions.

Seven Eras in the History of Business

In the roughly 400 years since the first European settlements appeared on the North American continent, amazing changes have occurred in the size, focus, and goals of U.S. businesses. As ▤ **Figure 1.2** indicates, U.S. business history is divided into seven distinct time periods: (1) the Colonial period, (2) the Industrial Revolution, (3) the age of industrial entrepreneurs,

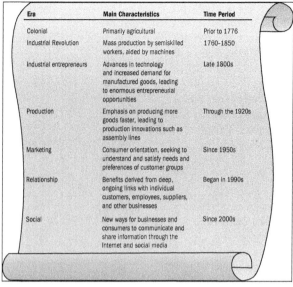

Era	Main Characteristics	Time Period
Colonial	Primarily agricultural	Prior to 1776
Industrial Revolution	Mass production by semiskilled workers, aided by machines	1760-1850
Industrial entrepreneurs	Advances in technology and increased demand for manufactured goods, leading to enormous entrepreneurial opportunities	Late 1800s
Production	Emphasis on producing more goods faster, leading to production innovations such as assembly lines	Through the 1920s
Marketing	Consumer orientation, seeking to understand and satisfy needs and preferences of customer groups	Since 1950s
Relationship	Benefits derived from deep, ongoing links with individual customers, employees, suppliers, and other businesses	Began in 1990s
Social	New ways for businesses and consumers to communicate and share information through the Internet and social media	Since 2000s

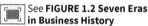
See **FIGURE 1.2 Seven Eras in Business History**

(4) the production era, (5) the marketing era, (6) the relationship era, and (7) the social era. The following sections describe how events in each of these time periods have influenced U.S. business practices.

The Colonial Period

Colonial society emphasized agricultural production. Colonial towns were small compared with European cities, and they functioned as marketplaces for farmers and craftspeople. The economic focus of the nation centered on rural areas because prosperity depended on the output of farms, orchards, and the like. The success or failure of crops influenced every aspect of the economy.

Colonists depended on England for manufactured items as well as financial backing for their infant industries. Even after the Revolutionary War (1775–1783), the United States maintained close economic ties with England. British investors continued to provide much of the financing for developing the U.S. business system, and this financial influence continued well into the 19th century.

The Industrial Revolution

The Industrial Revolution began in England around 1750. It moved business operations from an emphasis on independent, skilled workers who specialized in building products one by one to a factory system that mass-produced items by bringing together large numbers of semiskilled workers. The factories profited from the savings created by large-scale production, bolstered by increasing support from machines over time. As businesses grew, they could often purchase raw materials more cheaply in larger lots than before. Specialization of labor, limiting each worker to a few specific tasks in the production process, also improved production efficiency.

Influenced by these events in England, business in the United States began a time of rapid industrialization. Agriculture became mechanized, and factories sprang up in cities. During the mid-1800s, the pace of industrialization increased as newly built railroad systems provided fast, economical transportation. In California, for example, the combination of railroad construction and the Gold Rush fueled a tremendous demand for construction.

The Age of Industrial Entrepreneurs

Building on the opportunities created by the Industrial Revolution, entrepreneurship increased in the United States. Inventors created a virtually endless array of commercially useful products and new production methods. Many of them are famous today:

- Eli Whitney introduced the concept of interchangeable parts, an idea that would later facilitate mass production on a previously impossible scale.
- Robert McCormick designed a horse-drawn reaper that reduced the labor involved in harvesting wheat. His son, Cyrus McCormick, saw the commercial potential of the reaper and launched a business to build and sell the machine. By 1902, the company was producing 35 percent of the nation's farm machinery.
- Cornelius Vanderbilt (railroads), J. P. Morgan (banking), and Andrew Carnegie (steel), among others, took advantage of the enormous opportunities waiting for anyone willing to take the risk of starting a new business.

The entrepreneurial spirit of this golden age in business did much to advance the U.S. business system and raise the country's overall standard of living. That market transformation, in turn, created new demand for manufactured goods.

The Production Era

As demand for manufactured goods continued to increase through the 1920s, businesses focused even greater attention on the activities involved in producing those goods. Work became increasingly specialized, and huge, labor-intensive factories dominated U.S.

business. Assembly lines, introduced by Henry Ford, became commonplace in major industries. Business owners turned over their responsibilities to a new class of managers trained in operating established companies. Their activities emphasized efforts to produce even more goods through quicker methods.

During the production era, business focused attention on internal processes rather than external influences. Marketing was almost an afterthought, designed solely to distribute items generated by production activities. Little attention was paid to consumer wants or needs. Instead, businesses tended to make decisions about what the market would get. If you wanted to buy a Ford Model T automobile, your color choice was black—the only color produced by the company.

The Marketing Era

The Great Depression of the early 1930s changed the shape of U.S. business yet again. As incomes nosedived, businesses could no longer automatically count on selling everything they produced. Managers began to pay more attention to the markets for their goods and services, and sales and advertising took on new importance. During this period, selling was often synonymous with marketing.

Demand for all kinds of consumer goods exploded after World War II. After nearly five years of doing without new automobiles, appliances, and other items, consumers were buying again. At the same time, however, competition also heated up. Soon businesses began to think of marketing as more than just selling; they envisioned a process of first determining what consumers wanted and needed and then designing products to satisfy those needs. In short, they developed a **consumer orientation**.

Businesses began to analyze consumer desires before beginning actual production. Consumer choices skyrocketed. Car buyers, for example, could choose among a wide variety of colors and styles. Companies also discovered the need to distinguish their goods and services from those of competitors. **Branding**—the process of creating an identity in consumers' minds for a good, service, or company—is an important marketing tool. A **brand** can be a name, term, sign, symbol, design, or some combination that identifies the products of one firm and differentiates them from competitors' offerings.

Branding can go a long way toward creating value for a firm by providing recognition and a positive association between a company and its products. Some of the world's most famous—and enduring—brands include Apple, Google, Coca-Cola, IBM, Microsoft, GE, Samsung, Toyota, McDonald's, and Mercedes-Benz.[5]

The marketing era has had a tremendous effect on the way business is conducted today. Even the smallest business owners recognize the importance of understanding what customers want and the reasons they buy.

The Relationship Era

As business continues in the 21st century, a significant change is taking place in the ways companies interact with customers. Since the Industrial Revolution, most businesses have concentrated on building and promoting products in the hope that enough customers will buy them to cover costs and earn acceptable profits, an approach called **transaction management**.

In contrast, in the **relationship era**, businesses are taking a different, longer-term approach to their interactions with customers. Firms now seek ways to actively nurture customer loyalty by carefully managing their interactions with buyers. They earn enormous paybacks for their efforts. A company that retains customers over the long haul reduces its advertising and sales costs. Because customer spending tends to accelerate over time, revenues also grow. Companies with long-term customers often can avoid costly reliance on price discounts to attract new business, and they find that many new buyers come from loyal customer referrals.

Business owners gain several advantages by developing ongoing relationships with customers. Because it is much less expensive to serve existing customers than to find new ones, businesses that develop long-term customer relationships can reduce their overall costs. Long-term relationships with customers enable businesses to improve their understanding of what customers want and prefer from the company. As a result, businesses enhance their chances of sustaining real advantages through competitive differentiation.

The relationship era is an age of connections—between businesses and customers, employers and employees, technology and manufacturing, and even separate companies. The world economy is increasingly interconnected as businesses expand beyond their national boundaries. In this new environment, techniques for managing networks of people, businesses, information, and technology are critically important to contemporary business success.

The Social Era

The **social era** of business can be described as a new approach to the way businesses and consumers interact, connect, communicate, share, and exchange information with each other via various channels, including the Internet and social media platforms.

Based on the premise that organizations create value through connections with groups or networks of people with similar goals and interests, the social era offers businesses immense opportunities, particularly through the use of technology and **relationship management**—the collection of activities that build and maintain ongoing, mutually beneficial ties with customers and other parties.

Social media tools and technologies come in various shapes and sizes. They include weblogs, blogs, podcasts, and microblogs (such as Twitter); social and professional networks (such as Facebook and LinkedIn); picture-sharing platforms (such as Instagram and Tumblr); and content communities (such as YouTube), to name a few.[6]

As consumers continue to log fewer hours on computers and more time on mobile devices, companies are implementing mobile strategies using real-time data and location-based technology. Businesses use mobile social media applications to engage in marketing research, communications, sales promotions, loyalty programs, and other processes. In the social era, businesses tailor specific promotions to specific users in specific locations at specific times to build customer loyalty and long-term relationships.

Q | Answer the **Concept Check** questions.

Today's Business Workforce

A skilled and knowledgeable workforce is an essential resource for keeping pace with the accelerating rate of change in today's business world. Employers need reliable employees who are dedicated to fostering strong ties with customers and partners. They must build workforces capable of the efficient, high-quality production needed to compete in global markets. Savvy business leaders also realize that employee brainpower plays a vital role in a firm's ability to stay on top of new technologies and innovations. In short, a first-class workforce can be the foundation of a firm's competitive differentiation, providing important advantages over competing businesses.

Changes in the Workforce

Companies now face several trends that challenge their skills for managing and developing human resources. Those challenges include an aging population and a shrinking labor pool, growing diversity of the workforce, the changing nature of work, the need for flexibility and mobility, and the use of collaboration to innovate.

An Aging Population and Shrinking Labor Pool

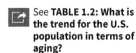
See **TABLE 1.2: What is the trend for the U.S. population in terms of aging?**

By 2030, the number of U.S. workers 65 or older will reach 72 million—double what it is today—and many of them will soon retire from the workforce, taking their experience and expertise with them. As **Table 1.2** shows, the U.S. population as a whole is trending older. Yet today, many members of the Baby Boomer generation—the huge number of people born between 1946 and 1964—are still hitting the peaks of their careers. At the same time, members of so-called Generation X (born from 1965 to 1981) and Generation Y (born from 1982 to 2005) are building their careers, so employers are finding more generations in the workforce simultaneously than ever before. This broad age diversity brings management challenges, such as accommodating a variety of work–life styles, changing expectations of work, and varying levels of technological expertise. Still, despite the widening age spectrum of the workforce, some economists predict the U.S. labor pool could soon fall short by as many as 10 million people as Baby Boomers retire.

More sophisticated technology has intensified the hiring challenge by requiring workers to have ever more advanced skills. Companies are increasingly seeking—and finding—talent at the extreme ends of the working-age spectrum. Teenagers are entering the workforce sooner, and some seniors are staying longer—or seeking a new career after retiring from their primary career. Many older workers work part-time or flexible hours. Meanwhile, for older employees who do retire, employers must administer a variety of retirement planning and disability programs and insurance benefits.

Increasingly Diverse Workforce

The U.S. workforce is growing more diverse, in age and in every other way. The two fastest-growing ethnic populations in the United States are Hispanics and people of Asian origin. By the year 2050, the number of Hispanics in the United States will grow from a current 35 million to 102 million, or 24 percent of the total population. The Asian population will increase from 10 million to 33 million, or 8 percent of the total U.S. population.[7] Considering that minority groups are growing, managers must learn to work effectively with diverse ethnic groups, cultures, and lifestyles to develop and retain a superior workforce for their company.

Diversity—the blending of individuals of different genders, ethnic backgrounds, cultures, religions, ages, and physical and mental abilities in a workforce—can enhance a firm's chances of success. In a recent list of top companies for diversity, the top ten were also leaders and innovators in their industries:

1. Novartis Pharmaceuticals Corporation
2. Sodexo
3. EY (Ernst & Young)
4. Kaiser Permanente
5. PricewaterhouseCoopers
6. MasterCard Worldwide
7. Procter & Gamble
8. Prudential Financial
9. Johnson & Johnson
10. AT&T[8]

Several studies have shown that diverse employee teams and workforces tend to perform tasks more effectively and develop better solutions to business problems than homogeneous employee groups. This result is due in part to the varied perspectives and experiences that foster innovation and creativity in multicultural teams.

Outsourcing and the Changing Nature of Work

Not only is the U.S. workforce changing, but so is the very nature of work. Manufacturing once accounted for most of U.S. annual output, but the balance has now shifted to services such as financial management and communications. This means firms must rely heavily on well-trained service workers with knowledge, technical skills, the ability to communicate and deal with people, and a talent for creative thinking. The Internet has made possible another business tool for staffing flexibility—**outsourcing**, or using outside vendors to produce goods or fulfill services and functions previously handled inhouse. At its best, outsourcing allows a firm to reduce costs and concentrate its resources in the areas it does best while gaining access to expertise it may not have. But outsourcing also brings challenges, such as differences in language or culture.

Offshoring, the relocation of business processes to lower-cost locations overseas, can include both production and services. In recent years, China has emerged as a popular location for production offshoring for many firms, while India has become the key player in offshoring services. Some U.S. companies are now structured so that entire divisions or functions are developed and staffed overseas. Another trend in some industries is **nearshoring**, outsourcing production or services to nations near a firm's home base. And in some cases, companies are **onshoring**—returning production to its original manufacturing location because of changes in costs or processes.

Flexibility and Mobility

Younger workers in particular are looking for something other than the work-comes-first lifestyle exemplified by the Baby Boomer generation. But workers of all ages are exploring different work arrangements, such as telecommuting from remote locations and sharing jobs with two or more employees. Employers are also hiring growing numbers of temporary and part-time employees, some of whom are more interested in using and developing their skills than climbing the career ladder. While the cubicle-filled office will likely never become entirely obsolete, technology makes productive networking and virtual team efforts possible by allowing people to work where they choose and easily share knowledge, a sense of purpose or mission, and a free flow of ideas across any geographical distance or time zone.

Managers of such far-flung workforces need to build and earn employees' trust in order to retain valued workers and to ensure that all members are acting ethically and contributing their share without the day-to-day supervision of a more conventional work environment. Managers and employees must be flexible and responsive to change while work, technology, and relationships continue to evolve.

Innovation through Collaboration

Some observers also see a trend toward more collaborative work in the future, as opposed to individuals working alone. Businesses using teamwork hope to build a creative environment where all members contribute their knowledge and skills to solve problems or seize opportunities. Businesses and individuals have also turned to crowdsourcing—the process of obtaining input, information, or services for a particular task or project from a large group of people, typically via the Internet.

The old relationship between employers and employees was pretty simple: every day, workers arrived at a certain hour, did their jobs, and departed at the same time. Companies rarely laid off workers, and employees rarely left for a job at another firm. But all that—and more—has changed. Employees are no longer likely to remain with a single company throughout their entire career and do not necessarily expect lifetime loyalty from the company they work for. They do not expect to give that loyalty, either; rather, they build their own career however and wherever they can. These changes mean that many firms now recognize the value of a partnership with employees that encourages creative thinking and problem solving and rewards risk taking and innovation.

Q Answer the **Concept Check** questions.

The 21st Century Manager

Today's companies look for managers who are intelligent, highly motivated people with the ability to create and sustain a vision of how an organization can succeed. The 21st century manager must also apply critical-thinking skills and creativity to business challenges and lead change.

Importance of Vision

To thrive in the 21st century, businesspeople need **vision**, the ability to perceive marketplace needs and what an organization must do to satisfy them.

Importance of Critical Thinking and Creativity

Critical thinking and creativity are essential characteristics of the 21st century workforce. Today's businesspeople need to look at a wide variety of situations, draw connections between disparate information, and develop future-oriented solutions. This need applies not only to top executives but to mid-level managers and entry-level workers as well.

Critical thinking is the ability to analyze and assess information to pinpoint problems or opportunities. The critical-thinking process includes activities such as determining the authenticity, accuracy, and worth of information, knowledge, and arguments. It involves looking beneath the surface for deeper meaning and connections that can help identify critical issues and solutions. Without critical thinking, a firm may encounter serious problems.

Creativity is the capacity to develop novel solutions to perceived organizational problems. Although most people think of it in relation to writers, artists, musicians, and inventors, that is a very limited definition. In business, creativity refers to the ability to see better and different ways of operating. A computer engineer who solves a glitch in a software program is thinking creatively. Creativity and critical thinking must go beyond generating new ideas, however. They must lead to action. In addition to creating an environment in which employees can nurture ideas, managers must give them opportunities to take risks and try new solutions.

Ability to Lead Change

Today's business leaders must guide their employees and organizations through the changes brought about by technology, marketplace demands, and global competition. Managers must be skilled at recognizing employee strengths and motivating people to move toward common goals as members of a team. Throughout this book, real-world examples demonstrate how companies have initiated sweeping change initiatives. Most, if not all, have been led by managers comfortable with the tough decisions that today's fluctuating conditions require.

Factors that require organizational change can come from both external and internal sources; successful managers must be aware of both. External forces might include feedback from customers, developments in the international marketplace, economic trends, and new technologies. Internal factors might arise from new company goals, emerging employee needs, labor union demands, or production challenges.

> **Q** Answer the **Concept Check** questions.

What Makes a Company Admired?

Who is your hero? Is it someone who has achieved great feats in sports, government, entertainment, or business? Why do you admire the person? Does he or she lead a company, earn a lot of money, or give back to the community and society? Every year, business magazines and organizations publish lists of companies that they consider to be "most admired." Companies, like individuals, may be admired for many reasons. Most people would mention solid profits, stable growth, a safe and challenging work environment, high-quality goods and services, and business ethics and social responsibility. *Business ethics* refers to the standards of conduct and moral values involving decisions made in the work environment. *Social responsibility* is a management philosophy that includes contributing resources to the community, preserving the natural environment, and developing or participating in nonprofit programs designed to promote the well-being of the general public. You'll find business ethics and social responsibility examples throughout this book, as well as a deeper exploration of these topics in Chapter 2.

As you read this text, you'll be able to make up your mind about why companies should—or should not—be admired. *Fortune* publishes two lists of most admired companies each year, one for U.S.-based firms and one for the world. The list is compiled from surveys and other research conducted by the Hay Group, a global management consulting firm. Criteria for making the list include innovation, people management, use of corporate assets, social responsibility, quality of management, and quality of products and services.[9] 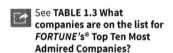 **Table 1.3** lists the top ten World's Most Admired Companies for a recent year.

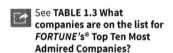 See **TABLE 1.3 What companies are on the list for FORTUNE's® Top Ten Most Admired Companies?**

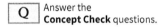 **Q** Answer the **Concept Check** questions.

> **WP LS** Go to your WileyPLUS Learning Space course for video episodes, examples, art, tables, Concept Checks, practice, and resources that will help you succeed in this course.

2

Reading for
BUSINESS ETHICS AND SOCIAL RESPONSIBILITY

WP LS Go to your WileyPLUS Learning Space course for video episodes, examples, art, tables, Concept Checks, practice, and resources that will help you succeed in this course.

See **FIGURE 2.1 Common Business Ethical Challenges**

Ethical Challenges

In both your personal and business life, you will sometimes be called on to weigh the ethics of decisions that can affect not just your own future but possibly the future of your fellow workers, your company, and its customers. As already noted, it's not always easy to distinguish between what is right and wrong in many business situations, especially when the needs and concerns of various parties conflict. Thus, the need for **business ethics** is critical.

Solving ethical dilemmas is not easy. In many cases, each possible decision can have both unpleasant consequences and positive benefits that must be evaluated. The ethical issues that confront manufacturers with unsold merchandise are just one example of many different types of ethical questions encountered in the workplace. **Figure 2.1** identifies the most common ethical challenges that businesspeople face.

Conflict of Interest

A **conflict of interest** occurs when a businessperson is faced with a situation in which an action benefiting one person or group has the potential to harm another. Conflicts of interest may pose ethical challenges when they involve the businessperson's own interests and those of someone to whom he or she has a duty or when they involve two parties to whom the businessperson has a duty. Lawyers, business consultants, or advertising agencies would face a conflict of interest if they represented two competing companies: a strategy that would benefit one of the client companies might harm the other client. A conflict of interest may also occur when one person holds two or more similar jobs in two different workplaces.

Ethical ways to handle conflicts of interest include (1) avoiding them and (2) disclosing them. Some companies have policies against taking on clients who are competitors of existing clients. Most businesses and government agencies have written policies prohibiting employees from accepting gifts or specifying a maximum gift value. Or a member of a board of directors or committee might abstain from voting on a decision in which he or she has a financial interest. In other situations, people state their potential conflict of interest so that the people affected can decide whether to get information or help they need from another source instead.

Honesty and Integrity

Employers value honesty and integrity. An employee who is honest can be counted on to tell the truth. An employee with integrity goes beyond truthfulness. Having **integrity** means adhering to deeply felt ethical principles in business situations. It includes doing what you say you will do and accepting responsibility for mistakes. Behaving with honesty and integrity inspires trust, and as a result, it can help build long-term relationships with customers, employers, suppliers, and the public. Employees, in turn, want their managers and the company as a whole to treat them honestly and with integrity.

Unfortunately, violations of honesty and integrity are all too common. Some people misrepresent their academic credentials on their résumés or job applications. Reputable organizations take these violations very seriously and often terminate employees for their actions.[1] Others steal from their employers by taking home supplies or products without permission or by carrying out personal business during the time they are being paid to work.

And many employees use company computers to surf the web for personal shopping, e-mail, gaming, and social networking. According to researchers, this misuse costs U.S. companies an estimated 40 percent loss in productivity on an annual basis.[2]

Loyalty versus Truth

Businesspeople expect their employees to be loyal and to act in the best interests of the company. But when the truth about a company is not favorable, an ethical conflict can arise. Individuals may have to decide between loyalty to the company and truthfulness in business relationships. People resolve such dilemmas in various ways. Some place the highest value on loyalty, even at the expense of truth. Others avoid volunteering negative information but answer truthfully if someone asks them a specific question. People may emphasize truthfulness and actively disclose negative information, especially if the cost of silence is high, as in the case of operating a malfunctioning aircraft or selling tainted food items.

Q Answer the **Concept Check** questions.

The Contemporary Ethical Environment

In today's business environment, individuals can make the difference in ethical expectations and behavior. As executives, managers, and employees demonstrate their personal ethical principles—or lack of ethical principles—the expectations and actions of those who work for and with them can change.

What is the current status of individual business ethics in the United States? Although ethical behavior can be difficult to track or define in all circumstances, evidence suggests that unfortunately some individuals act unethically or illegally on the job. And technology seems to have expanded the range and impact of unethical behavior. For example, anyone with computer access to data has the potential to steal or manipulate the data or to shut down the system, even from a remote location. Banks, insurance companies, and other financial institutions are often targeted for such attacks. Although some might shrug these occurrences away, in fact they have an impact on how investors, customers, and the general public view a firm. It is difficult to rebuild a tarnished image, and long-term customers may be lost.

Nearly every employee, at every level, wrestles with ethical questions at some point or another. Some rationalize questionable behavior by saying, "Everybody's doing it." Others act unethically because they feel pressured in their jobs or have to meet performance quotas. Yet some avoid unethical acts that don't mesh with their personal values and morals. To help you understand the differences in the ways individuals arrive at ethical choices, the next section focuses on how personal ethics and morals develop.

Development of Personal Ethics

An individual's stage in moral and ethical development is determined by a huge number of factors. Experiences help shape responses to different situations. A person's family, educational, cultural, and religious backgrounds can also play a role, as can the environment within the firm. Individuals can also have different styles of deciding ethical dilemmas, no matter what their stage of moral development.

Regardless of their ethical background, psychologist Lawrence Kohlberg identified that individuals typically develop ethical standards in the three stages shown in ▣ **Figure 2.2**: the pre-conventional, conventional, and post-conventional stages.[3]

In stage 1, the pre-conventional stage, individuals primarily consider their own needs and desires in making decisions. They obey external rules only because they are afraid of punishment or hope to receive rewards if they comply. For them, ethics is proscriptive in that they do not think about or evaluate unique ethical situations but rather just identify the rules and follow them (or not). A stage 1 ethical approach to taking something that doesn't belong to you—for example, food—would be saying that such an action is theft and is always wrong.

In stage 2, the conventional stage, individuals are aware of and act in response to their duty to others, including their obligations to family members, co-workers, and organizations. The expectations of these groups influence how they choose between what is acceptable and unacceptable in certain situations. In stage 2, individuals who take food without permission from a restaurant where they work could make the ethical argument that the

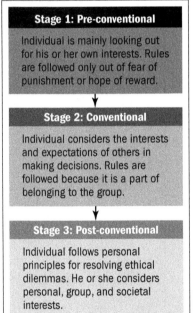

Stage 1: Pre-conventional

Individual is mainly looking out for his or her own interests. Rules are followed only out of fear of punishment or hope of reward.

Stage 2: Conventional

Individual considers the interests and expectations of others in making decisions. Rules are followed because it is a part of belonging to the group.

Stage 3: Post-conventional

Individual follows personal principles for resolving ethical dilemmas. He or she considers personal, group, and societal interests.

See **FIGURE 2.2 Stages of Moral and Ethical Development**

need to feed their family was an overriding concern, and taking food in such circumstances is not unethical. Self-interest, however, continues to play a role in decisions.

Stage 3, the post-conventional stage, represents the highest level of ethical and moral behavior. Individuals are able to move beyond mere self-interest and duty and take the larger needs of society into account as well. They have developed personal ethical principles for determining what is right and can apply those principles in a wide variety of situations.

Q | Answer the **Concept Check** questions.

How Organizations Shape Ethical Conduct

Regardless of where a person is in terms of ethical development, it is important to remember that no one makes decisions in a vacuum. Choices are strongly influenced by the standards of conduct established within the organizations where people work. Unfortunately, not all organizations are able to build a solid framework of business ethics. Because the damage from ethical misconduct can powerfully affect a firm's **stakeholders**—customers, investors, employees, and the public—pressure is exerted on businesses to act in acceptable ways.

 See **FIGURE 2.3 Johnson & Johnson Credo**

Ethical Awareness

The foundation of an ethical climate is ethical awareness. As we have already seen, ethical dilemmas occur frequently in the workplace. Employees need help identifying ethical problems when they occur and knowing how the firm expects them to respond.

One way for a firm to provide this support is to develop a **code of conduct**, a formal statement that defines how the organization expects employees to resolve ethical questions. Johnson & Johnson's credo, shown in **Figure 2.3**, is such a code. Recently Johnson & Johnson's CEO, Alex Gorsky, took the time at a shareholders' meeting to review the credo, pointing out along the way how each part illustrates how current Johnson & Johnson employees put the code into action each day.[4]

At the most basic level, a code of conduct may simply specify ground rules for acceptable behavior, such as identifying the laws and regulations that employees must obey. Other companies use their codes of conduct to identify key corporate values and provide frameworks that guide employees as they resolve moral and ethical dilemmas.

Ethical Education

Although a code of conduct can provide an overall framework, it cannot detail a solution for every ethical situation. Some ethical questions have black-and-white answers, but others do not. Businesses must provide employees the tools and training they need to evaluate the options and arrive at suitable decisions. Similar strategies are being used in many business school ethics programs, where case studies and practical scenarios work best. Convicted white-collar criminal Walter Pavlo, a former employee at telecommunications firm MCI, speaks at colleges and universities about his experiences in the firm and prison. Pavlo, who along with other MCI associates stashed money in offshore accounts, speaks about his actions in an effort to warn students of the consequences of cheating.[5]

Ethical Leadership

Executives must not only talk about ethical behavior but also demonstrate it in their actions. This requires top managers to be personally committed to the company's core values and be willing to base their actions on them. The recent recession exposed executive-level misdeeds that damaged or even destroyed entire organizations and wiped out many people's life savings. In the aftermath, some organizations and business leaders have made a commitment to demonstrate ethical leadership and increased social responsibility. It is imperative that executives demonstrate high ethical standards in their words and actions. Put another way, they must "walk the talk" when it comes to ethics. Employees and middle managers look to senior managers as examples of acceptable behavior within a company. If the bosses are less than ethical, it is likely their workers will be as well.

The current ethical environment of business also includes the appointment of new corporate officers specifically charged with deterring wrongdoing and ensuring that ethical standards are met. Ethics compliance officers, whose numbers are rapidly rising, are responsible for conducting employee training programs that help spot potential fraud and abuse within the firm, investigating sexual harassment and discrimination charges, and monitoring any potential conflicts of interest.

Whistle-Blowing

When individuals encounter unethical or illegal actions at work, they must decide what action to take. Sometimes it is possible to resolve the problem by working through channels within the organization. Resolving an ethical problem within the organization can be more effective than going outside of the organization—assuming, of course, that higher-level managers cooperate with the investigation. However, sometimes ethical violations involve an organization's management team; when this is the case, managers may not investigate the wrongdoing or, in extreme cases, suppress or cover up the allegations. When this happens, the individual should consider the potential damages to the company against the needs of the stakeholders to be informed as well as the greater public good. If the damage is significant, a person may conclude that the only solution is to blow the whistle. **Whistle-blowing** is an employee's disclosure to company officials, government authorities, or the media of illegal, immoral, or unethical practices.

State and federal laws protect whistle-blowers in certain situations, such as reports of discrimination, and the **Sarbanes-Oxley Act of 2002** now requires that firms in the private sector provide procedures for anonymous reporting of accusations of fraud. Shortly after this act was passed, the wrongdoings of three high-profile organizations were exposed by internal whistle-blowers. Ethical violations as well as illegal acts at WorldCom and Enron were exposed by employees after they tried to resolve the issues internally. To encourage whistle-blowing, the act makes it illegal for anyone to retaliate against an employee for taking concerns of unlawful conduct to a public official. In addition, whistle-blowers can seek protection under the False Claims Act, under which they can file a lawsuit on behalf of the government if they believe that a company has somehow defrauded the government. Charges against health care companies for fraudulent billing for Medicare or Medicaid are examples of this type of lawsuit.

Q | Answer the **Concept Check** questions.

Acting Responsibly to Satisfy Society

Companies that want to attract skilled and knowledgeable workers have wide-ranging responsibilities to their employees, both here and abroad. These include workplace safety, quality-of-life issues, ensuring equal opportunity on the job, avoiding age discrimination, and preventing sexual harassment and sexism.

Workplace Safety

A century ago, few businesses paid much attention to the safety of their workers. In fact, most business owners viewed employees as mere cogs in the production process. Workers, some of them young children, toiled in frequently dangerous conditions. In 1911, a fire at the Triangle Shirtwaist Factory in New York City killed 146 people, mostly young girls. Contributing to the massive loss of life were the sweatshop working conditions at the factory, including overcrowding, blocked exits, and a lack of fire escapes. This tragedy forced businesses to begin to recognize their responsibility for workers' safety.

Workplace safety is now an important business responsibility. The Occupational Safety and Health Administration (OSHA) is the main federal regulatory force in setting safety and health standards. Its mandates range from broad guidelines on storing hazardous materials to specific safety standards in industries such as construction, manufacturing, and mining. OSHA tracks and investigates workplace accidents and has the authority to fine employers found liable for injuries and deaths on the job.

Although most businesses strive to make their operations safe for all employees and customers, in some cases a business's need for workplace health and safety can conflict with an individual worker's personal beliefs. Take for example the case of an Indiana hospital that fired eight workers for failing to take a flu shot. A hospital spokeswoman said, "The flu has the highest death rate of any vaccine-preventable disease, and it would be irresponsible from our perspective for health care providers to ignore that." Many of the fired workers filed exemptions, claiming religious reasons for not taking the injections, but the hospital's need to provide a safe environment for its staff and patients outweighed these employees' concerns.[6]

Quality-of-Life Issues

Balancing work and family is becoming harder for many employees. They find themselves squeezed between working long hours and handling child-care problems, caring for elderly parents, and solving other family crises.

Many employers offer **family leave** to employees who need to deal with family matters. Under the Family and Medical Leave Act of 1993, employers with 50 or more employees must provide unpaid leave annually for any eligible employee who wants time off for the birth or adoption of a child; to become a foster parent; or to care for a seriously ill relative, spouse, or self if he or she has a serious health condition or injury. The law requires employers to grant up to 12 weeks of leave each year, and leave may be taken intermittently as medical conditions necessitate.

Ensuring Equal Opportunity on the Job

Businesspeople also face challenges managing an increasingly diverse workforce. Techno-logical advances are expanding the ways people with physical disabilities can contribute in the workplace. Businesses need to find ways to responsibly recruit and manage older work-ers and workers with varying lifestyles. In addition to their direct employees, companies may offer benefits such as health insurance to family members and unmarried domestic partners. More than 60 percent of *Fortune 500* companies currently offer domestic-partner benefits to their employees.[7]

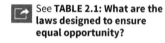
See **TABLE 2.1: What are the laws designed to ensure equal opportunity?**

To a great extent, efforts at managing diversity are regulated by law. The Civil Rights Act (1964) outlawed many kinds of discriminatory practices, and Title VII of the act specifically prohibits **discrimination**—biased treatment of a job candidate or employee—in the work-place. As shown in **Table 2.1**, other nondiscrimination laws include the Equal Pay Act (1963), the Age Discrimination in Employment Act (1967), the Equal Employment Oppor-tunity Act (1972), the Pregnancy Discrimination Act (1978), the Civil Rights Act of 1991, and numerous executive orders. The Americans with Disabilities Act (1990) protects the rights of physically challenged people. The Vietnam Era Veterans Readjustment Act (1974) protects the employment of veterans of the Vietnam War. The Genetic Information Nondiscrimina-tion Act (2008) prohibits discrimination on the basis of genetic tests or the medical history of an individual or that individual's family.

The **Equal Employment Opportunity Commission (EEOC)** was created to increase job opportunities for women and minorities and to help end discrimination based on race, color, religion, disability, gender, or national origin in any personnel action. To enforce fair-employment laws, it investigates charges of discrimination and harassment and files suit against violators. The EEOC can also help employers set up programs to increase job opportunities for women, minorities, people with disabilities, and people in other protected categories.

Age Discrimination

With the average age of U.S. workers steadily rising, more than half of the workforce is projected to be age 40 or older in a few years. Yet some employers find it less expensive to hire and retain younger workers, who generally have lower medical bills as well as lower salary and benefits packages. At the same time, many older workers have training and skills that younger workers have yet to acquire. The Age Discrimination in Employment Act of 1967 (ADEA) protects individuals who are age 40 or older, prohibiting discrimination on the basis of age and denial of benefits to older employees.

Legal issues aside, employers might do well to consider not only the experience that older workers bring to the workplace but also their enthusiasm. Many surveys report that older workers who remain on the job by choice—not because they are forced to do so for economic reasons—are often happy with their employment. But other studies show that aging Baby Boomers are dissatisfied with the workplace due to the falling value of their retirement investments and diminishing options such as relocation. Still, employees with decades of work experience can be a valuable asset to any firm.[8]

Sexual Harassment and Sexism

Every employer has a responsibility to ensure that all workers are treated fairly and are safe from sexual harassment. **Sexual harassment** refers to unwelcome and inappropriate actions of a sexual nature in the workplace. It is a form of sex discrimination that violates the Civil Rights Act of 1964, which gives both men and women the right to file lawsuits for intentional sexual harassment. About 7,000 sexual harassment complaints were filed with the EEOC in a recent year, of which more than 17 percent were filed by men.[9] Thousands of other cases are either handled internally by companies or never reported.

Two types of sexual harassment exist. The first type occurs when an employee is pressured to comply with unwelcome advances and requests for sexual favors in return for job security, promotions, and raises. The second type results from a hostile work environment in which an employee feels hassled or degraded because of unwelcome flirting, lewd comments, or obscene jokes. The courts have ruled that allowing sexually oriented materials in the workplace can create a hostile atmosphere that interferes with an employee's ability to do the job. Employers are also legally responsible to protect employees from sexual harassment by customers and clients. The EEOC's website informs employers and employees of criteria for identifying sexual harassment and how it should be handled in the workplace.

Sexual harassment is often part of the broader problem of **sexism**—discrimination against members of either sex, but primarily affecting women. One important sexism issue is equal pay for equal work.

U.S. Census statistics show that, overall, women still earn 78 cents for every 1 dollar earned by men. The number drops to 68 cents for African American women and 60 cents for Hispanic women. Education, occupation, work hours, and other factors don't seem to affect the gap, which remains unexplained other than the differences by gender.[10] In some extreme cases, differences in pay and advancement can become the basis for sex discrimination suits which, like sexual harassment suits, can be costly and time-consuming to settle. As in all business practices, it is better to act legally and ethically in the first place than to attempt to resolve these issues when they become the subject of litigation.

Q | Answer the **Concept Check** questions.

Ethical Responsibilities to the General Public

In a general sense, **social responsibility** is management's acceptance of the role that ethics plays in their business and their obligation to consider consumer satisfaction and societal well-being of equal value to profit in evaluating the firm's performance. Businesses may exercise social responsibility because such behavior is required by law, because it enhances the company's image, or because management believes it is the ethical course of action.

Historically, a company's social performance has been measured by its contribution to the overall economy and the employment opportunities it provides. Variables such as total wages paid often indicate social performance. Although profits and employment remain crucial, today many factors contribute to an assessment of a firm's social performance, including providing equal employment opportunities; respecting the cultural diversity of employees; responding to environmental concerns; providing a safe, healthy workplace; and producing high-quality products that are safe to use. The responsibilities of business to the general public include dealing with public health issues, protecting the environment, and developing the quality of the workforce.

Public-Health Issues

One of the most complex issues facing business as it addresses its ethical and social responsibilities to the general public is public health. Central to the public-health debate is the question of what businesses should do about dangerous products such as tobacco and alcohol. Tobacco products represent a major health risk, contributing to heart disease, stroke, and cancer among smokers. Families and co-workers of smokers share this danger as well, as their exposure to secondhand smoke increases their risks for cancer, asthma, and respiratory infections. CVS Health, the parent company of more than 7,700 CVS retail stores, recently made news by announcing it would no longer sell tobacco products, a move that could cost the company more than $2 billion in annual sales. The company's CEO remarked that ending the sale of cigarettes and other tobacco products was the right thing to do in an effort to help consumers improve their overall health.[11]

Heart disease, diabetes, and obesity have become major public health issues as the rates of these three conditions have been rising. According to the Centers for Disease Control and Prevention, the obesity rate for children between the ages of 6 and 11 in the United States has tripled over the last four decades. Three-quarters of obese teenagers will become obese adults at risk for diabetes and heart disease. Jared Fogle became famous for losing 245 pounds over a two-year period through exercise and a diet that included SUBWAY sandwiches. He has since set up the Jared Foundation with the goal of fighting childhood obesity by encouraging children to develop healthy diet and exercise habits. Spreading his message through speaking tours, grants to schools, and programs for children and their families, Fogle says, "My goal is to help children avoid the physical and emotional hardships I went through living with obesity." SUBWAY's website lists the nutritional values of its menu items and sources of diet and nutrition advice. The website also features a linked page supporting the Jared Foundation and its mission.[12]

Protecting the Environment

Businesses impact the environment in a variety of ways—through the energy they consume, the waste they produce, the natural resources they use, and more. Today, many businesses have taken significant steps toward protecting the environment. Some have even launched sustainability initiatives—operating in such a way that the firm not only minimizes its impact on the environment but actually regenerates or replaces used resources. Procter & Gamble and Kaiser Permanente maintain sustainability assessments of their suppliers, rating them on energy and water use, recycling, waste production, greenhouse gases produced, and other factors.[13]

For many managers, finding ways to minimize pollution and other environmental damage caused by their products or operating processes has become an important economic and legal issue as well as a social one. When Tesla Motors unveiled its Model S, the company's first premium five-door hatchback electric sedan, the car generated a lot of buzz. Running on a lithium battery, the Model S has a range of 270 miles.[14]

Despite the efforts of companies like Procter & Gamble, Kaiser Permanente, Tesla, and thousands of others, production and manufacturing methods still leave behind large quantities of waste materials that can further pollute the air, water, and soil. Some products themselves, such as electronics that contain lead and mercury, are difficult to recycle or reuse—although scientists and engineers are finding ways to do this. In other instances, the action (or lack of action) on the part of a firm results in an environmental disaster, as in the case of the explosion and large-scale spill from BP's offshore drilling rig in the Gulf of Mexico. The months-long spill affected not only the ocean and coastal environments but also the lives of residents and local economies.[15] Despite the difficulty, however, companies are finding that they can be environmentally friendly and profitable, too.

Another solution to the problems of pollutants is **recycling**—reprocessing of used materials for reuse. Recycling can sometimes provide much of the raw material that manufacturers need, thereby conserving the world's natural resources and reducing the need for landfills. Robert King founded King Diesel on the island of Maui in Hawaii. The company used conventional diesel fuel to run the generators at the Central Maui Landfill. After King became concerned at the large amounts of used cooking oil being dumped, he contacted Daryl Reece at the University of Idaho. Reece helped develop a process that converts used restaurant oils into biodiesel fuel. Together they founded Pacific Biodiesel, using biodiesel to run the generators at the landfill in one of America's first commercially viable, community-based biodiesel plants. Today, Robert King and his wife, Kelly, manage Pacific Biodiesel and its associated companies, producing and selling biodiesel and other biofuels and designing and building similar plants around the country.[16]

Corporate Philanthropy

As Chapter 1 pointed out, not-for-profit organizations play an important role in society by serving the public good. They provide the human resources that enhance the quality of life in communities around the world. To fulfill this mission, many not-for-profit organizations rely on financial contributions from the business community. Firms respond by donating billions of dollars each year to not-for-profit organizations. This **corporate philanthropy** includes cash contributions, donations of equipment and products, and support for the volunteer efforts of company employees. Recipients include cultural organizations, adopt-a-school programs, neighborhood sports programs, and housing and job training programs.

Responsibilities to Customers

Businesspeople share a social and ethical responsibility to treat their customers fairly and act in a manner that is not harmful to them. **Consumerism**—the public demand that a business consider the wants and needs of its customers in making decisions—has gained widespread acceptance. Consumerism is based on the belief that consumers have certain rights. A frequently quoted statement of consumer rights was made by President John F. Kennedy more than 50 years ago. ◼ **Figure 2.4** summarizes these consumer rights. Numerous state and federal laws have been implemented since then to protect these rights.

See **FIGURE 2.4 Consumer Rights as Proposed by President Kennedy**

The Right to Be Safe

Contemporary businesspeople must recognize obligations, both moral and legal, to ensure the safe operation and sale of their products. Consumers should feel assured that the products they purchase will not cause injuries in normal use. **Product liability** refers to the responsibility of manufacturers and sellers of those products for injuries and damages caused by their products. Items that lead to injuries, either directly or indirectly, can have disastrous consequences for the manufacturer or seller of that product.

Many companies rigorously test their products to avoid safety problems. Still, testing alone cannot foresee every eventuality. Companies must try to consider all possibilities and provide adequate warning of potential dangers. When a product does pose a threat to customer safety, a responsible manufacturer responds quickly to correct the problem or recall the product. Although we take for granted that our food and our pets' food is safe, sometimes contamination occurs, which can cause illness or even death. A recent concern about salmonella, a microorganism that produces dangerous infections, caused Tuffy's Pet Foods to voluntarily recall dry pet food. No illnesses or deaths were reported, but the company wanted to be certain its products were safe for pets.[17]

The Right to Be Informed

Consumers should have access to enough education and product information to make responsible buying decisions. In their efforts to promote and sell their goods and services, companies can easily neglect consumers' right to be fully informed. False or misleading advertising is a violation of the Wheeler-Lea Act, a federal law enacted in 1938. The Federal Trade Commission and other federal and state agencies have established rules and regulations that govern advertising truthfulness.

The Food and Drug Administration (FDA), which sets standards for advertising conducted by drug manufacturers, eased restrictions for prescription drug advertising on television. In print ads, drug makers are required to spell out potential side effects and the proper uses of prescription drugs. Because of the requirement to disclose this information, prescription drug television advertising was limited. Now, however, the FDA says drug ads on radio and television can directly promote a prescription drug's benefits if they provide a quick way, such as displaying a toll-free number or Internet address, for consumers to learn about side effects.

The responsibility of business to preserve consumers' right to be informed extends beyond avoiding misleading advertising. All communications with customers from salespeople's comments to warranties and invoices must be controlled to clearly and accurately inform customers. Most packaged-goods firms, personal computer makers, and makers of other products bought for personal use by consumers include toll-free customer service numbers on their product labels so that consumers can get answers to questions about a product.

The Right to Choose

Consumers should have the right to choose which goods and services they need and want to purchase. Socially responsible firms attempt to preserve this right, even if they reduce their own sales and profits in the process. Brand-name drug makers are engaged in a battle being waged by state governments, insurance companies, consumer groups, unions, and major employers such as General Motors and Verizon. These groups want to force down the rising price of prescription drugs by ensuring that consumers have the right and the opportunity to select cheaper, generic brands.

The Right to Be Heard

Consumers should be able to express legitimate complaints to appropriate parties. Many companies expend considerable effort to ensure full hearings for consumer complaints. The auction website eBay assists buyers and sellers who believe they were victimized in transactions conducted through the site, deploying employees to work with users and law enforcement agencies to combat fraud.[18]

Q Answer the **Concept Check** questions.

Responsibilities to Investors and the Financial Community

Although a fundamental goal of any business is to make a profit for its shareholders, investors and the financial community demand that businesses behave ethically and legally. When firms fail in this responsibility, thousands of investors and consumers can suffer.

Right to Fair Accounting

State and federal government agencies are responsible for protecting investors from financial misdeeds. At the federal level, the Securities and Exchange Commission (SEC) investigates suspicions of unethical or illegal behavior by publicly traded firms. It investigates accusations that a business is using faulty accounting practices to inaccurately portray its financial resources and profits to investors. Regulation FD ("Fair Disclosure") is an SEC rule that requires publicly traded companies to announce major information to the general public, rather than first disclosing the information to selected major investors. The agency also operates an Office of Internet Enforcement to target fraud in online trading and online sales of stock by unlicensed sellers.

Although pledges and codes of conduct are common in American business, not all organizations live up to them. In addition to provisions for protecting whistleblowing, the Sarbanes-Oxley Act of 2002 established new rules and regulations for securities trading and accounting practices. Companies are now required to publish their code of ethics, if they have one, and inform the public of any changes made to it. The law may actually motivate even more firms to develop written codes and guidelines for ethical business behavior. The federal government also created the U.S. Sentencing Commission to institutionalize ethics compliance programs that would establish high ethical standards and end corporate misconduct.

Q Answer the **Concept Check** questions.

WP LS **Go to your WileyPLUS Learning Space course for video episodes, examples, art, tables, Concept Checks, practice, and resources that will help you succeed in this course.**

Reading for
ECONOMIC CHALLENGES FACING
CONTEMPORARY BUSINESS

3

WP LS Go to your WileyPLUS Learning Space course for video episodes, examples, art, tables, Concept Checks, practice, and resources that will help you succeed in this course.

Microeconomics: The Forces of Demand and Supply

Think about your own economic activities. You shop for groceries, subscribe to a mobile phone service, pay college tuition, and fill your car with gas. Now think about your family's economic activities. When you were growing up, your parents might have owned a home or rented an apartment. Your parents may have shopped at discount clubs or local stores. Each of these choices relates to the study of **microeconomics**.

At the heart of every business transaction is an exchange between a buyer and a seller. The buyer recognizes that he or she needs or wants a particular good or service—whether it's a hamburger or a haircut—and is willing to pay a seller for it. The seller enters into the exchange to generate revenue and earn a profit. So, the exchange process involves both demand from consumers and supply from producers. Specifically, **demand** refers to the willingness and ability of buyers to purchase goods and services at different prices. The other side of the process is **supply**, the amount of goods and services for sale at different prices. Understanding the factors that determine demand and supply, as well as how the two interact, can help you understand many actions and decisions of individuals, businesses, and government. This section takes a closer look at these concepts.

Factors Driving Demand

For most of us, economics amounts to choices we make with our scarce resources, principally money and time. Each person must therefore choose how much money to save (for future consumption) and how much to spend (current consumption). If we use our money for current consumption, we must decide among all the goods and services competing for our attention. Suppose you wanted to purchase a smart phone. You'd have to choose from a variety of brands and models. You'd also have to decide where you wanted to buy one. After shopping around, you might decide you didn't want a smart phone at all. Instead, you might purchase something else or save your money. All of these choices are part of the landscape that is microeconomics.

Demand for any good or service is driven by a number of factors that influence how people decide to spend their money, by outside circumstances, or larger economic events such as the recent recession. Typically, consumers will tend to purchase more of a good if the price is lower and less of a good if the price is higher (think about items on sale, where lower prices often attract more buyers). A **demand curve** is a graph of the amount of a product that buyers will purchase at different prices. Demand curves typically slope downward, meaning that lower and lower prices attract larger and larger purchases.

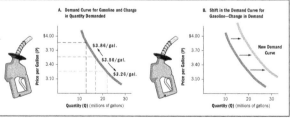

See **FIGURE 3.1 Demand Curves for Gasoline**

Gasoline provides a classic example of how demand curves work. The left side of ▦ **Figure 3.1** shows a possible demand curve for the total amount of gasoline that people will purchase at different prices. The prices shown may not reflect the actual price in your location at this particular time, but they still demonstrate the concept. When gasoline is priced at $3.56 a gallon, drivers may fill up their tanks once or twice a week. However, when the price of gasoline goes up—say, to $3.86 a gallon—many consumers start economizing. They may combine errands or carpool to work. So, the quantity of gasoline demanded at $3.86 a gallon is lower than the amount demanded at $3.56 a gallon. The opposite happens at $3.26 a gallon. More gasoline is sold at $3.26 a gallon than at $3.56 a gallon, as people opt to take a weekend trip.

Movement along a demand curve is caused by changes in the price of the good. However, the overall demand for a product at any price can change as well, increasing or decreasing demand at all prices. Many factors can combine to determine the overall demand for a product—that is the shape and position of the demand curve. These influences include customer preferences and income, the prices of substitute and complementary items, whether the good is a necessity or a luxury, the number of buyers in a market, and the strength of their optimism regarding the future. Changes in any of these factors produce a new demand curve. Changes in household income also change demand. As consumers have more money to spend, firms can sell more services and merchandise at every price. This means the demand curve has shifted to the right. When income shrinks, nearly everyone suffers, and the demand curve shifts to the left. **Table 3.1** describes how a demand curve is likely to respond to each of these changes.

See **TABLE 3.1: How does a demand curve respond to expected shifts?**

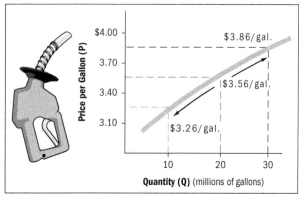

See **FIGURE 3.2 Supply Curve for Gasoline**

See **TABLE 3.2: How do changes in various factors affect the supply curve?**

Factors Driving Supply

As consumers are willing to buy more goods at lower prices, sellers are willing to produce more products if they can sell them at higher prices. A **supply curve** shows the relationship between different prices and the quantities that sellers will offer for sale, regardless of demand. Movement along the supply curve is the opposite of movement along the demand curve. As prices rise, the quantity that sellers are willing to supply also rises. At progressively lower prices, the quantity supplied decreases. In **Figure 3.2**, a possible supply curve for gasoline shows that increasing prices for gasoline should bring increasing supplies to market.

Table 3.2 summarizes how changes in various factors can affect the supply curve. Sometimes forces of nature can affect the supply curve.

How Demand and Supply Interact

Separate shifts in demand and supply have obvious effects on prices and the availability of products. In the real world, factors affecting the supply and demand often change at the same time—and they keep changing. Sometimes such changes cause contradictory pressures on prices and quantities. In other cases, the final direction of prices and quantities reflects the factor that has changed the most.

Figure 3.3 shows the interaction of both supply and demand curves for gasoline on a single graph. Notice that the two curves intersect at *P*. The law of supply and demand states that prices (*P*) are set by the intersection of the supply and demand curves. The point where the two curves meet identifies the **equilibrium price**, the prevailing market price at which you can buy an item. It is important to note that the equilibrium price is an imaginary point, as prices and quantities are constantly changing. Every purchase moves the point slightly and causes a ripple effect as both consumers and producers react to the new market prices.

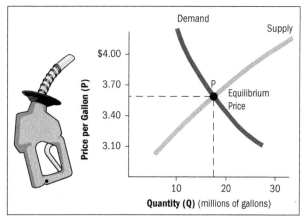

See **FIGURE 3.3 Law of Supply and Demand**

Q Answer the **Concept Check** questions.

As pointed out earlier, the forces of demand and supply can be affected by a variety of factors. One important variable is the larger economic environment. The next section explains how macro-economics and economic systems influence market forces and, ultimately, demand, supply, and prices.

Macroeconomics: Issues for the Entire Economy

Macroeconomics is the study of a country's overall economic issues. Each nation's policies and the choices their citizens make help determine its economic system, and although some are similar, no two countries have exactly the same economic system. In general, however, these systems can be classified into three categories: private enterprise systems; planned economies; or combinations of the two, referred to as mixed market economies. As business becomes an increasingly global undertaking, it is important to understand the primary features of the various economic systems operating around the world.

Capitalism: The Private Enterprise System and Competition

Most industrialized nations operate economies based on the *private enterprise system,* also known as *capitalism* or a *market economy.* A private enterprise system rewards businesses for meeting the needs and demands of consumers. Government tends to favor a hands-off attitude toward controlling business ownership, profits, and resource allocations. Instead, competition regulates economic life, creating opportunities and challenges that business-people must handle to succeed.

The relative competitiveness of a particular industry is an important consideration for every firm because it determines the ease and cost of doing business within that industry. Four basic types of competition take shape in a private enterprise system: pure competition, monopolistic competition, oligopoly, and monopoly. **Table 3.3** highlights the main differences among these types of competition.

See **TABLE 3.3: What are some of the characteristics among different types of competition?**

Pure competition is a market structure, like that of small-scale agriculture or fishing, in which large numbers of buyers and sellers exchange homogeneous products and no single participant can significantly influence price. Instead, prices are set by the market as the forces of supply and demand interact. Firms can easily enter or leave a purely competitive market because no single company dominates. Also, in pure competition, buyers see little difference between the goods and services offered by competitors.

Monopolistic competition is a market structure, like that of retailing, in which large numbers of buyers and sellers exchange differentiated (heterogeneous) products, so each participant has some control over price. Sellers can differentiate their products from competing offerings on the basis of price, quality, or other features. In an industry that features monopolistic competition, it is relatively easy for a firm to begin or stop selling a good or service. The success of one seller often attracts new competitors to such a market. Individual firms also have some control over how their goods and services are priced.

One example of monopolistic competition is the market for pet food. Consumers can choose from private-label products (store brands such as Walmart's Ol' Roy) and brand-name products like Purina. Producers of pet food and the stores that sell it have wide latitude in setting prices. Consumers can choose the store or brand with the lowest prices, or sellers can convince them that a more expensive offering—for example, the Fromm brand—is worth more because it offers better nutrition or other benefits.

An **oligopoly** is a market situation in which relatively few sellers compete and high start-up costs serve as barriers to new competitors. In some oligopolistic industries, such as paper and steel, competitors offer similar products. In others, such as aircraft and auto-mobiles, they sell different models and features. The huge investment required to enter an oligopoly market tends to discourage new competitors. The limited number of sellers also enhances the control these firms exercise over price. Competing products in an oligopoly usually sell for very similar prices because substantial price competition would reduce profits for all firms in the industry. So a price cut by one firm in an oligopoly will typically be met by its competitors. However, prices can vary from one market to another, as from one country to another.

The final type of market structure is a **monopoly**, in which a single seller dominates the trade of a good or service for which buyers can find no close substitutes. A pure monopoly occurs when a firm possesses characteristics so important to competition in its industry that they form barriers to prevent entry by would-be competitors. There are a number of companies once thought to dominate their respective markets, but disruptive technology, a new technology that unexpectedly replaces an existing one, has changed that. PayPal's e-commerce payment system, Google's search engine, Facebook's social networking platform, and Apple's iTunes no longer dominate their respective markets as they once did.[1]

Because a monopoly market lacks the benefits of competition, many governments regulate monopolies. For example, the U.S. government prohibits most pure monopolies through antitrust legislation such as the Sherman Act and the Clayton Act. The government has applied these laws against monopoly behavior by Microsoft and by disallowing proposed mergers of large companies in some industries. In other cases, the government permits certain monopolies in exchange for regulating their activities.

Many firms create short-term monopolies when research breakthroughs permit them to receive exclusive patents on new products. In the pharmaceuticals industry, drug giants such as Merck and Pfizer invest billions in research and development programs. When the research leads to successful new drugs, the companies can enjoy the benefits of their patents: the ability to set prices without fear of competitors undercutting them. Once the patent expires, however, generic substitutes enter the market, driving down prices.

With **regulated monopolies**, a local, state, or federal government grants exclusive rights in a certain market to a single firm. Pricing decisions—particularly rate increase requests—are subject to control by regulatory authorities such as state public service commissions. An example is the delivery of first-class mail, a monopoly held by the U.S. Postal Service (USPS). The USPS is a self-supporting corporation wholly owned by the federal government. Its postal rates are set by a postal commission and approved by a board of governors.

During the 1980s and 1990s, the U.S. government trended away from regulated monopolies and toward deregulation. Regulated monopolies that have been deregulated include transportation, energy, and communications. The idea was to improve customer service and reduce prices through increased competition. The Federal Communications Commission (FCC) recently announced regulations that affect "net neutrality"—the idea that all traffic on the Internet should be treated equally. These rules are not without controversy, however. Some Internet providers, such as AT&T and Comcast, are unhappy with the latest FCC regulations because they now reclassify broadband services under the same strict guidelines that govern telephone networks.[2]

Planned Economies: Socialism and Communism

In a **planned economy**, government **controls** determine business ownership, profits, and resource allocation to accomplish government goals rather than those set by individual firms. Two forms of planned economies are socialism and communism.

Socialism is characterized by government ownership and operation of major industries such as communications. Socialists argue that major industries like medical care are too important to a society to be left in private hands, and that government-owned businesses can serve the public's interest better than private firms. However, socialism allows private ownership in industries considered less crucial to social welfare, such as retail shops, restaurants, and certain types of manufacturing facilities. Scandinavian countries such as Denmark, Sweden, and Finland have many socialist features in their societies, as do some African nations and India.

The writings of Karl Marx in the mid-1800s formed the basis of communist theory. Marx believed that private enterprise economies created unfair conditions and led to worker exploitation because business owners controlled most of society's resources and reaped most of the economy's rewards. Instead, he suggested an economic system called **communism**, in which all property would be shared equally by the people of a community under the direction of a strong central government. Marx believed that elimination of private ownership of property and businesses would ensure the emergence of a classless society that would benefit all. Each individual would contribute to the nation's overall economic success, and resources would be distributed according to each person's needs. Under communism, the central government owns the means of production, and the people work for state-owned enterprises. The government determines what people can buy because it dictates what is produced in the nation's factories and farms.

Several nations adopted communist-like economic systems during the early 20th century in an effort to correct what they saw as abuses in their existing systems. In practice, however, under these new governments individuals typically found less freedom of choice in regard to jobs and purchases. Consider the former Soviet Union, where large government bureaucracies controlled nearly every aspect of daily life. Shortages became chronic because producers had little or no incentive to satisfy customers. The quality of goods and services also suffered for the same reason. When Mikhail Gorbachev became the last president of the dying Soviet Union, he tried to improve the quality of Soviet-made products. Effectively shut out of trading in the global marketplace and caught up in a treasury-depleting arms race with the United States, the Soviet Union faced severe financial problems. Eventually, these events led to the collapse of Soviet communism and the breakup of the Soviet Union itself.

Today, communist-like systems exist in just a few countries, such as North Korea. By contrast, the People's Republic of China has shifted toward a more market-oriented economy. The national government has given local government and individual plant managers more say in business decisions and has permitted some private businesses. Households now have more control over agriculture, in contrast to the collectivized farms introduced during an earlier era. In addition, Western products such as McDonald's restaurants and Coca-Cola soft drinks are now part of Chinese consumers' lives, and Chinese workers manufacture products for export to other countries.

Mixed Market Economies

Private enterprise systems and planned economies adopt basically opposite approaches to operating their economies. In reality though, many countries operate **mixed market economies**, economic systems that mix both types of economies, to different degrees. In nations generally considered to have a private enterprise economy, government-owned firms frequently operate alongside private enterprises.

France has blended socialist and free enterprise policies for hundreds of years. The nation's energy production, public transportation, and defense industries are operated as nationalized industries, controlled by the government. Meanwhile, a market economy operates in other industries. Over the past two decades, the French government has loosened its reins on state-owned companies, inviting both competition and private investment into industries previously operated as government monopolies.

The proportions of private and public enterprise can vary widely in mixed economies, and the mix frequently changes. Dozens of countries have converted government-owned and operated companies into privately held businesses in a trend known as **privatization**. Even the United States has seen proposals to privatize everything from the postal service to Social Security.

Governments may privatize state-owned enterprises in an effort to raise funds and improve their economies. The objective is to cut costs and run the operation more efficiently. One example is the Student Loan Marketing Association (SLMA), also known informally as Sallie Mae. Originally a government-sponsored enterprise, it is now a publicly traded company and the largest originator of federally insured student loans in the country. After going through a successful privatization process, SLMA originates, services, and collects payments on student loans.[3] **Table 3.4** compares the alternative economic systems on the basis of ownership and management of enterprises, rights to profits, employee rights, and worker incentives.

See **TABLE 3.4: What are the system features of alternative economic systems?**

Q Answer the **Concept Check** questions.

Evaluating Economic Performance

Ideally, an economic system should provide two important benefits for its citizens: a stable business environment and sustained growth. In a stable business environment, the overall supply of needed goods and services is aligned with the overall demand for these items. No wild fluctuations in price or availability make economic decisions complicated. Consumers and businesses not only have access to ample supplies of desired products at affordable prices but also have money to buy the items they demand.

Growth is another important economic goal. An ideal economy incorporates steady change directed toward continually expanding the amount of goods and services produced from the nation's resources. Growth leads to expanded job opportunities, improved wages, and a rising standard of living.

Flattening the Business Cycle

A nation's economy tends to flow through various stages of a business cycle: prosperity, recession, depression, and recovery. Decisions made by businesses and consumers differ at each stage of the business cycle. In periods of economic prosperity, unemployment is typically low, confidence about the future is high, and consumers make more purchases. In response to increased demand, businesses expand—by hiring more employees, investing in new technology, and making similar purchases—to take advantage of new opportunities.

While we all enjoy times of prosperity, there comes a point in the economic cycle when consumers begin to pull back on their purchases. Either they are concerned about their rising debt level or some economic event happens to shake their confidence. When this happens,

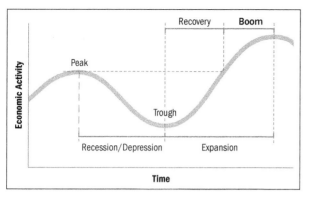

See **FIGURE 3.4 Phases of the Business Cycle**

consumers begin to postpone their major purchases and shift buying patterns toward basic, low-priced products. Businesses mirror these changes by slowing production, postponing expansion plans, reducing inventories, and often cutting the size of their workforce. As economic activity slows down, the rate of economic growth is reduced. If the economic contraction lasts for six months or longer, the country is said to be in **recession**. ▣ **Figure 3.4** illustrates the various elements of the business cycle, showing economic recessions, expansions, recoveries, and booms.

During recessions, people facing layoffs and depletions of household savings become much more conservative in their spending, postponing luxury purchases and vacations. They often turn to lower-priced retailers like Dollar Tree and Dollar General for the goods they need. And they may have sold cars, jewelry, and stocks to make ends meet. They have also sold everything from old books to artwork to kitchenware on eBay.

A **depression** can occur if the economic slowdown continues for an extended period of time or is particularly severe (significant drop in gross domestic product [GDP]). Many Americans have grown up hearing stories about their great-grandparents who lived through the Great Depression of the 1930s, when food and other basic necessities were scarce and jobs were even scarcer.

In the recovery stage of the business cycle, the economy emerges from recession and consumer spending picks up. Even though businesses often continue to rely on part-time and other temporary workers during the early stages of recovery, unemployment begins to decline as business activity accelerates and firms seek additional workers to meet growing production demands. Gradually, the concerns of recession begin to disappear, and consumers start eating out at restaurants, booking vacations, and purchasing new cars again.

Productivity and the Nation's Gross Domestic Product

An important concern for every economy is **productivity**, the relationship between the goods and services produced in a nation each year and the inputs needed to produce them. In general, as productivity rises, so does an economy's growth and the wealth of its citizens. In a recession, productivity stalls or even declines.

Productivity describes the relationship between the number of units produced and the number of human and other production inputs necessary to produce them. Productivity is a ratio of output to input. When a constant amount of inputs generates increased outputs, an increase in productivity occurs.

Total productivity considers all inputs necessary to produce a specific amount of outputs. Stated in equation form, it can be written as follows:

$$\text{Total Productivity} = \frac{\text{Output (goods or services produced)}}{\text{Input (human/natural resources, capital)}}$$

Many productivity ratios focus on only one of the inputs in the equation: labor productivity or output per labor-hour. An increase in labor productivity means that the same amount of work produces more goods and services than before. Many of the gains in U.S. productivity can be attributed to technology.

Productivity is a widely recognized measure of a company's efficiency. In turn, the total productivity of a nation's businesses has become a measure of its economic strength and standard of living. Economists refer to this measure as a country's **gross domestic product (GDP)**— the sum of all goods and services produced within its boundaries. The GDP is based on a country's per-capita output—in other words, total national output divided by the number of citizens. As ▣ **Figure 3.5** shows, the United States has the highest estimated GDP: $16.7 trillion. The European Union comes in second behind the United States, with its 28 member nations and estimated GDP of $15.8 trillion.[4] In the United States, GDP is tracked by the Bureau of Economic Analysis (BEA), a division of the U.S. Department of Commerce. Current updates and historical data on the GDP are available at the BEA's website (http://www.bea.gov).

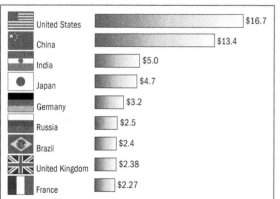

United States		$16.7
China		$13.4
India	$5.0	
Japan	$4.7	
Germany	$3.2	
Russia	$2.5	
Brazil	$2.4	
United Kingdom	$2.38	
France	$2.27	

See **FIGURE 3.5 Nations with Highest Gross Domestic Products**

Price Level Changes

An important indicator of an economy's stability is the general level of prices. For the last 100 years, economic decision makers concerned themselves with **inflation**, rising prices caused by a combination of excess consumer demand and increases in the costs of raw materials, component parts, human resources, and other factors of production. The **core inflation rate** is the inflation rate of an economy after energy and food prices are removed. This measure is often an accurate prediction of the inflation rate that consumers, businesses, and other organizations can expect to experience during the near future.

America's most severe inflationary period during the last half of the 20th century peaked in 1980, when general price levels jumped almost 14 percent in a single year. In extreme cases, an economy may experience **hyperinflation**—an economic situation characterized by soaring prices. This situation has occurred in Zimbabwe, Argentina, and countries that once formed the Soviet Union (for example, Belarus).

Inflation devalues money as persistent price increases reduce the amount of goods and services people can purchase with a given amount of money. This is bad news for people whose earnings do not keep up with inflation, who live on fixed incomes, or who have most of their wealth in investments paying a fixed rate of interest. Inflation can be good news for people whose income is rising or those with debts at a fixed rate of interest.

The opposite situation—**deflation**—occurs when prices continue to fall. In Japan, where deflation has been a reality for several years, shoppers pay less for a variety of products ranging from groceries to homes. While this situation may sound ideal to consumers, it can weaken the economy. For instance, if consumers believe that prices will be cheaper in the future, they are likely to postpone their purchases. When all consumers do this, it then becomes self-fulfilling as producers react to the lower demand by further reducing their prices. Seeing the reduced prices, consumers are willing to postpone their purchases once again. And so the cycle goes. Without predictable prices, industries such as housing and auto manufacturing cannot operate effectively, and weak demand in these sectors tends to depress the rest of the economy.

In the United States, the government tracks changes in price levels with the **Consumer Price Index (CPI)**, which measures the monthly average change in prices of goods and services. The federal Bureau of Labor Statistics (BLS) calculates the CPI monthly based on prices of a "market basket," a compilation of the goods and services most commonly purchased by urban consumers. ▣ **Figure 3.6** shows the categories included in the CPI market basket. Each month, BLS representatives visit thousands of stores, service establishments, rental units, and doctors' offices across the United States to price the many items in the CPI market basket. From these data they create the CPI, providing a running measurement of changes in consumer prices.

See **FIGURE 3.6 Contents of the CPI Market Basket**

Employment Levels

People need money to buy the goods and services produced in an economy. Because most consumers earn that money by working, the number of people in a nation who currently have jobs is an important indicator of how well the economy is doing. In general, employment dropped during the recent U.S. recession, although it recently has rebounded. Areas that have seen gains include professional and technical services, as well as construction, retail, and health care.[5]

Economists refer to a nation's unemployment rate as an indicator of its economic health. The **unemployment rate** is usually expressed as a percentage of the total workforce actively seeking work but who are currently unemployed. The total labor force includes all people who are willing and available to work at the going market wage, whether they currently have jobs or are seeking work. The U.S. Department of Labor, which tracks unemployment rates, also measures so-called discouraged workers and "underemployed" workers. Discouraged workers are individuals who want to work but have given up looking for jobs. Underemployed workers are individuals who have taken lower-paying positions than their qualifications would suggest. Unemployment can be grouped into the four categories: frictional, seasonal, cyclical, and structural.

Frictional unemployment is experienced by members of the workforce who are temporarily not working but are looking for jobs. This pool of potential workers includes new graduates, people who have left jobs for any reason and are looking for other employment, and former workers who have decided to return to the labor force. Service personnel who have recently left the military fall into this category as well. However, for some of them, finding employment may have gotten a bit easier, as Walmart recently announced that they would hire 100,000 veterans.[6]

Seasonal unemployment is the joblessness of people in a seasonal industry. Construction workers, farm laborers, fishing boat operators, and landscape employees may contend with bouts of seasonal unemployment when conditions make work unavailable.

Cyclical unemployment includes people who are out of work because of a cyclical contraction in the economy. During periods of economic expansion, overall employment is likely to rise, but as growth slows and a recession begins, unemployment levels commonly rise. At such times, even workers with good job skills may face temporary unemployment.

Structural unemployment applies to people who remain unemployed for long periods of time, often with little hope of finding new jobs like their old ones. This situation may arise because these workers lack the necessary skills for available jobs or because the skills they have are no longer in demand, such as some types of factory workers.

Q Answer the **Concept Check** questions.

Managing the Economy's Performance

Government can use both monetary policy and fiscal policy in its efforts to fight unemployment, increase business and consumer spending, and reduce the length and severity of economic recessions. For instance, the Federal Reserve System can increase or reduce interest rates, and the federal government can enact tax cuts and rebates or propose other reforms.

Monetary Policy

A common method of influencing economic activity is **monetary policy**, government actions to increase or decrease the money supply and change banking requirements and interest rates to influence spending by altering bankers' willingness to make loans. An **expansionary monetary policy** increases the money supply in an effort to cut the cost of borrowing, which encourages business decision makers to make new investments, in turn stimulating employment and economic growth. By contrast, a **restrictive monetary policy** reduces the money supply to curb rising prices, overexpansion, and concerns about overly rapid economic growth.

In the United States, the Federal Reserve System ("the Fed") is responsible for formulating and implementing the nation's monetary policy. It is headed by a chairman and board of governors, all of whom are nominated by the president. The current chair is Janet Yellen, the first woman to head the central bank in its history. All national banks must be members of this system and keep some percentage of their checking and savings funds on deposit at the Fed.

The Fed's board of governors uses a number of tools to regulate the economy. By changing the required percentage of checking and savings accounts that banks must deposit with the Fed, the governors can expand or shrink funds available to lend. The Fed also lends money to member banks, which in turn make loans at higher interest rates to business and individual borrowers. By changing the interest rates charged to commercial banks, the Fed affects the interest rates charged to borrowers and, consequently, their willingness to borrow.

Fiscal Policy

Governments also influence economic activities by making decisions about taxes and spending. Through revenues and expenses, the government implements **fiscal policy**, a set of decisions designed to control inflation, reduce unemployment, improve the general standard of living, and encourage economic growth.

The Federal Budget

Each year, the president proposes a **budget** for the federal government, a plan for how it will raise and spend money during the coming year, and presents it to Congress for approval. A typical federal budget proposal undergoes months of deliberation and many modifications before receiving approval. The federal budget includes a number of different spending categories, ranging from defense and Social Security to interest payments on the national debt (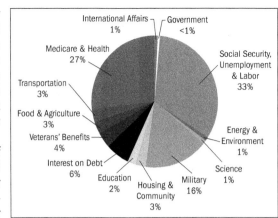 **Figure 3.7**). The decisions about what to include in the budget have a direct effect on various sectors of the economy. For example, during a recession, the federal government may approve increased spending on interstate highway repairs to improve transportation and increase employment in the construction industry. During prosperity, the government may allocate more money for scientific research.

The primary sources of government funds to cover the costs of the annual budget are taxes, fees, and borrowing. Both the overall amount of these funds and their specific combination have major effects on the economic well-being of the nation. One way governments raise money is to impose taxes on sales, income, and other sources. But increasing taxes leaves people and businesses with less money to spend. This might reduce inflation, but overly high taxes can also slow economic growth. Governments then try to balance taxes to give people necessary services without slowing economic growth.

Taxes don't always generate enough funds to cover every spending project the government hopes to undertake. When the government spends more than the amount of money it raises through taxes, it creates a **budget deficit**. To cover the deficit, the U.S. government borrows money by selling Treasury bills, Treasury notes, and Treasury bonds to investors. All of this borrowing makes up the **national debt**. If the government takes in more money than it spends, it is said to have a **budget surplus**. A **balanced budget** means total revenues raised by taxes equal the total proposed spending for the year.

Achieving a balanced budget—or even a budget surplus—does not erase the national debt. U.S. legislators continually debate how to use revenues to reduce its debt. Most families want to wipe out debt—from credit cards, automobile purchases, and college, to name a few sources. To put the national debt into personal perspective, with roughly 320 million people in the United States, each person owes about $56,635 as his or her share.[7]

But for the federal government, the decision is more complex. When the government raises money by selling Treasury bills, it makes safe investments available to investors worldwide. If foreign investors cannot buy Treasury notes, they might turn to other countries, reducing the amount of money flowing into the United States. U.S. government debt has also been used as a basis for pricing riskier investments. If the government issues less debt, the interest rates it commands are higher, raising the overall cost of debt to private borrowers. In addition, the government uses the funds from borrowing, at least in part, to pay for such public services as education and scientific research.

See **FIGURE 3.7 United States Federal Budget**

Q Answer the **Concept Check** questions.

WP LS Go to your WileyPLUS Learning Space course for video episodes, examples, art, tables, Concept Checks, practice, and resources that will help you succeed in this course.

Reading for
COMPETING WORLD MARKETS

WP LS Go to your WileyPLUS Learning Space course for video episodes, examples, art, tables, Concept Checks, practice, and resources that will help you succeed in this course.

Why Nations Trade

As domestic markets mature and sales growth slows, companies in every industry recognize the increasing importance of efforts to develop business in other countries. **Exports** are domestically produced goods and services sold in other countries. **Imports** are foreign-made products purchased by domestic consumers. Walmart operates stores in Mexico, Boeing sells jetliners in Asia, and Apple sells iPads in Germany. These are only a few of the thousands of U.S. companies taking advantage of large populations, substantial resources, and rising standards of living abroad to boost sales of their goods and services. Likewise, the U.S. market, with the world's greatest purchasing power, attracts thousands of foreign companies looking to increase their sales.

International Sources of Factors of Production

Business decisions to operate abroad depend on the availability, price, and quality of labor, natural resources, capital, and entrepreneurship—the basic factors of production—in the foreign country. For example, Indian colleges and universities produce thousands of highly qualified computer scientists and engineers each year. To take advantage of this talent, many U.S. computer software and hardware firms have set up operations in India, and many others are outsourcing information technology and customer service jobs there.

Trading with other countries also allows a company to spread risk because different nations may be at different stages of the business cycle or in different phases of development. If demand falls off in one country, the company may still enjoy strong demand in other nations. Companies such as Kellogg's and IKEA have long used international sales to offset lower domestic demand.

Size of the International Marketplace

As developing nations expand their involvement in global business, the potential for reaching new groups of customers dramatically increases. Firms looking for new revenue are inevitably attracted to giant markets such as China and India, with respective populations of more than 1.3 billion and 1.2 billion. However, people alone are not enough to create a market. Consumer demand also requires purchasing power. As 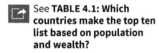 **Table 4.1** shows, population size is no guarantee of economic prosperity. Of the ten most populous countries, only the United States appears on the list of those with the highest per-capita GDPs.

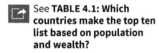
See **TABLE 4.1: Which countries make the top ten list based on population and wealth?**

Although people in developing nations have lower per-capita incomes than those in the highly developed economies of North America and Western Europe, their huge populations do represent lucrative markets. Even when the higher-income segments are only a small percentage of the entire country's population, their sheer numbers may still represent significant and growing markets.

In addition to large populations, many developing countries have posted high rates of annual GDP growth. In the United States, GDP generally averages between 2 and 4 percent growth per year. By contrast, GDP growth in less developed countries is greater—China's GDP growth rate averaged nearly 8 percent over a recent three-year period, and India's averaged 5 percent.[1] These markets represent opportunities for global businesses, even though their per-capita incomes lag behind those in more developed countries. Many firms are establishing operations in these and other developing countries to position themselves to benefit from local sales driven by expanding economies and rising standards of living. Walmart is one of those companies. As the world's largest retailer, Walmart employs 2.2 million workers worldwide. Walmart International is growing fast, with more than 6,290 stores and 900,000 employees in 27 countries as far-ranging as Lesotho and Swaziland in Africa.[2]

The United States trades with many other nations. As ◼ **Figure 4.1** shows, the top five U.S. trading partners are Canada, China, Mexico, Japan, and Germany. With the United Kingdom, South Korea, France, Brazil, and Taiwan, they represent nearly two-thirds of U.S. imports and exports every year.[3] Within the United States, foreign trade makes up a large portion of the business activity in many individual states. Texas exports more than $289 billion of goods annually, and California exports more than $174 billion. Other big exporting states include Florida, Illinois, New York, and Washington.[4]

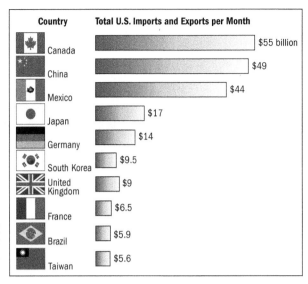

See **FIGURE 4.1 Top Ten Trading Partners with the United States**

Absolute and Comparative Advantage

Few countries can produce all the goods and services their people need. For centuries, trading has been the way that countries can meet consumer demands. If a country focuses on producing what it does best, it can export surplus domestic output and buy foreign products that it lacks or cannot efficiently produce. The potential for foreign sales of a particular item depends largely on whether the country has an absolute advantage or a comparative advantage.

A country has an **absolute advantage** in making a product if it can maintain a monopoly in the production of that product or if it can consistently produce the product at a lower cost than any competitor.

A nation can develop a **comparative advantage** if it can supply its products more efficiently—at a lower price—than it can supply other goods. Beyond the production of goods, ensuring that its people are well educated is another way a nation can develop a comparative advantage. For example, India offers the services of its educated tech workers at a lower wage.

To see the differences between a comparative and absolute advantage, consider the following example. An accountant operates a CPA firm where she bills $200 per hour doing accounting work. In addition to being an excellent accountant, she is also a pretty good typist able to type 80 words per minute. As her business grows, she decides to hire an administrative assistant specifically to help with the typing. To find suitable candidates she posts an ad on Craigslist: "Wanted: administrative assistant for growing CPA firm. Pay $20 per hour." After interviewing several candidates, she finds that the best candidate can type only 40 words per minute. Should she hire this person?

It is clear that the accountant has an absolute advantage in typing compared to her administrative assistant candidate. However, the administrative assistant has a comparative advantage when it comes to typing. This is true because of the accountant's **opportunity cost** (the difference between what she could earn doing accounting work versus what she saves by doing her own typing). Even though she can type twice as fast as the assistant, she is much better off focusing on accounting work and letting her assistant handle the typing. And so it goes with international trade, where comparative advantages and opportunity costs form the basis for most trade between nations.

Q Answer the **Concept Check** questions.

Measuring Trade between Nations

Clearly, engaging in international trade provides tremendous competitive advantages to both the countries and individual companies involved. But how do we measure global business activity? To understand what the trade inflows and outflows mean for a country, we need to examine the concepts of balance of trade and balance of payments. Another important factor is currency exchange rates for each country.

A nation's **balance of trade** is the difference between its exports and imports. If a country exports more than it imports, it achieves a positive balance of trade, called a **trade surplus**. If it imports more than it exports, it produces a negative balance of trade, called a **trade deficit**. The United States has run a trade deficit for years. Despite being one of the world's top exporters, the United States has an even greater appetite for foreign-made goods, which creates a trade deficit.

A nation's balance of trade plays a central role in determining its **balance of payments**—the overall flow of money into or out of a country. Other factors also affect the balance of payments, including overseas loans and borrowing, international investments, profits from such investments, and foreign aid payments. To calculate a nation's balance of payments, subtract the monetary outflows from the monetary inflows. A positive balance of payments, or a *balance-of-payments surplus,* means more money has moved into a country than out of it. A negative balance of payments, or a *balance-of-payments deficit,* means more money has gone out of the country than entered it.

Major U.S. Exports and Imports

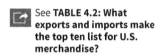

See **TABLE 4.2: What exports and imports make the top ten list for U.S. merchandise?**

The United States, with combined exports and imports of about $4.9 trillion, leads the world in the international trade of goods and services. As listed in **Table 4.2**, the leading categories of goods exchanged by U.S. exporters and importers range from machinery and vehicles to crude oil and chemicals. Strong U.S. demand for imported goods is partly a reflection of the nation's prosperity and diversity.

With annual imports of nearly $2.3 trillion, the United States is by far the world's leading importer. American tastes for foreign-made goods for everything from clothing to consumer electronics show up as huge trade deficits with the consumer goods–exporting nations of China and Japan.

Although the United States imports more goods than it exports, the opposite is true for services. U.S. exporters sell more than $700 billion in services annually. Much of that money comes from travel and tourism—money spent by foreign nationals visiting the United States.[5] U.S. service exports also include business and technical services such as engineering, financial services, computing, legal services, and entertainment, as well as royalties and licensing fees. Major service exporters include Citibank, Walt Disney, Allstate Insurance, and Federal Express, as well as retailers such as McDonald's and Starbucks.

Businesses in many foreign countries want the expertise of U.S. financial and business professionals. Accountants are in high demand in Russia, China, the Netherlands, and Australia—Sydney has become one of Asia's biggest financial centers. Entertainment is another major growth area for U.S. service exports. The Walt Disney Company already has theme parks in Europe and Asia and is building Shanghai Disney Resort, a multi-billion-dollar park in China.[6]

Exchange Rates

The value of a nation's currency is an important "thermometer" reflecting the state of a nation's economic health. A country with a strong currency can generally purchase more goods and services in the international market than one with a weaker currency. An **exchange rate** is a measure of the strength of the local currency as a nation's money is exchanged for the currencies of other nations. For example, roughly 15 Mexican pesos are needed to exchange for one U.S. dollar. A Canadian dollar can be exchanged for approximately $1 in the United States. The euro, the currency used in most of the European Union (EU) member countries, has made considerable moves in exchange value during its years in circulation. European consumers and businesses use the euro to pay bills by check, credit card, or bank transfer. Euro coins and notes are also used in many EU member-countries.

Foreign exchange rates are influenced by a number of factors, including domestic economic and political conditions, central bank intervention, balance-of-payments position, and speculation over future currency values. Currency values fluctuate, or "float," depending on the supply and demand for each currency in the international market. In this system of *floating exchange rates,* currency traders create a market for the world's currencies based on each country's relative trade and investment prospects. In theory, this market permits exchange rates to vary freely according to supply and demand. In practice however, exchange rates do not float in total freedom: national governments often intervene in currency markets to adjust their exchange rates.

Exchange rate changes can quickly create—or wipe out—a competitive advantage, so they are important factors in decisions about whether to invest abroad. In Europe, a declining dollar means that a price of ten euros is worth more, so companies are pressured to lower prices. **Devaluation** describes a drop in a currency's value relative to other currencies or to a fixed standard. At the same time, if the dollar falls it makes European vacations less affordable for U.S. tourists because their dollars are worth less relative to the euro.

Currencies that owners can easily convert into other currencies are called *hard currencies.* Examples include the euro, the U.S. dollar, and the Japanese yen. The Russian ruble and many central European currencies are considered soft currencies because they cannot be readily converted to other currencies. Exporters trading with these countries sometimes prefer to barter, accepting payment in oil, timber, or other commodities that they can resell for hard currency.

The foreign currency market is the largest financial market in the world, with a daily volume of about $5.3 trillion in U.S. dollars.[7] This is more than ten times the size of all the world's stock markets combined, so the foreign exchange market is one of the largest, most efficient financial markets in the world.

Q Answer the **Concept Check** questions.

Barriers to International Trade

Whether they sell only to local customers or trade in international markets, all businesses encounter challenges—barriers—to their operations. For example, countries such as Australia and New Zealand regulate the hours and days retailers may be open. International companies may have to reformulate their products to accommodate different tastes in new locations. Some of the challenges shown in **Figure 4.2** are easily overcome, but others require major changes in a company's business strategy. To successfully compete in global markets, companies and their managers must understand not only how these barriers affect international trade but also how to overcome them.

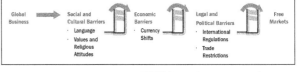

See **FIGURE 4.2 Barriers to International Trade**

Social and Cultural Differences

The social and cultural differences among nations range from language and customs to educational background and religious holidays. Understanding and respecting these differences are critical to international business success. Businesspeople with knowledge of host countries' cultures, languages, social values, and religious attitudes and practices are well equipped for the marketplace and the negotiating table. Sensitivity to such elements as local attitudes, forms of address, and expectations regarding dress, body language, and timeliness also helps them win customers and achieve their business objectives.

Language

Understanding a business colleague's primary language may prove to be the difference between closing an international business transaction and losing the sale to someone else. Company representatives operating in foreign markets must not only choose correct and appropriate words but also translate words correctly to convey the intended meanings. Firms may also need to rename products or rewrite slogans for foreign markets.

Values

U.S. society places a higher value on business efficiency and low unemployment than does European society, where employee benefits are more valued. The U.S. government does not regulate vacation time, and in the U.S. employees typically have limited or no paid vacation during their first year of employment, then two weeks vacation, and eventually up to three or four weeks if they stay with the same employer for many years. In contrast, the EU mandates a minimum paid vacation of four weeks per year, and most Europeans get five or six weeks. In these countries, a U.S. company that opens a manufacturing plant would not be able to hire any local employees without offering vacations in line with a nation's business practices.

Economics

Business opportunities are flourishing in densely populated countries such as China and India, as local consumers eagerly buy Western products. Although such prospects might tempt American firms, managers must first consider the economic factors involved in doing business in these markets. A country's size, per-capita income, and stage of economic development are among the economic factors to consider when evaluating it as a candidate for an international business venture. Tata Motors, for instance, has an eye on Western auto buyers, even as it markets its low-priced Nano car for the home market in India.

Political and Legal Differences

Like social, cultural, and economic differences, legal and political differences in host countries can pose barriers to international trade. To compete in today's world marketplace, managers involved in international business must be well versed in legislation that affects their industries. Some countries impose general trade restrictions. Others have established detailed rules that regulate how foreign companies can operate. An important factor in any international business investment is the stability of the political climate. The political structures of many nations promote stability similar to that in the United States. Other nations, such as Indonesia, Thailand, and Congo, feature quite different—and frequently changing—structures. Host nations often pass laws designed to protect their own interests, sometimes at the expense of foreign businesses.

Legal Environment

When conducting business internationally, managers must be familiar with three dimensions of the legal environment: U.S. law, international regulations, and the laws of the countries in which they plan to do business. Some laws protect the rights of foreign companies to compete in the United States. Others dictate actions allowed for U.S. companies doing business in foreign countries.

The Foreign Corrupt Practices Act forbids U.S. companies from bribing foreign officials, political candidates, or government representatives. Although the law has been in effect since 1977, in the past few years the U.S. government has increased its enforcement, including major proceedings in the pharmaceutical, medical device, and financial industries. The United States, United Kingdom, France, Germany, and 37 other countries have signed the Organization for Economic Cooperation and Development Anti-Bribery Convention. Still, corruption continues to be an international problem. Its pervasiveness, combined with U.S. prohibitions, creates a difficult obstacle for U.S. businesspeople who want to do business in many foreign countries. Chinese pay *huilu,* and Russians rely on *vzyatka.* In the Middle East, palms are greased with *baksheesh.*

Types of Trade Restrictions

Trade restrictions such as taxes on imports and complicated administrative procedures create additional barriers to international business. They may limit consumer choices while increasing the costs of foreign-made products. Trade restrictions are also imposed to protect citizens' security, health, and jobs. A government may limit exports of strategic and defense-related goods to unfriendly countries to protect its security, ban imports of insecticide-contaminated farm products to protect health, and restrict imports to protect domestic jobs in the importing country.

Other restrictions are imposed to promote trade with certain countries. Still others protect countries from unfair competition. Regardless of the political reasons for trade restrictions, most take the form of tariffs. In addition to tariffs, governments impose a number of nontariff—or administrative—barriers. These include quotas and embargoes.

Tariffs

A tax, surcharge, or duty on foreign products is referred to as a **tariff**. Governments may assess two types of tariffs—revenue and protective tariffs—both of which make imports more expensive for domestic buyers. Revenue tariffs generate income for the government. Upon returning home, U.S. leisure travelers who are out of the country more than 48 hours and who bring back goods purchased abroad may pay import taxes on the goods' value depending on the country of origin. This duty goes directly to the U.S. Treasury. The sole purpose of a protective tariff is to raise the retail price of imported products to match or exceed the prices of similar products manufactured in the home country. In other words, protective tariffs seek to limit imports and provide advantages for domestic competitors.

Nontariff Barriers

Nontariff, or administrative, trade barriers restrict imports in more subtle ways than tariffs. These measures may take such forms as quotas on imports, restrictive standards for imports, and export subsidies. Because many countries have recently substantially reduced tariffs or eliminated them entirely, they increasingly use nontariff barriers to control flows of imported products.

A **quota** limits the amount of a particular product that countries can import during specified time periods. Limits may be set as quantities, such as number of cars or bushels of wheat, or as values, such as dollars' worth of cigarettes. Governments regularly set quotas for agricultural products and sometimes for imported automobiles. The United States, for example, sets a quota on imports of sugar. Imports under the quota amount are subject to a lower tariff than shipments above the quota. However, sugar and related products imported at the higher rate may enter the country in unlimited quantities.[8]

Quotas help prevent **dumping**. In one form of dumping, a company sells products abroad at prices below its cost of production. In another, a company exports a large quantity of a product at a lower price than the same product in the home market and drives down the price of the domestic product. Dumping benefits domestic consumers in the importing market, but it hurts domestic producers. It also allows companies to gain quick entry to foreign markets.

More severe than a quota, an **embargo** imposes a total ban on importing a specified product or even a total halt to trading with a particular country.

> **Q** Answer the **Concept Check** questions.

Reducing Barriers to International Trade

Although tariffs and administrative barriers still restrict trade, overall the world is moving toward free trade. Several types of organizations ease barriers to international trade, including groups that monitor trade policies and practices and institutions that offer monetary assistance. Another type of federation designed to ease trade barriers is the multinational economic community, such as the European Union. This section looks at the roles these organizations play.

Organizations Promoting International Trade

For the 60-plus years of its existence, the **General Agreement on Tariffs and Trade (GATT)**, an international trade accord, sponsored a series of negotiations, called rounds, which substantially reduced worldwide tariffs and other barriers. Major industrialized nations founded the multinational organization in 1947 to work toward reducing tariffs and relaxing import quotas. The last set of completed negotiations—the Uruguay Round—cut average tariffs by one-third, in excess of $700 billion; reduced farm subsidies; and improved protection for copyright and patent holders. In addition, international trading rules now apply to various service industries. Finally, the new agreement established the **World Trade Organization (WTO)** to succeed GATT. This organization includes representatives from 160 countries.

World Trade Organization

Since 1995, the WTO has monitored GATT agreements among the member nations, mediated disputes, and continued the effort to reduce trade barriers throughout the world. Unlike provisions in GATT, the WTO's decisions are binding on parties involved in disputes.

The WTO has grown more controversial in recent years as it issues decisions that have implications for working conditions and the environment in member nations. Concerns have been expressed that the WTO's focus on lowering trade barriers encourages businesses to keep costs down through practices that may increase pollution and human rights abuses. Particularly worrisome is the fact that the organization's member-countries must agree on policies, and developing countries tend not to be eager to lose their low-cost advantage by enacting stricter labor and environmental laws. Other critics claim that if well-funded U.S. firms such as fast food chains, entertainment companies, and Internet retailers can freely enter foreign markets, they will wipe out smaller foreign businesses serving the distinct tastes and practices of other countries' cultures.

World Bank

Shortly after the end of World War II, industrialized nations formed an organization to lend money to less developed and developing countries. The **World Bank** primarily funds projects that build or expand nations' infrastructure such as transportation, education, and medical systems and facilities. The World Bank and other development banks also provide advice and assistance to developing nations. Often, in exchange for granting loans, the World Bank imposes requirements intended to build the economies of borrower nations.

Although the World Bank provides many benefits to developing countries, it is not without its critics. For example, it has been criticized for making loans with conditions that ultimately hurt the borrower nations. When developing nations are required to balance government budgets, they are sometimes forced to cut vital social programs. Critics also say that the World Bank should consider the impact of its loans on the environment and working conditions.

International Monetary Fund

Established a year after the World Bank, the **International Monetary Fund (IMF)** was created to promote trade through financial cooperation and, in the process, eliminate barriers. The IMF makes short-term loans to member nations that are unable to meet their expenses. It operates as a lender of last resort for troubled nations. In exchange for these emergency loans, IMF lenders frequently require significant commitments from borrowing nations to address the problems that led to the crises. These steps may include curtailing imports or even devaluing currencies. Throughout its existence, the IMF has worked to prevent financial crises by warning the international business community when countries encounter problems meeting their financial obligations. Often, the IMF lends to countries to keep them from defaulting on prior debts and to prevent economic crises in particular countries from spreading to other nations.

International Economic Communities

International economic communities reduce trade barriers and promote regional economic integration. In the simplest approach, countries may establish a *free-trade area* in which they trade freely among themselves without tariffs or trade restrictions. Each maintains its own tariffs for trade outside this area. A *customs union* sets up a free-trade area and specifies a uniform tariff structure for members' trade with nonmember nations. In a *common market,* or economic union, members go beyond a customs union and try to bring all of their trade rules into agreement.

One example of a free-trade area is the **North American Free Trade Agreement (NAFTA)** enacted by the United States, Canada, and Mexico. Other examples of regional trading blocs include the MERCOSUR customs union (joining Brazil, Argentina, Paraguay, Uruguay, Chile, and Bolivia) and the ten-country Association of South East Asian Nations (ASEAN).

NAFTA

NAFTA became effective in 1994, creating the world's largest free-trade zone with the United States, Canada, and Mexico. With a combined population of more than 473 million and a total GDP of more than $20 trillion, North America represents one of the world's most attractive markets. By eliminating all trade barriers and investment restrictions among the United States, Canada, and Mexico over a 15-year period, NAFTA opened more doors for free trade. The agreement also eased regulations governing services, such as banking, and established uniform legal requirements for protection of intellectual property. The three nations can now trade with one another without tariffs or other trade barriers, simplifying shipments of goods across the partners' borders. Standardized customs and uniform labeling regulations create economic efficiencies and smooth import and export procedures. Trade among the partners has increased steadily, more than doubling since NAFTA took effect.

CAFTA-DR

The **Central America–Dominican Republic Free Trade Agreement (CAFTA-DR)** created a free-trade area among the United States, Costa Rica, the Dominican Republic (the DR of the title), El Salvador, Guatemala, Honduras, and Nicaragua. The agreement—the first of its kind between the United States and these smaller developing economies—ends tariffs on the nearly $60 billion in products traded between the United States and its Latin American neighbors. Agricultural producers such as corn, soybean, and dairy farmers stand to gain under the relaxed trade rules. Overall, CAFTA-DR's effects have increased both exports and imports substantially, much as NAFTA did.[9]

European Union

Perhaps the best-known example of a common market is the **European Union (EU)**. The EU combines 28 countries, over 511 million people, and a total GDP of roughly $16 trillion to form a huge common market. ▣ **Figure 4.3** shows the member countries. Current candidates for membership are Albania, Iceland, Montenegro, Serbia, Turkey, and Macedonia.[10]

The EU's goals include promoting economic and social progress, introducing European citizenship as a complement to national citizenship, and giving the EU a significant role in international affairs. To achieve its goal of a borderless Europe, the EU is removing barriers to free trade among its members. This highly complex process involves standardizing business regulations and requirements, standardizing import duties and taxes, and eliminating customs checks so that companies can transport goods from England to Italy or Poland as easily as from New York to Boston.

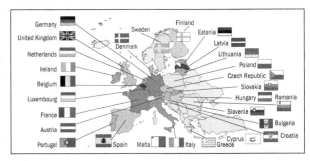

Unifying standards and laws can contribute to economic growth. But just as NAFTA sparked fears in the United States about free trade with Mexico, some people in Western Europe worried that opening trade with such countries as Poland, Hungary, and the Czech Republic would cause jobs to flow eastward to lower-wage economies.

The EU also introduced the euro to replace currencies such as the French franc and Italian lira. For the 19 member-states that have adopted the euro, potential benefits include eliminating the economic costs of currency exchange and simplifying price comparisons.

See **FIGURE 4.3 The 28 Nations of the European Union**

 Answer the **Concept Check** questions.

Going Global

While expanding into overseas markets can increase profits and marketing opportunities, it also introduces new complexities to a firm's business operations. Before deciding to go global, a company faces a number of key decisions, beginning with the following:

- determining which foreign market(s) to enter
- analyzing the investment required to enter a new market
- deciding the best way to organize the overseas operations

These issues vary in importance depending on the level of involvement a company chooses. Education and employee training in the host country would be much more important for an electronics manufacturer building an Asian factory than for a firm that is simply planning to export American-made products.

The choice of which markets to enter usually follows extensive research focusing on local demand for the firm's products, availability of needed resources, and ability of the local workforce to produce world-class quality. Other factors include existing and potential competition, tariff rates, currency stability, and investment barriers. A variety of government and other sources are available to facilitate this research process. A good starting place is the CIA's *World Factbook,* which contains country-by-country information on geography, population, government, economy, and infrastructure.

U.S. Department of Commerce counselors working at district offices offer a full range of international business advice, including computerized market data and names of business and government contacts in dozens of countries. As ◨ **Table 4.3** shows, the Internet provides access to many resources for international trade information.

See **TABLE 4.3: What are some international trade research resources on the Internet?**

Levels of International Involvement

After a firm has completed its research and decided to do business overseas, it can choose one or more strategies:

- exporting or importing
- entering into contractual agreements such as franchising, licensing, and subcontracting deals
- direct investment in the foreign market through acquisitions, joint ventures, or establishment of an overseas division

Although the company's risk increases with the level of its involvement, so does its overall control of all aspects of producing and selling its goods or services.

Importers and Exporters

When a firm brings in goods produced abroad to sell domestically, it is an importer. Conversely, companies are exporters when they produce—or purchase—goods at home and sell them in overseas markets. An importing or exporting strategy provides the most basic level of international involvement, with the least risk and control.

Firms engage in exporting of two types: indirect and direct. A company engages in indirect exporting when it produces a product, such as an electronic component, that becomes part of another product that is ultimately sold in foreign markets. The second method, direct exporting, occurs as the name implies when a company directly sells its products in markets outside its own country. Often the first step for companies entering foreign markets, direct exporting is the most common form of international business. Firms that succeed at this may then move to other strategies.

Contractual Agreements

Once a company gains experience in international sales, it may decide to enter into contractual agreements with local parties. These arrangements can include franchising, foreign licensing, and subcontracting.

Common among U.S. companies and fast food brands like McDonald's and KFC, franchising can work well for companies seeking to expand into international markets. A **franchise**, as described in detail in Chapter 6, is a contractual agreement in which a wholesaler or retailer (the franchisee) gains the right to sell the franchisor's products under that company's brand name if it agrees to the related operating requirements.

Advantageous for a small manufacturer eager to launch a well-known product overseas, a **foreign licensing agreement** occurs when one firm allows another to produce or sell its product or use its trademark, patent, or manufacturing processes, in a specific geographical area. In return, the firm gets a royalty or other compensation.

Another type of contractual agreement, **subcontracting**, involves hiring local companies to produce, distribute, or sell goods or services. This move allows a foreign firm to take advantage of the subcontractor's expertise in local culture, contacts, and regulations. Many companies simply modify their domestic business strategies by translating promotional brochures and product-use instructions into the languages of the host nations.

International Direct Investment

Investing directly in production and marketing operations in a foreign country is the ultimate level of global involvement. Over time, a firm may become successful at conducting business in other countries through exporting and contractual agreements. Its managers may then decide to establish manufacturing facilities in those countries, open branch offices, or buy ownership interests in local companies. Making the decision to directly invest in another country can carry significant risks for the investing company. Political instability, currency devaluation, and changes in the competitive environment are but a few of the issues that a firm must consider before making a direct investment.

One type of direct investment is the **joint venture**, which allows companies to share risks, costs, profits, and management responsibilities with one or more host country nationals. By setting up such an arrangement, a company can conduct a significant amount of its business overseas while reducing the risk of "going it alone" in a foreign country.

 See **TABLE 4.4: World's largest multinational companies**

From Multinational Corporation to Global Business

A **multinational corporation (MNC)** is an organization with significant foreign operations. As  **Table 4.4** shows, the top ten largest multinational companies are evenly split between the United States and China as the site for their headquarters. Also note that the top two industries continue to be banking and oil and gas operations.

Many U.S. multinationals, including Nike and Walmart, have expanded their overseas operations because they believe that domestic markets are peaking and foreign markets offer greater sales and profit potential. Other MNCs are making substantial investments in developing countries in part because these countries provide low-cost labor compared with the United States and Western Europe. In addition, many MNCs are locating high-tech facilities in countries with large numbers of technical school graduates.

 Answer the **Concept Check** questions.

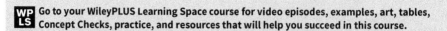 Go to your WileyPLUS Learning Space course for video episodes, examples, art, tables, Concept Checks, practice, and resources that will help you succeed in this course.

Reading for
SMALL BUSINESS AND FORMS OF BUSINESS OWNERSHIP

5

WP LS Go to your WileyPLUS Learning Space course for video episodes, examples, art, tables, Concept Checks, practice, and resources that will help you succeed in this course.

Most Businesses are Small Businesses

Although many people associate the term *business* with corporate giants such as Walmart, 3M, and ExxonMobil, most people do not know that 99.7 percent of all U.S. companies are considered small businesses. These firms have generated 65 percent of new jobs over the past two decades and employ half of all private-sector (nongovernment) workers.[1] Small business is also the launching pad for new ideas and products. Small businesses hire 43 percent of high-tech workers such as scientists, engineers, and computer programmers, who devote their time to developing new goods and services.[2]

What Is a Small Business?

How can you tell a small business from a large one? The Small Business Administration (SBA), the federal agency most directly involved with this sector of the economy, defines a **small business** as an independent business having fewer than 500 employees. However, those bidding for government contracts or applying for government assistance may vary in size according to industry. For example, small manufacturers fall in the 500-worker range, whereas wholesalers must employ fewer than 100. Retailers may generate up to $7 million in annual sales and still be considered small businesses, whereas farms or other agricultural businesses must generate less than $750,000 annually to be designated as small.[3]

Typical Small-Business Ventures

Small businesses have experienced steady erosion in some industries as larger firms have bought them out and replaced them with larger operations. The number of independent home improvement stores, for example, has fallen dramatically as Lowe's, Home Depot, and other large brands have increased the size and number of their stores. But as ▣ **Table 5.1** reveals, the businesses least likely to be gobbled up are those that sell personalized services, rely on certain locations, and keep their overhead costs low.

As ▣ **Figure 5.1** shows, small businesses provide most jobs in the construction, agricultural services, wholesale trade, services, and retail trade industries. Retailing to the consumer is another important industry for small firms. Retailing giants such as Amazon and Macy's may be the best-known firms, but smaller stores and websites outnumber them. And these small firms can be very successful, often because they can keep their overhead expenses low.

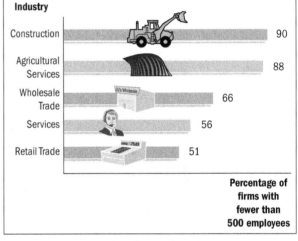

Industry	Percentage of firms with fewer than 500 employees
Construction	90
Agricultural Services	88
Wholesale Trade	66
Services	56
Retail Trade	51

See **FIGURE 5.1 Industries Dominated by Small Businesses**

Source: U.S. Small Business Administration, Office of Advocacy, "Small Business Profile: United States," www.sba.gov, accessed February 24, 2015.

See **TABLE 5.1: Which business sectors are most dominated and least dominated by small firms?**

Q Answer the **Concept Check** questions.

Contributions of Small Business to the Economy

Creating New Jobs

One impressive contribution that small business makes to the U.S. economy is the number of new jobs created each year. On average, companies with fewer than 500 employees are responsible for creating two of every three new jobs in a year.[4] The smallest companies—those with four or fewer employees—are responsible for a significant share of those jobs. Over the last several years, the SBA has provided more than $100 billion in loans to small businesses to allow access to capital and increased growth.[5]

Even if you never plan to start your own company, you will probably work for a small business at some point in your career, particularly at the beginning. Small firms often hire the youngest workers. Most of us will spend some time working in areas dominated by small business such as construction, retail, or food service.

Innovation

Small businesses are adept at developing new and improved goods and services. Innovation is often the entire reason for the founding of a new business. In a typical year, small firms develop twice as many product innovations per employee as larger firms. They also produce over 16 times more patents per employee than larger firms.[6]

Creating New Industries

See **TABLE 5.2: Can you list some of the new job opportunities within these emerging industries?**

Small firms give businesspeople the opportunity and outlet for developing their new ideas. Sometimes these innovations become entirely new industries. **Table 5.2** illustrates some of the newest jobs within emerging industries, many of which can be found in small businesses. Many of today's largest and most successful firms, such as Whole Foods, Google, and Mattel, began as small businesses. Facebook co-founders Mark Zuckerberg, Dustin Moskovitz, Chris Hughes, and Eduardo Saverin launched their new business from their college dorm room. Within a few years, Facebook had logged more than 500 million active users, positioned itself as a leader in the new industry of social networking, and prompted others to start their own businesses. Facebook recently passed more than 1.3 billion active users.[7]

Q Answer the **Concept Check** questions.

Out of Business Within 2 to 10 Years

Gone Out of Business

	2 yrs.	4 yrs.	6 yrs.	10 yrs.
	33%	50.4%	61.5%	82%

See **FIGURE 5.2 Rate of Business Failures**

*Data includes companies that have changed their names, changed their legal structure, merged into another firm, or been sold.
Source: Office of Advocacy, U.S. Small Business Administration, "Frequently Asked Questions: Advocacy Small Business Statistics and Research," www.sba.gov, accessed February 24, 2015.

Why Small Businesses Fail

As we have seen, small businesses play a huge role in the U.S. economy. However, owning or even working in a small business is often more challenging than in a large firm. Some of the advantages of small business, such as lower costs, can also be disadvantages. For example, suppose a firm has lower costs because it doesn't have a human resources department. In this case, the owner must deal with all human resource issues as well as all other duties. This same concept applies to other areas within a small business as well, from accounting to production to marketing and sales. The owner and the staff have to perform many duties, often without the resources of larger firms. To succeed, a small business owner must have a clear focus, stick to a plan, and hope for a bit of luck. However, even in the best case, owning a small business can be difficult. Some of the more common issues that plague small firms include management inexperience, inadequate financing, and the challenge of meeting government regulations.

As **Figure 5.2** shows, seven out of ten new businesses survive at least two years and about half make it to the four-year mark. But by the tenth year, 82 percent will have closed.[8] Let's look a little more closely at why this happens.

Management Shortcomings

Management shortcomings may include lack of people skills, inadequate knowledge of finance, inability to track inventory or sales, poor assessment of the competition, or simply the lack of time to do everything required. As we have seen, large firms often have the resources to recruit specialists in areas such as marketing and finance, whereas the owner of a small business often must wear many hats.

Inadequate Financing

Many of the challenges that small businesses face can be traced to inadequate financing. Money is the foundation of any business. Every business, large or small, needs a certain amount of financing in order to operate, grow, and thrive. First-time business owners often assume their firms will generate enough funds from initial sales to finance continuing operations. But building a business takes time. Products need to be developed, employees have to be hired, a website must be constructed, a distribution strategy has to be determined, office or retail space might have to be secured, and so forth. Most small businesses—even those with minimal start-up costs—sometimes don't turn a profit for months or even years.[9]

Government Regulation

Small-business owners cite their struggle to comply with government regulations as one of the biggest challenges they face. Some firms falter because of this burden alone. Paperwork costs account for billions of small-business dollars each year. A large company can better cope with requirements for forms and reports. Larger firms often find it makes economic sense to hire or contract with specialists in specific types of regulation, such as employment law and workplace safety regulations. By contrast, small businesses often struggle to absorb the costs of government paperwork because of their smaller staff and budgets. The smallest firms—those with fewer than 20 employees—spend 45 percent more per employee than larger firms just to comply with federal regulations.[10]

[Q] Answer the **Concept Check** questions.

Available Assistance for Small Businesses

An important part of organizing a small business is financing its activities. Once a business plan has been created, various sources can be tapped for loans and other types of financing. These include government agencies as well as private investors.

Small Business Administration

Not all government involvement in small business is burdensome. Small businesses can benefit from using the resources provided by the U.S. government's **Small Business Administration (SBA)**. The SBA is the principal agency concerned with helping small U.S. firms, and it is the advocate for small businesses within the federal government. Several thousand employees staff the SBA's Washington D.C. headquarters and its 1,800 regional and field offices. The SBA's mission statement declares that "Small business is critical to our economic recovery and strength, to building America's future, and to helping the United States compete in today's global marketplace."[11]

Contrary to popular belief, the SBA seldom provides direct business loans or outright grants to start or expand small businesses. Rather, the SBA guarantees small-business loans made by private lenders, including banks and other institutions. To qualify for an SBA-backed loan, borrowers must be unable to secure conventional commercial financing on reasonable terms and be a "small business" as defined by SBA size standards.[12] Direct SBA loans are available in only a few special situations, such as natural disaster recovery, energy conservation, or development programs.

Start-ups and other small firms can obtain an SBA-guaranteed **microloan** of up to $35,000, with the average being $13,000 with a maximum term of six years.[13] Microloans may be used to buy equipment or operate a business but not to buy real estate or pay off other loans. These loans are available from nonprofit organizations located in most states. Other sources of microloans include the federal Economic Development Administration; some state governments; and certain private lenders, such as credit unions and community development groups. The most frequent suppliers of credit to small firms are banks.

Small-business loans are also available through a Small Business Investment Company (SBIC), an SBA-licensed organization operated by experienced venture capitalists. SBICs use their own capital, supplemented with government loans, to invest in small businesses. Like banks, SBICs are profit-making enterprises, but they are likely to be more flexible than banks in their lending decisions.

Small-Business Opportunities for Women and Minorities

Like male business owners, women have a variety of reasons for owning their own companies. Some have a unique business idea that they want to bring to life. Others decide to form a business when they lose their jobs or become frustrated with the bureaucracies in large

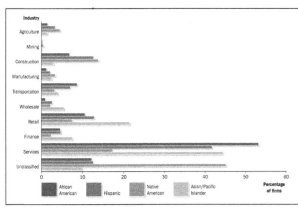

See **FIGURE 5.3 Types of Businesses Owned by Racial and Ethnic Minorities**

Source: Data from Office of Advocacy, U.S. Small Business Administration, "Minorities in Business," http://www.sba.gov/advocacy, accessed February 24, 2015.

Q Answer the **Concept Check** questions.

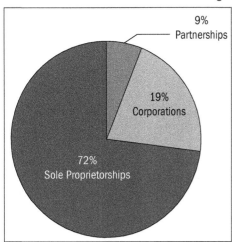

See **FIGURE 5.4 Forms of Business Ownership**

Source: Data from U.S. Census Bureau, "Business Enterprise: Sole Proprietorships, Partnerships, Corporations, Table 744," *Statistical Abstract of the United States*, http://www.uscensus.gov, accessed February 24, 2015.

companies. In some cases, women leave large corporations when they feel blocked from opportunities for advancement—when they hit the so-called "glass ceiling." Because women are more likely than men to be their family's primary caregiver, many seek self-employment as a way to achieve flexible working hours so they can spend more time with their families.

Business ownership is also an important opportunity for America's racial and ethnic minorities. In recent years, the growth in the number of businesses owned by African Americans, Hispanics, and Asian Americans has far outpaced the overall growth of U.S. businesses. ▦ **Figure 5.3** shows the percentages of minority ownership in major industries. The relatively strong presence of minorities in the services and retail industries is especially significant because these industries contain the greatest number of businesses.

Forms of Private Business Ownership

Regardless of its size, every business is organized according to one of three categories of legal structure: sole proprietorship, partnership, or corporation. Each legal structure offers unique advantages and disadvantages. But because there is no universal formula for every situation, U.S. state governments have created or adopted a variety of organizational structures. Business owners can then choose the structure that best meets their needs. For example, within the corporate organizational form there are C corporations, S corporations, and, depending on size and other factors, limited liability companies (LLC). Within partnerships, there are general partnerships, limited partnerships, and limited liability partnerships. And there are even variations on sole proprietors, such as a single person LLC. ▦ **Figure 5.4** shows the breakdown of organizational forms, with sole proprietorships being the most common form of business ownership, accounting for more than 70 percent of all firms in the United States.

Sole Proprietorships

The most common form of business ownership, the **sole proprietorship** is also the oldest and the simplest. In a sole proprietorship, no legal distinction separates the sole proprietor's status as an individual from his or her status as a business owner. Although sole proprietorships are common in a variety of industries, they are concentrated primarily among small businesses such as repair shops, small retail stores, and service providers such as plumbers, hair stylists, and photographers.

A sole proprietorship offers some unique advantages. Because such businesses involve a single owner, they are easy to form and dissolve. A sole proprietorship gives the owner maximum management flexibility, along with the right to all profits after payment of business-related bills and taxes. A highly motivated owner of a sole proprietorship directly reaps the benefits of his or her hard work.

Minimal legal requirements simplify creating a sole proprietorship. The owner registers the business or trade name—to guarantee that two firms do not use the same name—and takes out any necessary licenses. Local governments require certain licenses for businesses such as restaurants, motels or hotels, and retail stores. In addition, some occupational licenses require business owners to obtain specific insurance such as liability coverage.

Sole proprietorships are also easy to dissolve. This advantage is particularly important to temporary or seasonal businesses that set up for a limited period of time. It's also helpful if the owner wants or needs to close the business for any reason—say, to relocate or to accept a full-time position with a larger firm.

Management flexibility is another advantage of a sole proprietorship. The owner can make decisions without reporting to a manager, take quick action, and keep trade secrets.

A sole proprietorship always bears the individual stamp or flair of its owner, whether it's a discount loyalty program or extended warranty.

The greatest disadvantage of the sole proprietorship is the owner's personal financial liability for all debts of the business. Also, the business must operate with financial resources limited to the owner's personal funds and money that he or she can borrow. Such financing limitations can keep the business from expanding.

Partnerships

Another option for organizing a business is to form a partnership. The Uniform Partnership Act, which regulates this ownership form in most states, defines a **partnership** as an association of two or more persons who operate a business as co-owners by voluntary legal agreement. Many small businesses begin as partnerships between co-founders.

Partnerships are easy to form. All the partners need to do is register the business name and obtain any necessary licenses. Having a partner generally means greater financial capability and someone to share in the tasks and decision making of a business. It's even better if one partner has a particular skill, such as design, while the other has a knack for financials.

Most partnerships have the disadvantage of being exposed to unlimited financial liability. Each partner bears full responsibility for the debts of the firm, and each is legally liable for the actions of the other partners. If the firm fails and is left with debt—no matter who is at fault—every partner is responsible for those debts. If one partner defaults, the others are responsible for the firm's debts, even if it means dipping into personal funds. To avoid these problems, many firms establish a limited partnership or a limited-liability partnership, which limits the liability of partners to the value of their interests in the company. In the case of a limited partnership, the general partners have complete liability, while the liability of limited partners is limited to the amount of their investment. Limited-liability partnerships go a step further in limiting the liability for all partners to the assets of the partnership.

Breaking up a partnership is more complicated than dissolving a sole proprietorship. Rather than simply withdrawing funds from the bank, the partner who wants out may need to find someone to buy his or her interest in the firm. The death of a partner also threatens the survival of a partnership. A new partnership must be formed, and the estate of the deceased is entitled to a share of the firm's value. To ease the financial strains of such events, business planners often recommend life insurance coverage for each partner, combined with a buy–sell agreement. The insurance proceeds can be used to repay the deceased partner's heirs and allow the surviving partner to retain control of the business. Because partnerships are vulnerable to personal conflicts that can quickly escalate, it's important for partners to choose each other carefully—not just because they are friends—and try to plan for the future.

Corporations

A **C corporation** is a legal organization with assets and liabilities separate from those of its owner(s). A corporation can be a large or small business. It can be Ford Motor Company or a local auto repair shop.

Corporate ownership offers considerable advantages. Because a corporation is a separate legal entity, its stockholders have only limited financial risk. If the firm fails, stockholders lose only the money they invested. This applies to the firm's managers and executives as well. Because they are not the sole proprietors or partners in the business, their personal savings are not at risk if the company folds or goes bankrupt. This protection also extends to legal risk. Class-action suits involving automakers, drug manufacturers, and food producers are filed against the companies, not the owners of those companies. Target experienced a class-action lawsuit due to a data breach; however, its employees and stockholders were not required to pay the settlements from their own bank accounts.[14]

Corporations offer other advantages. They gain access to expanded financial capabilities based on the opportunity to offer direct outside investments such as stock sales. A large corporation can legally generate internal financing for many projects by transferring money from one part of the corporation to another.

One major disadvantage for a corporation is the double taxation of corporate earnings. After a corporation pays federal, state, and local income taxes on its profits, its owners (stockholders) also pay personal taxes on any distributions of those profits they receive from the corporation in the form of dividends.

S Corporations and Limited-Liability Corporations

To avoid double taxation of business income while minimizing financial liability for their owners, many smaller firms (those with fewer than 100 stockholders) organize as an **S corporation**. An S corporation can elect to pay federal income taxes as a partnership while retaining the liability limitations typical of corporations. S corporations are only taxed once. Unlike regular corporations, S corporations do not pay corporate taxes on their profits. Instead, the untaxed profits of S corporations are paid directly as dividends to shareholders, who then pay the individual tax rate. This tax advantage has resulted in a tremendous increase in the number of S corporations. Consequently, the IRS closely monitors S corporations because some businesses don't meet the legal requirements to form S corporations.[15]

Business owners may also form a **limited-liability company (LLC)** to secure the corporate advantage of limited liability while avoiding the double taxation characteristic of corporations. An LLC combines the pass-through taxation of a partnership or sole proprietorship with the limited liability of a corporation.

Some for-profit organizations are choosing a newer corporate form called a Benefit Corporation, or B corporation for short. Companies with a culture, structure, and decision making centered around creating a meaningful impact on the environment have chose this form of business ownership.

Employee-Owned Corporations

Another alternative for creating a corporation is **employee ownership**, in which workers buy shares of stock in the company that employs them. The corporate organization stays the same, but most stockholders are also employees. The popularity of this form of corporation is growing, with the number of employee ownership plans increasing dramatically. Today about 20 percent of all employees of for-profit companies report owning stock in their companies; approximately 25 million Americans own employer stock through employee stock ownership plans (ESOPs), options, stock purchase plans, 401(k) plans, and other programs.

Not-for-Profit Corporations

The same business concepts that apply to commercial companies also apply to the **not-for-profit corporation**—an organization whose goals do not include pursuing a profit. About 1.4 million not-for-profits operate in the United States, including charitable groups, social-welfare organizations, government agencies, and religious congregations. This sector also includes museums, libraries, hospitals, conservation groups, private schools, and the like.

City Year Inc., a not-for-profit organization, supports the community service efforts of people in their late teens and early twenties. The organization offers a number of programs in which volunteers can participate. Its signature program, the City Year Youth Corps, invites 6,000 volunteers between the ages of 17 and 24 to commit to a year of full-time community service in activities such as mentoring and tutoring inner-city school children, helping to restore and reclaim public spaces, and staffing youth summer camps. The organization also partners with for-profit corporations such as Microsoft, Cisco, and Pepsi to fund and implement its efforts.[16]

Q Answer the **Concept Check** questions.

Public and Collective Ownership of Business

One alternative to private ownership is some form of public ownership owned and operated by a government unit or agency. In the United States, local governments often own parking structures and water systems.

Collective ownership establishes an organization referred to as a cooperative (or co-op), whose owners join forces to operate all or part of the activities in their firm or industry. Currently, about 250 million people worldwide are employed by cooperatives.[17] Cooperatives allow small businesses to pool their resources on purchases, marketing, equipment, distribution, and the like. Discount savings can be split among members. Cooperatives can share equipment and expertise. During difficult economic times, members find a variety of ways to support each other. Ocean Spray is an example of an agricultural cooperative.

Q Answer the **Concept Check** questions.

Organizing a Corporation

A corporation is a legal structure, but it also requires a certain organizational structure that is more complex than the structure of a sole proprietorship or a partnership. This is why people often think of a corporation as a large entity, even though it does not have to be a specific size.

Types of Corporations

Corporations fall into three categories: domestic, foreign, and alien. A firm is considered a domestic corporation in the state where it is incorporated. When a company does business in states other than the one where it has filed incorporation papers, it is registered as a foreign corporation in each of those states. A firm incorporated in one nation that operates in another is known as an alien corporation where it operates. Many firms—particularly large corporations with operations scattered around the world—may operate under all three of these designations.

The Corporate Charter

Each state has a specific procedure for incorporating a business. Most states require at least three incorporators—the individuals who create the corporation. In addition, the new corporation must select a name that is different from names used by other businesses. ▣ **Figure 5.5** lists the ten elements that most states require for chartering a corporation.

The information provided in the articles of incorporation forms the basis on which a state grants a corporate charter, which is the legal document that formally establishes a corporation. After securing the charter, the owners prepare the company's bylaws, which describe the rules and procedures for its operation.

Corporate Management

Regardless of its size, every corporation has levels of management and ownership. ▣ **Figure 5.6** illustrates those that are typical—although a smaller firm might not contain all five of these. These levels range from stockholders down to supervisory management.

Stock Ownership and Stockholder Rights

At the top of Figure 5.6 are **stockholders**. They buy shares of stock in the corporation, becoming part owners. Some companies, such as family businesses, are owned by relatively few stockholders, and the stock is generally unavailable to outsiders. In such a firm, known as a private, closed, or closely held corporation, the stockholders also control and manage all of the company's activities.

In contrast, an open corporation, also called a publicly held corporation, sells stock to the general public, establishing diversified ownership and often leading to a broader scope of operations than those of a closed corporation. Publicly held corporations usually hold annual stockholders' meetings. During these meetings, managers report on corporate activities, and stockholders vote on any decisions that require their approval, including elections of officers. Walmart holds the nation's largest stockholder meeting at the University of Arkansas Bud Walton Arena; approximately 16,000 people attend.

Stockholders' role in the corporation depends on the class of stock they own. Shares are usually classified as common or preferred stock. Although owners of **preferred stock** have limited voting rights, they are entitled to receive dividends before holders of common stock. If the corporation is dissolved, they have first claims on assets, once debtors are repaid. Owners of **common stock** have voting rights but only residual claims on the firm's assets, which means they are last to receive any income distributions. Because one share is typically worth only one vote, small stockholders generally have little influence on corporate management actions.

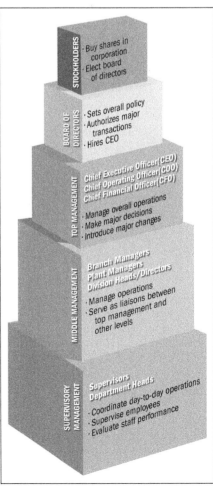

· Name and Address of the Corporation
· Corporate Objectives
· Type and Amount of Stock to Issue
· Expected Life of the Corporation
· Financial Capital at the Time of Incorporation
· Provisions for Transferring Shares of Stock among Owners
· Provisions for Regulating Internal Corporate Affairs
· Address of the Business Office Registered with the State of Incorporation
· Names and Addresses of the Initial Board of Directors
· Names and Addresses of the Incorporators

See **FIGURE 5.5 Traditional Articles of Incorporation**

STOCKHOLDERS
· Buy shares in corporation
· Elect board of directors

BOARD OF DIRECTORS
· Sets overall policy
· Authorizes major transactions
· Hires CEO

TOP MANAGEMENT
Chief Executive Officer (CEO)
Chief Operating Officer (COO)
Chief Financial Officer (CFO)
· Manage overall operations
· Make major decisions
· Introduce major changes

MIDDLE MANAGEMENT
Branch Managers
Plant Managers
Division Heads/Directors
· Manage operations
· Serve as liaisons between top management and other levels

SUPERVISORY MANAGEMENT
Supervisors
Department Heads
· Coordinate day-to-day operations
· Supervise employees
· Evaluate staff performance

See **FIGURE 5.6 Levels of Management in a Corporation**

Board of Directors

Stockholders elect a **board of directors**—the corporation's governing body. The board sets overall policy, authorizes major transactions involving the corporation, and hires the chief executive officer (CEO). Most boards include both inside directors (corporate executives) and outside directors—people who are not otherwise employed by the organization. Sometimes the corporation's top executive also chairs the board. Generally, outside directors are also stockholders, so they have a financial stake in the company's performance.

Corporate Officers and Managers

The CEO and other members of top management—such as the chief operating officer (COO), chief financial officer (CFO), and chief information officer (CIO)—make most major corporate decisions. Managers at the middle management level handle the company's ongoing operational functions. At the first tier of management, supervisory personnel coordinate day-to-day operations, assign specific tasks to employees, and evaluate job performance.

Today's CEOs and CFOs are bound by stricter regulations than in the past. They must verify in writing the accuracy of their firm's financial statements, and the process for nominating candidates for the board has become more complex. In short, more checks and balances are in place for the governance of corporations.

Q Answer the **Concept Check** questions.

When Businesses Join Forces

Today's business environment contains many complex relationships among businesses as well as not-for-profit organizations. Two firms may team up to develop a product or co-market products. One company may buy out another. Large corporations may split into smaller units. The list of alliances is as varied as the organizations themselves, but the major trends in corporate ownership include mergers and acquisitions and joint ventures.

Mergers and Acquisitions (M&A)

In recent years, mergers and acquisitions among U.S. corporations hit an all-time high. Airlines, financial institutions, telecommunications companies, and media corporations are just a few of the types of businesses that merged into giants. For example, American Airlines merged with US Airways to form one entity known as American Airlines. The merger will create savings and new revenue as the two companies consolidate. Together, the airlines form the largest carrier in the world.[18]

The terms *merger* and *acquisition* are often used interchangeably, but their meanings are different. In a **merger**, two or more firms combine to form one company. In an **acquisition**, one firm purchases the other. This means that not only does the buyer acquire the firm's property and assets; it also takes on any debt obligations.

Mergers can be classified as vertical, horizontal, or conglomerate. A **vertical merger** combines firms operating at different levels in the production and marketing process—the combination of a manufacturer and a large retailer, for instance. A vertical merger pursues one of two primary goals: (1) to ensure adequate flows of raw materials and supplies needed for a firm's products or (2) to increase distribution.

A **horizontal merger** joins firms in the same industry. This is done for the purpose of diversification, increasing customer bases, cutting costs, or expanding product lines. This type of merger is particularly popular in the auto and health care industries. Volkswagen now owns the Porsche brand, while CVS Health purchased another firm's Medicaid prescription business.

A **conglomerate merger** combines unrelated firms. The most common reasons for a conglomerate merger are to diversify, spur sales growth, or spend a cash surplus that might otherwise make the firm a tempting target for a takeover effort. Conglomerate mergers may join firms in totally unrelated industries. General Electric is, in fact, well known for its conglomerate mergers, including its ownership of health care services and airplane engines. Experts debate whether conglomerate mergers are beneficial. The usual argument in favor of such mergers is that a company can use its management expertise to succeed in a variety of industries. But the obvious drawback is that a huge conglomerate can spread its resources too thin to be dominant in any one market.

Joint Ventures: Specialized Partnerships

A **joint venture** is a partnership between companies formed for a specific undertaking. Sometimes a company enters into a joint venture with a local firm, sharing the operation's costs, risks, management, and profits with its local partner. This is particularly common when a firm wants to enter into business in a foreign market. French carmaker Renault recently won approval from Chinese authorities to begin production of SUVs in China in a joint venture with Dongfeng Motor Group, allowing Renault entry into the world's largest auto market.[19]

Joint ventures between for-profit firms and not-for-profit organizations are becoming more and more common. These partnerships provide great benefits for both parties. Not-for-profit organizations receive the funding, marketing exposure, and sometimes manpower they might not otherwise generate.

Q Answer the **Concept Check** questions.

WP LS Go to your WileyPLUS Learning Space course for video episodes, examples, art, tables, Concept Checks, practice, and resources that will help you succeed in this course.

Reading for
STARTING YOUR OWN BUSINESS

WP LS Go to your WileyPLUS Learning Space course for video episodes, examples, art, tables, Concept Checks, practice, and resources that will help you success in this course.

What Is an Entrepreneur?

An **entrepreneur** is a person who seeks a profitable opportunity and takes the necessary risks to set up and operate a business. The history of business is full of examples of entrepreneurs who through their innovation and hard work created very successful companies. From John Deere (Deere and Company) to Thomas Edison (General Electric), Henry Ford (Ford Motor Company), Sam Walton (Walmart), and Steve Jobs (Apple), these entrepreneurs' visions for the future were the driving force behind revolutions in farming, manufacturing, retailing, and computer technology.

Entrepreneurs differ from many small-business owners. Although many small-business owners possess the same drive, creative energy, and desire to succeed, what makes entrepreneurs different is that one of their major goals is expansion and growth. By contrast, small-business owners without a strong entrepreneurial spirit may prefer to keep their businesses small. For them, maintaining a small, profitable enterprise may be more important than growth.

Entrepreneurs also differ from managers. Managers are employees of a firm who direct the efforts of others to achieve the organization's goals. Entrepreneurs may also perform a managerial role, but their overriding responsibility is to use the resources of their organizations to accomplish their goals. Those resources may include:

- employees
- money
- equipment
- facilities

Studies have identified certain personality traits and behaviors common to entrepreneurs that differ from those required for managerial success. One of these traits is the willingness to assume the risks involved in starting a new venture. Others want a challenge or a different quality of life. And still others want to pursue their vision. Regardless of their motivation, entrepreneurs are a breed apart from traditional business managers, for they are the ones whose drive, energy, and creativity create new jobs, new businesses, and even whole new industries. The characteristics of successful entrepreneurs are examined in detail later in this chapter.

Q Answer the
Concept Check questions.

The Environment for Entrepreneurs

When considering a new venture, entrepreneurs are wise to consider broader socioeconomic trends as well as those connected with their particular business. Several ongoing trends that support and expand the opportunities for entrepreneurs are globalization, education, and information technology. Each of these factors is discussed in the following sections.

Globalization

The next time you look into your closet, reach for your smart phone, or bend down to tie your shoes, you are likely experiencing one of the results of globalization: low-cost, high-quality products produced in developing nations. These products and a host of others are often created by companies founded by entrepreneurs.

Education

You don't have to major in business to become an entrepreneur, but students who do major in entrepreneurship or take entrepreneurship courses are more likely to start their own business or help someone else start one.[1] The past two decades have brought tremendous growth in the number of educational opportunities for would-be entrepreneurs. Today, many U.S. universities offer full-fledged majors in entrepreneurship, dozens of others offer an emphasis in entrepreneurship, and hundreds more offer one or two courses in how to start a business. In fact, you don't have to wait for graduation to develop your first start-up. FedEx, Facebook, Microsoft, and Google were all conceived by college students. And who would have thought that student housing was the best place to start a company? Michael Dell did exactly that, turning his University of Texas dorm room into the first company headquarters for Dell Computer.[2] Learning about business is important for entrepreneurs, but the opportunity to put your ideas into practice is—as they say in the MasterCard commercials—"priceless."

Information Technology

The explosion in information technology (IT) has provided one of the biggest boosts for entrepreneurs, such as Jack Dorsey of Twitter. As computer and communications technologies have merged and dropped dramatically in cost, entrepreneurs have gained tools that help them compete with large companies. IT helps entrepreneurs

- work quickly and efficiently
- provide immediate and attentive customer service
- increase sales

In fact, technology has leveled the playing field to the point that, with the use of smart phones and other wireless devices, along with instant distribution on the web, a dorm room innovator can compete with a much larger firm.

Social networking has further transformed the business environment for entrepreneurs. Mark Zuckerberg's entrepreneurial venture Facebook opened up vast new opportunities for other entrepreneurs. According to a recent study, more than 90 percent of successful companies now use at least one social media tool. One entrepreneur who embraces the full impact of social media on her business is Brandi Temple, who started an online children's clothing company called Lolly Wolly Doodle. Based in North Carolina, this retailer does more business on Facebook than many global brands. With over $11 million in annual sales, Temple's strategy is simple. Children's clothing items are posted on the company's website as well as on Facebook, where customers (mostly busy moms) do their shopping. Lolly Wolly Doodle has more than 1 million followers on its Facebook page.[3]

Q Answer the **Concept Check** questions.

The Process of Starting a New Venture

The examples of entrepreneurs presented so far have introduced many different types of businesses. This section discusses the process of choosing an idea for a new venture and transforming the idea into a working business.

Selecting a Business Idea

In choosing an idea for your business, the two most important considerations are (1) finding something you are passionate about and (2) determining whether your idea can satisfy a need in the marketplace. People willingly work hard doing something they love, and the experience will bring personal fulfillment. Success also depends on customers, so would-be entrepreneurs must also be sure that the idea they choose has interest in the marketplace. The most successful entrepreneurs tend to operate in industries in which a great deal of change is taking place and in which customers have difficulty pinpointing their precise needs. These industries allow entrepreneurs to capitalize on their strengths (such as creativity, hard work, and vision) to build customer relationships.

Nevertheless, examples of outstanding entrepreneurial success occur in every industry. Whether you want to build a business based on your grandmother's cookie recipes or know that you have a better idea for tax-preparation software, you are more likely to succeed if you ask yourself the right questions from the beginning.

Consider the following guidelines as you think about your business ideas:

- List your interests and abilities. Include your values and beliefs, your goals and dreams, things you like and dislike doing, and your job experiences.

- Make another list of the types of businesses that match your interests and abilities.
- Read newspapers and business and consumer magazines to learn about demographic and economic trends that identify future needs for products that no one yet offers.
- Carefully evaluate existing goods and services, looking for ways you can improve them.
- Decide on a business that matches what you want and offers profit potential.
- Conduct marketing research to determine whether your business idea will attract enough customers to earn a profit.
- Learn as much as you can about your industry, your goods or service, and your competitors.
- Read surveys that project growth in various industries.

Creating a Business Plan

Large or small, every business needs a plan in order to succeed. While there are tales of firms launched from an idea scribbled on a napkin at a restaurant or sketched out on graph paper on a college campus, the idea must be backed by a solid plan in order to become reality. A **business plan** is a written document that provides an orderly statement of a company's goals, the methods by which it intends to achieve these goals, and the standards by which it will measure its achievements. The business plan is often the document that secures financing for a firm and creates a framework for the organization.

In the past, many entrepreneurs launched their ventures without creating formal business plans. Although planning is an integral part of managing in contemporary business, what often defines entrepreneurs is the ability to seize opportunities as they arise and change course as necessary. Flexibility seems to be the key to business start-ups, especially in rapidly changing markets. However, due to the inherent risks of starting a business, it has become apparent that at least some planning is not only advisable but necessary, particularly if an entrepreneur is seeking funds from outside sources. Business plans give the organization a sense of purpose. They identify the firm's mission and goals. They create measurable standards and outline a strategy for reaching company objectives.

The Business Plan

A typical business plan includes the following sections:

- An *executive summary* that briefly answers the who, what, where, when, why, and how questions for the firm.
- *The company's mission and the vision.* For an example of a firm's mission statement, visit a business's website.
- *An outline of what makes the company unique.* Why start a business that's just like hundreds of others? An effective business plan describes what distinguishes the firm and its products from the rest of the pack. For example, TOMS Shoes illustrates a unique business model with its "one-for-one" donation program.
- *Customers.* A business plan identifies the company's prospective customers and how it will serve their needs.
- *Competition.* A business plan addresses the firm's existing and potential competitors as legitimate entities, with a strategy for creating superior or unique offerings. Studying the competition can provide valuable information about what works and what doesn't in the marketplace.
- *Financial evaluation of the industry and market conditions.* This knowledge helps develop a credible financial forecast and budget.
- *Assessment of the risks.* Every business undertaking involves risks. A solid business plan acknowledges these and outlines a strategy for dealing with them.
- *Résumés of principals*—especially in plans written to obtain financing.

Whether a firm's intention is to revolutionize an entire industry on a global scale or improve the lives of children by providing them with shoes, the business plan is a major factor in its success.

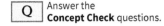
Answer the **Concept Check** questions.

Financing Your Venture

A key issue in any business plan is financing. Requirements for **seed capital**, the funds used to launch a company, depend on the nature of the business. Seed capital can range from as high as several million dollars—say, for the purchase of a McDonald's franchise in a lucrative area—to as low as $1,000 for website design. Many entrepreneurs rely on personal savings or loans from business associates, family members, or even friends for start-up funds. ⬛ **Table 6.1** lists the common sources of start-up capital.

See **TABLE 6.1: Where does funding come from for entrepreneurial start-ups?**

Self-Financing

Financing a venture using your own funds has many advantages over other methods. Since the funds belong to you as the entrepreneur, they can be used without restrictions or conditions. There also is no need to repay the funds, nor must you give up ownership of the venture in exchange for funding. At the very earliest stages of a new venture, entrepreneurs should use their own funds to advance their ideas and business processes. Not only does it help validate the entrepreneur's ideas, but it demonstrates commitment to the project and shows prospective investors that the entrepreneur has "skin in the game." Spending their own money also forces entrepreneurs to be more creative in the use of the funds.

However, at some point the cash demands of a growing business may exceed an entrepreneur's resources, and he or she will have to seek out additional sources of funds. **Other People's Money (OPM)** is the general term for the funds businesspeople raise from others. By using OPM, entrepreneurs can leverage their own investment, allowing their businesses to grow faster while sharing financial risks with others. Outside funds can be raised in a number of ways including traditional debt financing, equity financing, and more recently crowdfunding. The following sections detail each of these methods.

Debt Financing

When entrepreneurs use **debt financing**, they borrow money that they must repay. Loans from banks, finance companies, credit-card companies, and family or friends are all sources of debt financing. Although some entrepreneurs charge business expenses to personal credit cards because they are relatively easy to obtain, high interest rates make this source of funding expensive.

Many banks turn down requests for loans to fund start-ups, fearful of the high risk such ventures entail. This has been particularly true over the last several years. Only a small percentage of start-ups raise seed capital through bank loans, although some new firms can get Small Business Administration (SBA)–backed loans, as discussed in Chapter 5. Applying for a bank loan requires careful preparation. Bank loan officers want to see a business plan and will evaluate the entrepreneur's credit history. Because a start-up has not yet established a business credit history, banks often base lending decisions on evaluations of entrepreneurs' personal credit histories. Banks are more willing to make loans to entrepreneurs who have been in business for a while, show a profit on rising revenues, and need funds to finance expansion. Some entrepreneurs find that local community banks are more interested in business than are major national banks.

Equity Financing

To secure **equity financing**, entrepreneurs exchange a share of ownership in their company for money supplied by one or more investors. Entrepreneurs invest their own money along with funds supplied by other people and firms that become co-owners of the start-ups. An entrepreneur does not have to repay equity funds. Instead, investors share in the success of the business. Sources of equity financing include family and friends, business partners, venture capital firms, and private investors.

A **venture capitalist** is a business organization or a group of private individuals that invests in early-stage, high-potential, and growth companies. Venture capitalists often back companies in high-technology industries such as biotechnology. ⬛ **Figure 6.1**

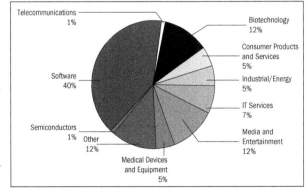

See **FIGURE 6.1 Venture Capital Investments**

Source: Data from PwC: MoneyTree™ Report, 2014. Data: Thomson Reuters, https://www.pwcmoneytree.com, accessed February 13, 2015.

details venture capital investment by sector during a recent period. In exchange for taking a risk with their own funds, these investors expect high rates of return, along with a stake in the company. Typical terms for accepting venture capital include agreement on how much the company is worth, how much stock both the investors and the founders will retain, control of the company's board, payment of dividends, and the period of time during which the founders are prohibited from seeking further investors. When investing, venture capitalists look for a combination of extremely rare qualities, such as innovative technology, potential for rapid growth, a well-developed business model, and an impressive management team.

An **angel investor**, a wealthy individual who invests money directly in new ventures in exchange for equity, represents another source of investment capital for start-up firms. In contrast to venture capitalists, angels focus primarily on new ventures and, because most entrepreneurs have trouble finding wealthy private investors, angel networks are formed to match business angels with start-ups in need of capital. One such network of angel investors is Keiretsu Forum, an association with worldwide affiliates.[4]

New Financing Methods

In addition to more traditional funding sources, a number of interesting new ways exist to raise funds for entrepreneurial ventures. The Internet has made these methods possible by **crowdfunding**, effectively linking entrepreneurs directly with their supporters.

A growing list of web-based businesses has been established specifically to facilitate these exchanges, which include direct donations, patronage, and advanced orders.[5] For many years, philanthropic groups have raised money for their causes by soliciting online donations. Social entrepreneurs may use this approach to help raise money for victims of natural disasters. Alternatively, a musical group or other artist may use a web-based appeal to raise money to pursue his or her career. This approach is a replay of the patronage model from centuries ago, when wealthy individuals would pay an artist to create art for them. Much of the great art and music of the Renaissance was produced this way. Entrepreneurs can also use crowdfunding sites to obtain pre-orders for their products. In this approach, an individual or group will make an appeal for funds to start or expand their business in exchange for their product.

Government Support for New Ventures

Federal, state, and local governments support new ventures in a number of ways, as discussed in Chapter 5. Through the SBA, state and local agencies offer entrepreneurs information, resources, and sometimes access to financing. Some community agencies interested in encouraging business development have implemented a concept called a **business incubator** to provide low-cost shared business facilities to small start-up ventures. A typical incubator might section-off space in an abandoned plant and rent it to various small firms. Tenants often share clerical staff and other business services. The objective is that, after a few months or years, the fledgling business will be ready to move out and operate on its own. More than 1,250 business incubator programs operate in the United States, with about 7,000 worldwide. Ninety-four percent are run by not-for-profit organizations focused on economic development. Nearly half of all incubators focus on new technology businesses, and more than half operate in urban areas.[6]

Another way to encourage entrepreneurship is through *enterprise zones,* specific geographic areas designated for economic revitalization. Enterprise zones encourage investment, often in distressed areas, by offering tax advantages and incentives to businesses locating within the boundaries of the zone. The state of Florida, for example, has 65 enterprise zones and allows a business located within urban zones to take tax credits for 20 or 30 percent of wages paid to new employees who reside within the urban enterprise zone. Colorado has 16 zones, and Ohio has over 360 active zones.

The government may also support new ventures through direct procurement of goods and services. The *Commerce Business Daily* is a U.S. government publication that lists opportunities for entrepreneurs to obtain government contracts. Many government agencies such as NASA, the Department of Defense (DOD), and the Department of Energy (DOE) have active research programs and support entrepreneurs and business organizations working in their areas of responsibility.[7]

Q Answer the **Concept Check** questions.

Reasons to Choose Entrepreneurship

People choose to become entrepreneurs for many reasons. Some are motivated by dissatisfaction with the traditional work world—they want a more flexible schedule or freedom to make all the decisions. Others launch businesses to fill a gap in goods or services that they could use themselves. Still others start their own firms out of financial necessity. Regardless of the particular motivation, entrepreneurs seem to share the following characteristics.

Pursuing Your Vision

Entrepreneurs generally begin with a *vision*—an overall idea for how to make their business idea a success. And they pursue this vision with relentless passion. Russell Simmons, a successful entrepreneur, is credited with bringing hip-hop culture to the mainstream and to every facet of business, media, and fashion. His company, Rush Communications, has grown to include music, film, video games, publishing, fashion, television, and even financial services. It is one of the largest African American–owned entertainment companies in the United States. Simmons was recently named of the top 25 most influential people of the last 25 years by *USA Today*.[8] However, just making a discovery is not enough; entrepreneurs must know how to turn their vision into a profitable business. Although Sir Alexander Fleming discovered penicillin, he was unable to turn his discovery into a cure for bacterial infections. It took others to develop the process to produce usable quantities of the drug.[9]

Being Your Own Boss

The freedom to make all the decisions—being your own boss—is one of the biggest lures of entrepreneurship. When Michael Grondahl purchased a struggling gym, little did he know that more than two decades later, he would be disrupting the fitness industry's model of locked-in annual membership contracts and high monthly fees. Based in New Hampshire, Planet Fitness offers its members a no "gymtimidation," judgment-free zone and a unique environment where anyone can be comfortable. Offering the same equipment and amenities as its competitors, Planet Fitness does not require a contract for sometimes-fickle gym members. For a $10 monthly fee, members join without the pressure of an annual commitment. A national brand partner of NBC's reality TV hit, *The Biggest Loser,* Planet Fitness has more than 850 locations.[10]

Achieving Financial Success

Entrepreneurs are wealth creators. Many start their ventures with the specific goal of becoming rich—or at least financially successful. Often they believe they have an idea for a superior product and they want to be the first to bring it to market, reaping the financial rewards as a result. Entrepreneurs believe they won't achieve their greatest success by working for someone else, and they're generally right. Of course, the downside is that, when they fail, they don't have the cushion of employment.

> Q Answer the **Concept Check** questions.

Categories of Entrepreneurs

Entrepreneurs apply their talents in different situations. These differences can be classified into distinct categories:

- classic entrepreneurs
- serial entrepreneurs
- social entrepreneurs

A **classic entrepreneur** identifies business opportunities and allocates available resources to tap those markets. Dana Hood is a classic entrepreneur. She recognized that dog owners want special attention for their pets when they leave those animals in the care of others. She also knew that pet owners spent close to $6 billion for boarding and daycare centers during a recent year. So, when she founded For the Love of Dogs, a canine daycare center, she made certain that her services stood out from the average kennel. Hood's firm offers customized services such as grooming and anesthesia-free teeth-cleaning, a treadmill, swimming pools, and water misters to cool off customers' pets during hot weather. In addition, pet owners can purchase high-end organic foods and treats, beds, toys, and other retail goods.[11]

While a classic entrepreneur starts a new company by identifying a business opportunity and allocating resources to tap a new market, a **serial entrepreneur** starts one business, runs it, and then starts and runs additional businesses in succession.

Some entrepreneurs focus on solving society's challenges through their businesses. A **social entrepreneur** recognizes a societal problem and uses business principles to develop innovative solutions. Social entrepreneurs are pioneers of innovations that benefit humanity. Conscious Commerce, co-founded by actress and social entrepreneur Olivia Wilde, encourages companies to become better corporate citizens. Conscious Commerce pairs a company's brand with a cause. Consumers may choose from among a number of participating companies, such as TOMS Shoes, Method cleaning products, Anthropologie, Aveda, and Kiehl's. Wilde's company recently raised $100,000 for New Light India, a community-development project serving women and children in Kolkata, India.[12]

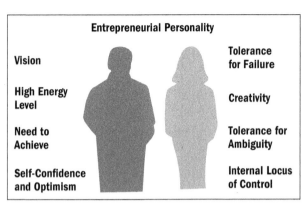

Entrepreneurial Personality

Vision

High Energy Level

Need to Achieve

Self-Confidence and Optimism

Tolerance for Failure

Creativity

Tolerance for Ambiguity

Internal Locus of Control

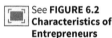 See **FIGURE 6.2 Characteristics of Entrepreneurs**

Characteristics of Successful Entrepreneurs

People who start businesses are pioneers in their own right. They aren't satisfied with the status quo and want to achieve certain goals on their own terms. They also tend to possess specific personality traits. Researchers who study successful entrepreneurs report that they are more likely to be curious, passionate, self-motivated, honest, courageous, and flexible. The eight traits summarized in ■ **Figure 6.2** are especially important for people who want to succeed as entrepreneurs.

Entrepreneurs work hard because they want to excel. Their strong competitive drive helps them enjoy the challenge of reaching difficult goals and promotes dedication to personal success. Entrepreneurs believe in their ability to succeed, and they instill their optimism in others. Often their optimism resembles fearlessness in the face of difficult odds. They see opportunities where others see danger lurking. Entrepreneurs often succeed by sheer will and the ability to try and try again when others would give up. They also view setbacks and failures as learning experiences and are not easily discouraged or disappointed when things don't go as planned. When things go well, it's easy to take personal credit. But when poor business decisions result in failure, it's a bit more difficult. Truly successful entrepreneurs are willing to take responsibility for their mistakes.

Entrepreneurs work long and hard to realize their visions. Many entrepreneurs work full-time at their regular day jobs and spend weeknights and weekends launching their start-ups. Entrepreneurs often work alone or with a very small staff, which means that they often wear most—if not all—of the hats required to get the business going. Most entrepreneurs spend at least 70 hours a week on their new business.[13] Thus they need a high level of energy in order to succeed.

If this sounds like you, then you may have what it takes to be an entrepreneur.

[Q] Answer the **Concept Check** questions.

The Franchising Alternative

While we might all like to think we can come up with the next "new big thing," the reality is that many entrepreneurs are not able to transform their business ideas into successful enterprises.[14] As we will see in Chapter 12, businesspeople face significant challenges in turning new ideas into successful products. And not only must entrepreneurs worry about developing their products; they also have to work diligently to

- establish their business operations
- hire employees
- obtain financing
- contract with suppliers
- set up product distribution, marketing, and promotion

Failure in any one of these areas can lead to failure of the entire venture.

To reduce these risks, some entrepreneurs may choose to follow business models that have been developed and successfully implemented by others. Franchising is just such an approach, where an entrepreneur acquires a license to use a company's name, suppliers, know-how, and advertising in his or her own business. For entrepreneurs, franchises often combine the best of both worlds, offering them the ability to develop their own business while at the same time enjoying the advantages of being part of a larger organization. **Franchising** is a contractual business arrangement between a manufacturer or another supplier and a dealer, such as a restaurant operator or a retailer. The contract specifies the methods by which the dealer markets the product of the supplier. Franchises can involve both goods and services, such as food staff and servers. The top ten franchises from *Entrepreneur*'s Franchise 500 are shown in ▨ **Table 6.2**. The ranking is based on a set of criteria developed by *Entrepreneur,* and the annual list is in its 36th year.

See **TABLE 6.2: Can you name the Top Ten Franchises?**

The Franchising Sector

Franchised businesses are a huge part of the U.S. economy, accounting for nearly 9 million jobs in the U.S. workforce. The International Franchise Association reported that franchising is responsible for more than 780,000 businesses at a gross value of $890 billion. Business sectors currently experiencing the most growth are quick-service restaurants, retail food, and personal and business services.[15]

Franchising overseas is also a growing trend for businesses whose goal is to expand into foreign markets. It seems that, anywhere you go in the world, you can get a McDonald's burger. But other international franchises are also common. Baskin-Robbins—owned by Dunkin' Brands—has more than 7,300 stores worldwide in such countries as Australia, Canada, China, Japan, Malaysia, and India.[16]

Franchising Agreements

The two principals in a franchising agreement are the franchisee and the franchisor. The individual or business firm purchasing the franchise is called the **franchisee**. This business owner agrees to sell the goods or services of the franchisor under certain terms. The **franchisor** is the firm whose products are sold by the franchisee. For example, McDonald's Corp. is a franchisor. Your local McDonald's restaurant owner is most likely a franchisee.

Franchise agreements can be complex. They involve an initial purchase fee plus agreed-on start-up costs. Because the franchisee is representing the franchisor's brand, the franchisor usually stipulates the purchase of certain ingredients or equipment, pricing, and marketing efforts. The total start-up cost for a SUBWAY franchise may be as low as $78,600.[17] In contrast, McDonald's is one of the more expensive franchises—total start-up costs can run well over $1 million. For this reason, businesspeople interested in purchasing a more expensive franchise often group together.

Benefits and Challenges of Franchising

Like any other type of business arrangement, franchising has its benefits and drawbacks. Benefits for the franchisor include opportunities for expansion that might not otherwise be available. A franchised business can move into new geographic locations, including overseas, employing workers with knowledge of local preferences. A good franchisor can manage a much larger and more complex business—with fewer direct employees—than could be handled without the franchise option.

Franchising can also have its downside—for both franchisors and franchisees. For the franchisor, if its franchisees fail in any way, that failure reflects on the brand as well as the bottom line. The same holds true for the franchisee: A firm that is mismanaged at the top level can spell doom for the people who are actually running the individual units. Of course, in offering franchise opportunities, the franchisor—often the founder of what was once a small business—loses absolute control over every aspect of the business. This uncertainty can make the process of selecting the right franchisees to carry out the company's mission a difficult one.[18]

Because franchises are so closely linked to their brand, franchisors and franchisees must work well together to maintain standards of quality in their goods and services. If customers are unhappy with their experience at one franchise location, they might avoid stopping at another one several miles away, even if the second one is owned and operated by someone else. This is especially true where food is involved. The discovery of tainted meat or produce at one franchise restaurant can negatively affect the entire chain. A potential franchisee

Q | Answer the
Concept Check questions.

would be wise to thoroughly research the financial performance and reputation of the franchisor, using resources such as other franchisees and the Federal Trade Commission.

Promoting Intrapreneurship

Franchising illustrates one way to integrate entrepreneurs into established businesses. Companies can also try to foster an entrepreneurial spirit in their employees by encouraging **intrapreneurship**, the process of promoting innovation within their organizational structures. Today's fast-changing business climate compels established firms to innovate continually to maintain their competitive advantages. Another form of intrapreneurship is a **skunkworks**, a project initiated by an employee who conceives an idea, convinces top management of its potential, and then recruits human and other resources from within the company to turn that idea into a commercial project.

Many companies encourage intrapreneurship—some organizations, including Google, have formalized the role of the intrapreneur through official positions such as the "Entrepreneur In Residence" (EIR) or "Chief Innovation Officer."[19]

Q | Answer the
Concept Check questions.

WP LS Go to your WileyPLUS Learning Space course for video episodes, examples, art, tables, Concept Checks, practice, and resources that will help you success in this course.

MANAGEMENT, LEADERSHIP, AND INTERNAL ORGANIZATION

7

What Is Management?

Management is the process of achieving organizational objectives through people and other resources. The manager's job is to combine human and technical resources in the best way possible to achieve the company's goals. Management principles and concepts apply to not-for-profit organizations as well as profit-seeking firms. A city mayor, the executive director of Goodwill Industries International, and a superintendent of schools all perform the managerial functions described later in this chapter. Management happens at many levels, from that of the manager of a family-owned restaurant to a national sales manager for a major manufacturer.

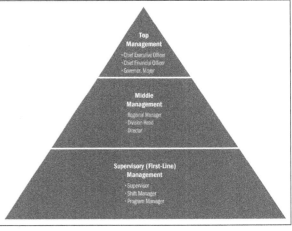

The Management Hierarchy

A firm's management usually has three levels: top, middle, and supervisory. These levels of management form a management hierarchy, as shown in 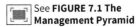 **Figure 7.1**. The hierarchy is the traditional structure found in most organizations. Managers at each level perform different activities. This hierarchy is often shown as a pyramid to illustrate that, at the top of the pyramid, the company president is supported by many other managers, with the numbers increasing as the job titles go from top to middle to supervisor.

See **FIGURE 7.1 The Management Pyramid**

The highest level of management is *top management*. Top managers include such positions as chief executive officer (CEO), chief financial officer (CFO), and executive vice president. Top managers devote most of their time to developing long-range plans for their organizations. They make decisions such as whether to introduce new products, purchase other companies, or enter new geographical markets. Top managers set a direction for their organization and inspire the company's executives and employees to achieve their vision for the company's future.

Middle management, the second tier in the management hierarchy, includes positions such as general managers, plant managers, division managers, and unit managers. Middle managers' attention focuses on specific operations, products, or customer groups within an organization. They are responsible for developing detailed plans and procedures to implement the firm's strategic plans. If top management decided to broaden the distribution of a product, a sales manager would be responsible for determining the number of sales personnel required. Middle managers are responsible for targeting the products and customers who are the source of the sales and profit growth expected by their CEOs. To achieve these goals, middle managers might budget money for product development, identify new uses for existing products, and improve the ways they train and motivate salespeople. Because they are more familiar with day-to-day operations than CEOs, middle managers often come up with new ways to increase sales or solve company problems.

Supervisory management, or first-line management, includes positions such as supervisor, shift manager, and team leader. These managers are directly responsible for assigning nonmanagerial employees to specific jobs and evaluating their performance. Managers at this first level of the hierarchy work directly with the employees who produce and sell the firm's goods and services. They are responsible for implementing middle managers' plans by motivating workers to accomplish daily, weekly, and monthly goals. A recent survey by the marketing research firm Temkin Group rated customer service at U.S. companies. All of the top-ranked firms have first-line managers who implement the firms' strategies to provide superior customer service.[1]

Skills Needed for Managerial Success

Managers at every level in the management hierarchy must exercise three basic types of skills: technical, human, and conceptual. All managers must acquire these skills in varying proportions, although the importance of each skill changes at different management levels.

Technical skills are the manager's ability to understand and use the techniques, knowledge, and tools and equipment of a specific discipline or department. Technical skills are especially important for first-line managers and become less important at higher levels of the management hierarchy. But most top executives started out as technical experts. The résumé of a vice president for information systems probably lists experience as a computer analyst, and that of a vice president for marketing usually shows a background in sales. Many firms, including Procter & Gamble and Marriott International, have increased training programs for first-line managers to boost technical skills and worker productivity.

Human skills are interpersonal skills that enable managers to work effectively with and through people. Human skills include the ability to communicate with, motivate, and lead employees to complete assigned activities. Managers need human skills to interact with people both inside and outside the organization. It would be tough for a manager to succeed without such skills, even though they must be adapted to different forms—for instance, mastering and communicating effectively with staff through e-mail, smart phones, videoconferencing, and text messaging, all of which are widely used in today's offices.

Conceptual skills determine a manager's ability to see the organization as a unified whole and to understand how each part of the overall organization interacts with other parts. These skills involve an ability to see the big picture by acquiring, analyzing, and interpreting information. Conceptual skills are especially important for top-level managers, who must develop long-range plans for the future direction of their organization.

Q | Answer the **Concept Check** questions.

Managers as Leaders

Above all else, business executives must demonstrate **leadership**, directing or inspiring people to attain certain goals. Great leaders do not all share the same qualities, but three traits are often mentioned: empathy (the ability to imagine yourself in someone else's position), self-awareness, and objectivity. Although it might seem as if empathy and objectivity are opposite traits, they do balance each other. Many leaders share other traits—courage, passion, commitment, innovation, and flexibility, to name a few.

Leadership involves the use of influence or power. This influence may come from one or more sources. One source of power is the leader's position in the company. A national sales manager has the authority to direct the activities of the sales force. Another source of power is a leader's expertise and experience. A first-line supervisor with expert machinist skills will most likely be respected by employees in the machining department.

Some leaders derive power from their personalities. Employees may admire a leader because they recognize an exceptionally kind, fair, humorous, energetic, or enthusiastic person. Admiration, inspiration, and motivation are especially important during difficult economic times or when a leader has to make tough decisions for the company.

Leadership Styles

The way a person uses power to lead others determines his or her leadership style. Leadership styles range along a continuum with autocratic leadership at one end and free-rein leadership at the other. *Autocratic leadership* focuses on the boss. Autocratic leaders make decisions on their own without consulting employees. They reach decisions, communicate them to subordinates, and expect automatic implementation.

Democratic leadership includes subordinates in the decision-making process. This leadership style centers on employees' contributions. Democratic leaders delegate assignments, ask employees for suggestions, and encourage participation. An important outgrowth of democratic leadership in business is **empowerment**, giving employees shared authority, responsibility, and decision making with their managers.

At the other end of the continuum is *free-rein leadership*. Free-rein leaders believe in minimal supervision and allow subordinates to make most of their own decisions. Free-rein leaders communicate with employees frequently, as the situation warrants. For the first decade of its existence, Google was proud of its free-rein leadership style. Engineers were encouraged to pursue any and all ideas; teams formed or disbanded on their own; employees spent as much or as little time as they wanted to on any given project. But as the firm entered its second decade, it became apparent that not every innovation was worth pursuing—and some valuable ideas were getting lost in the chaos. Concerned that some of the biggest ideas were getting squashed, the firm established a process for reviewing new project ideas in order to identify those most likely to succeed.[2]

Which Leadership Style Is Best?

No single leadership style is best for every firm in every situation. Sometimes leadership styles require change in order for a company to grow, as has been the case for Google. In a crisis, an autocratic leadership style might save the company—and sometimes the lives of customers and employees. This was the case when US Airways flight 1549 was forced to ditch into the Hudson River after hitting a wayward flock of Canada geese. Quick, autocratic decisions made by the pilot, Captain Chesley Sullenberger, resulted in the survival of everyone on board the flight. Yet, on the ground US Airways practiced a democratic style of leadership in which managers at many levels were empowered to take actions to help passengers and their families. For example, one executive arrived on the scene with a bag of emergency cash for passengers and credit cards for employees so they could purchase medicines, food, or anything else survivors needed.[3] A company that recognizes which leadership style works best for its employees, customers, and business conditions is most likely to choose the best leaders for its particular needs.

| Q | Answer the **Concept Check** questions. |

Leading by Setting a Vision for the Firm

All businesses begin with a **vision**, its founder's perception of what the organization wants to be or how it wants the world to be in an idealized way. Typically, a vision is a long-term view of the future. A vision statement is often emotive and inspirational.[4] The best vision statements serve as the target for a firm's actions, helping direct the company toward opportunities and differentiating it from its competitors. In articulating his vision for Apple Computer, founder Steve Jobs is reported to have said "An Apple on every desk."

Whether one is the president of a Fortune 500 company or a small business, a key part of a leader's vision for the firm is the **corporate culture**, an organization's system of principles, beliefs, and values. A corporate culture is typically shaped by the leaders who founded and developed the company and by those who succeed them. Although Google grew by leaps and bounds after its launch, the firm still tries to maintain the culture of innovation, creativity, and flexibility that co-founders Larry Page and Sergey Brin promoted from the beginning. Google now has offices around the world, staffed by thousands of workers who speak a multitude of languages.

Managers use symbols, rituals, ceremonies, and stories to reinforce corporate culture. The corporate culture at the Walt Disney Company is almost as famous as the original Disney characters themselves. In fact, Disney employees are known as cast members. All new employees attend training seminars in which they learn the language, customs, traditions, stories, product lines—everything there is to know about the Disney culture and its original founder, Walt Disney.[5]

Corporate culture can be strong and enduring, but sometimes it is forced to change to meet new demands in the business environment. A firm steeped in tradition and bureaucracy might have to shift to a leaner, more flexible culture in order to respond to shifts in technology or customer preferences. A firm that grows quickly—like Google—generally has to make some adjustments in its culture to accommodate more customers and employees.

| Q | Answer the **Concept Check** questions. |

Managers as Decision Makers

Managers make decisions every day. **Decision making** is the process of recognizing a problem or opportunity, evaluating alternative solutions, selecting and implementing an alternative, and assessing the results.

Delegating Work Assignments

One decision managers make involves assigning work to employees, a process called **delegation**. Employees might be responsible for answering customer calls, scooping ice cream, processing returns, making deliveries, opening or closing a store, cooking or serving food, contributing to new-product design, calculating a return on investment, or any of thousands of other tasks. Just as important, employees are given a certain amount of authority to make decisions.

As employees receive greater authority, they also must be accountable for their actions and decisions—they receive credit when things go well and must accept responsibility when they don't. Managers also must figure out the best way to delegate responsibilities to employees from different age groups, who may have very different interests and motivation.

Span of Management

The *span of management,* or span of control, is the number of employees a manager supervises. These employees are often referred to as direct reports. First-line managers have a wider span of management, monitoring the work of many employees. The span of management depends on many factors, including employees' training and the type of work performed. In recent years, a growing trend has resulted in wider spans of control as companies have reduced their layers of management to flatten their organizational structures, in the process increasing the decision-making responsibility they give employees.

Centralization and Decentralization

How widely should managers disperse decision-making authority throughout an organization? A company that emphasizes *centralization* retains decision making at the top of the management hierarchy. A company that emphasizes *decentralization* encourages decision making at lower levels. A trend toward decentralization has pushed decision making down to operating employees in many cases. Firms that have decentralized decision making believe that the change can improve their ability to serve customers. For example, the front-desk clerk at a hotel is much better equipped to fulfill a guest's request for a crib or a wake-up call than the hotel's general manager.

Managers as Planners

Planning is the process of anticipating future events and conditions and determining courses of action for achieving organizational objectives. Effective planning helps a business focus its vision, avoid costly mistakes, and seize opportunities. Planning should be flexible and responsive to changes in the business environment and should involve managers from all levels of the organization. As global competition intensifies, technology expands, and the speed at which firms bring new innovations to market increases, planning for the future becomes even more critical. For example, a CEO and other top-level managers need to plan for succession—those who will follow in their footsteps.

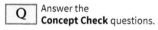
Answer the **Concept Check** questions.

Importance of Planning

Although some firms manage to launch without a clear strategic plan, they won't last long if they don't map out a future. Facebook founder Mark Zuckerberg claims he didn't have a major plan for the site at the beginning. But Facebook's global reach—and membership of more than 1.3 billion—means that Zuckerberg must plan the firm's next moves in order to outrun competitors and avoid major stumbles.

Types of Planning

Planning can be categorized by scope and breadth. Some plans are very broad and long range, whereas others are short range and very narrow, affecting selected parts of the organization rather than the company as a whole. Planning can be divided into the following categories: strategic, tactical, operational, and contingency, with each step including more specific information than the last. From the mission statement (described in the next section) to objectives to specific plans, each phase must fit into a comprehensive planning framework. The framework also must include narrow, functional plans aimed at individual employees and work areas relevant to individual tasks. These plans must fit within the firm's overall planning framework and help it reach objectives and achieve its mission.

- *Strategic planning* is the most far-reaching level of planning—the process of determining the primary objectives of an organization and then acting and allocating resources to achieve those objectives. Generally, a company's top executives have responsibility for strategic planning.
- *Tactical planning* involves implementing the activities specified by strategic plans. Tactical plans guide the current and near-term activities required to implement overall strategies. As part of a strategy to increase profitability, a firm may develop tactical plans around building sales revenue, reducing expense, or developing new products. Business executives often look at tactical plans as blueprints for the organization they want to create and the performance they want to achieve.
- *Operational planning* creates the detailed standards that guide implementation of tactical plans. This activity involves choosing specific work targets and assigning employees and teams to carry out plans. Unlike strategic planning, which focuses on the organization as a whole, operational planning deals with developing and implementing tactics in specific functional areas. The operation plan for Whole Foods' seafood labeling program includes partnering with the Safina Center (formerly Blue Ocean Institute) and Monterey Bay Aquarium and developing color-coded sustainability ratings for wild-caught seafood in collaboration with the Marine Stewardship Council.[6]
- *Contingency planning* takes into account all the possibilities that actual planning cannot foresee. Major accidents, natural disasters, and rapid economic downturns can throw even the best-laid plans into chaos. Many firms use contingency planning to address the possibility of business disruption from such events, allowing them to resume operations as quickly and as smoothly as possible while communicating with the public about what happened.

[Q] Answer the **Concept Check** questions.

The Strategic Planning Process

Strategic planning often makes the difference between an organization's success and failure. Strategic planning has formed the basis of many fundamental management decisions. Successful strategic planners typically follow the six steps shown in 🖩 **Figure 7.2**.

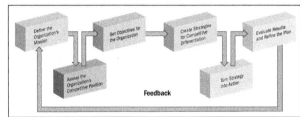

Defining the Organization's Mission

The first step in strategic planning is to translate the firm's vision into a **mission statement**—a written description of an organization's business intentions and aims. It is an enduring statement of a firm's purpose, possibly highlighting the scope of operations, the market it seeks to serve, and the ways it will attempt to set itself apart from competitors. A mission statement guides the actions of employees and publicizes the company's reasons for existence.

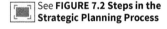 See **FIGURE 7.2 Steps in the Strategic Planning Process**

Assessing Your Competitive Position

Once a mission statement has been created, the next step in the planning process is to determine the firm's current—or potential—position in the marketplace. The company's founder or top managers evaluate the factors that could help it grow or cause it to fail. A frequently used tool in this phase of strategic planning is the **SWOT analysis**. SWOT is an acronym for *strengths, weaknesses, opportunities*, and *threats*. By systematically evaluating all four of these factors, a firm can then develop the best strategies for gaining a competitive advantage. The framework for a SWOT analysis appears in 🖩 **Figure 7.3**.

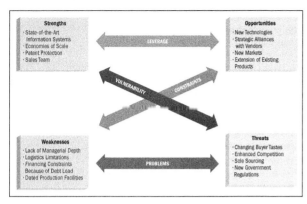

See **FIGURE 7.3 Elements of SWOT Analysis**

To evaluate their firm's strengths and weaknesses, managers may examine the functional areas—such as finance, marketing, information technology, and human resources—or each office, plant, or store. Entrepreneurs may focus on the individual skills and experience they bring to a new business.

SWOT analysis defines a firm's opportunities and threats. Threats might include an economic recession—during which consumers are not willing to pay a premium for products—or a change in federal regulations.

A SWOT analysis isn't carved in stone. Strengths, weaknesses, opportunities, and threats may shift over time. A strength may eventually become a weakness, and a threat may turn into an opportunity. But the analysis gives managers a place to start.

Setting Objectives for the Organization

In the next step in planning, a firm's leadership develops objectives. **Objectives** set guideposts by which managers define the organization's desired performance in such areas as new-product development, sales, customer service, growth, environmental and social responsibility, and employee satisfaction. Though the mission statement identifies a company's overall goals, objectives are more concrete and usually involve measurable (quantitative) outcomes.

Creating Strategies for Competitive Differentiation

Developing a mission statement and setting objectives point a business in a specific direction. But the firm needs to identify the strategies it will use to reach its destination ahead of the competition. The underlying goal of strategy development is *competitive differentiation*—the unique combination of a company's abilities and resources that set it apart from its competitors. A firm might differentiate itself by being the first to introduce a product such as the iPad to a widespread market; or by offering exceptional customer service, as Nordstrom does; or by offering values, as Costco does. College student Jack McDermott launched Balbus Speech, which developed apps with proven speech technology to help those with speech impediments. Downloaded thousands of times, the apps cost a fraction of what traditional competitors have charged in the past.[7]

Implementing the Strategy

Once the first four phases of the strategic planning process are complete, managers are ready to put those plans into action. Often, it's the middle managers or supervisors who actually implement a strategy. However, top company officials in some companies may still be reluctant to empower managers and employees with the authority to make decisions that could benefit the company. Companies that are willing to empower all employees generally reap the benefits. When Tony Hsieh, the CEO of Zappos, decided to sell the company to Amazon, he wanted to keep in place the customer service strategies that had made Zappos a success. Among those strategies is hiring people who want to "create fun and a little weirdness." Unlike most other companies, Zappos sets no time limit on how long customer service reps speak with customers; their chief goal is to empathize and take care of each customer's needs. The company values excellent customer service over the number of calls taken by its customer service staff.[8]

Monitoring and Adapting Strategic Plans

The final step in the strategic planning process is to monitor and adapt plans when the actual performance fails to meet goals. Monitoring involves securing feedback about performance. Managers might compare actual sales against forecasts; compile information from surveys; listen to complaints from the customer hotline; interview employees who are involved; and review reports prepared by production, finance, marketing, or other company units. If an Internet promotion doesn't result in enough response or sales, managers might evaluate whether to continue the advertisement, change it, or discontinue it. If a retailer observes customers buying more jeans when they are displayed near the front door, likely the display area will stay near the door—and perhaps be enlarged. Ongoing use of such tools as SWOT analysis and forecasting can help managers adapt their objectives and functional plans as changes occur.

Q | Answer the **Concept Check** questions.

Organizational Structures

Once plans have been developed, the next step in the management process typically is **organizing**—the process of blending human and material resources through a formal structure of tasks and authority: arranging work, dividing tasks among employees, and coordinating them to ensure implementation of plans and accomplishment of objectives. Organizing involves classifying and dividing work into manageable units with a logical structure. Managers staff the organization with the best possible employees for each job. Sometimes the organizing function requires studying a company's existing structure and determining whether to restructure it in order to operate more efficiently, cost effectively, or sustainably.

An **organization** is a structured group of people working together to achieve common goals. An organization features three key elements: human interaction, goal-directed activities, and structure. The organizing process, much of which is led by managers, should result in an overall structure that permits interactions among individuals and departments needed to achieve company goals.

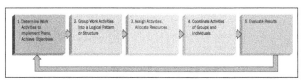

The steps involved in the organizing process are shown in **▦ Figure 7.4**. Managers first determine the specific activities needed to implement plans and achieve goals. Next, they group these work activities into a logical structure. Then they assign work to specific employees and give the people the resources they need to complete it. Managers coordinate the work of different groups and employees within the firm. Finally, they evaluate the results of the organizing process to ensure effective and efficient progress toward planned goals. Evaluation sometimes results in changes to the way work is organized.

See **FIGURE 7.4 Steps in the Organizing Process**

Many factors influence the results of organizing. The list includes a firm's goals and competitive strategy, the type of product it offers, the way it uses technology to accomplish work, and its size. Small firms typically use very simple structures. The owner of a dry-cleaning business generally is the top manager who hires several employees to process orders, clean the clothing, and make deliveries. The owner handles the functions of purchasing supplies such as detergents and hangers, hiring and training employees and coordinating their work, preparing advertisements for the local newspaper, and keeping accounting records.

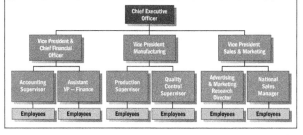

As a company grows, its structure increases in complexity. With increased size comes specialization and growing numbers of employees. A larger firm may employ many salespeople, along with a sales manager to direct and coordinate their work or organize an accounting department.

An effective structure is one that is clear and easy to understand: employees know what is expected of them and to whom they report. They also know how their jobs contribute to the company's mission and overall strategic plan. An *organization chart* can help clarify the structure of a firm. **▦ Figure 7.5** illustrates a sample organization chart.

See **FIGURE 7.5 Sample Organization Chart**

Not-for-profit organizations also organize through formal structures so they can function efficiently and carry out their goals. These organizations, such as the Salvation Army and the American Society for the Prevention of Cruelty to Animals (ASPCA), sometimes have a blend of paid staff and volunteers in their organizational structure.

Departmentalization

Departmentalization is the process of dividing work activities into units within the organization. In this arrangement, employees specialize in certain jobs—such as marketing, finance, or design. Depending on the size of the firm, usually an executive runs the department, followed by middle-level managers and supervisors. The five major forms of departmentalization subdivide work by product, geographical area, customer, function, and process.

- *Product departmentalization* organizes work units based on the goods and services a company offers. California's Activision Blizzard Inc. is organized by product. The video game publisher is divided into four divisions: Call of Duty, Skylanders, Diablo, and World of Warcraft.[9]

• *Geographical departmentalization* organizes units by geographical regions within a country or, for a multinational firm, by region throughout the world. The website Petswelcome.com makes it easy for traveling pet owners to locate hotel chains, rentals, amusement parks, and other recreational locations around the country that welcome pets. Users can search by type of lodging, route planned, and destination.[10]

• *Customer departmentalization* targets its goods and services at different types of customers. Procter & Gamble divides its management across four business units: Beauty, Hair, and Personal Care; Baby, Feminine, and Family Care; Fabric and Home Care; and Health and Grooming.[11]

• *Functional departmentalization* organizes work units according to business functions such as finance, marketing, human resources, and production. An advertising agency may create departments for creative personnel (say, copywriters), media buyers, and account executives.

• *Process departmentalization* organizes a firm by steps in a production process. For example, a manufacturer may set up separate departments for cutting material, heat-treating it, forming it into its final shape, and painting it.

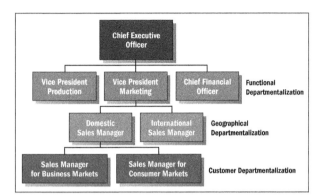

See **FIGURE 7.6**
Different Forms of Departmentalization within One Company

As ◾ **Figure 7.6** illustrates, a single company may implement several different departmentalization schemes. In deciding on a form of departmentalization, managers take into account the type of product they produce, the size of their company, their customer base, and the locations of their customers.

Types of Organization Structures

The four basic types of organization structures are line, line-and-staff, committee, and matrix. While some companies do follow one type of structure, most use a combination.

• *Line organization*, the oldest and simplest organization structure, establishes a direct flow of authority from the chief executive to employees. The line organization defines a simple, clear chain of command, or hierarchy of managers and workers. With a clear chain of command, everyone knows who is in charge and decisions can be made quickly. While line organization is particularly effective in a crisis, it has its drawbacks. Each manager has complete responsibility for a range of activities; in a midsize or large organization, however, this person can't possibly be an expert in all of them. In a small organization such as a local hair salon or dentist's office, a line organization is probably the most efficient way to run the business.

• *Line-and-staff organization* combines the direct flow of authority of a line organization with staff departments that support the line departments. Line departments participate directly in decisions that affect the core operations of the organization. Staff departments lend specialized technical support. ◾ **Figure 7.7** illustrates a line-and-staff organization. Accounting, engineering, and human resources are typical staff departments that support the line authority extending from the plant manager to the production manager and supervisors.

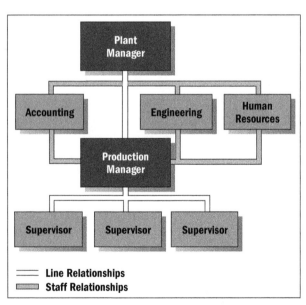

See **FIGURE 7.7 Line-and-Staff Organization**

A line manager and a staff manager differ significantly in their authority relationships. A line manager forms part of the primary line of authority that flows throughout the organization. Line managers interact directly with the functions of production, financing, or marketing—the functions needed to produce and sell goods and services. A staff manager provides information, advice, or technical assistance to aid line managers. Staff managers do not have authority to give orders outside their own departments or to compel line managers to take action.

The line-and-staff organization is common in midsize and large organizations. It is an effective structure because it combines the line organization's capabilities for rapid decision making and direct communication with the expert knowledge of staff specialists.

- *Committee organization* places authority and responsibility jointly in the hands of a group of individuals rather than a single manager. This model typically appears as part of a regular line-and-staff structure.

  Committees also work in areas such as new-product development. A new-product committee may include managers from such areas as accounting, engineering, finance, manufacturing, marketing, and technical research. By including representatives from all areas involved in creating and marketing products, such a committee generally improves planning and employee morale because decisions reflect diverse perspectives. Committees tend to act slowly and conservatively, however, and may make decisions by compromising conflicting interests rather than by choosing the best alternative. The definition of a camel as "a racehorse designed by committee" provides an apt description of some limitations of committee decisions.

- *Matrix organization* links employees from different parts of the firm to work together on specific projects. In a matrix structure, each employee reports to two managers: one line manager and one project manager. Employees chosen to work on a special project receive instructions from the project manager (horizontal authority), but they continue as employees in their permanent functional departments (vertical authority). The term *matrix* comes from the intersecting grid of horizontal and vertical lines of authority.

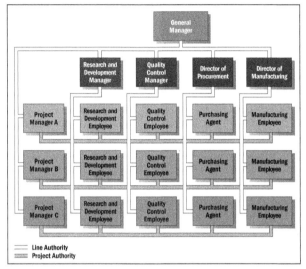

🔲 **Figure 7.8** depicts a matrix structure in which a project manager assembles a group of employees from different functional areas. The employees keep their ties to the line-and-staff structure, as shown in the vertical white lines. As the horizontal gold lines show, employees are also members of project teams. When the project is completed, employees return to their regular jobs.

See **FIGURE 7.8 Matrix Organization**

The matrix structure is popular at high-technology and multinational corporations, as well as hospitals and consulting firms. Both Dow Chemical and Procter & Gamble have used matrix structures. The major benefits of the matrix structure come from its flexibility in adapting quickly to rapid changes in the environment and its capability of focusing resources on major problems or products. It also provides an outlet for employees' creativity and initiative. However, it challenges project managers to integrate the skills of specialists from many departments into a coordinated team. It also means that team members' permanent functional managers must adjust their employees' regular workloads.

The matrix structure is most effective when company leaders empower project managers to use whatever resources are available to achieve the project's objectives. Good project managers know how to make the project goals clear and keep team members focused. A firm that truly embraces the matrix structure also nurtures a project culture by making sure staffing is adequate, the workload is reasonable, and other company resources are available to project managers.

Managerial Functions

In addition to planning and organizing, managers need to be able to perform a multitude of other functions. These include hard skills such as technical analysis, operating computer software, and reading financial statements. Managers must also perfect soft skills such as public speaking, networking, and writing. Of the additional skills a manager requires, two stand out as critical to a manager's success: directing and controlling.

Directing Once an organization has been established, managers focus on **directing**, or guiding and motivating employees to accomplish organizational objectives. Directing might include training (or retraining), setting up schedules, delegating certain tasks, and monitoring progress. To fulfill the objective of reducing the office electricity bill, an office manager might have incandescent light bulbs replaced by compact fluorescents, ask employees to turn off the lights when they leave a room or use occupancy sensors, and direct the IT staff to program all the office computer screens to turn off after 10 or 15 minutes of inactivity.

Often when managers take time to listen to their employees, the manager gains insight and the employee gets a motivational boost. Fashion designer Eileen Fisher says, "Share information and your own ideas. Be present. Be accessible. Listen."[12]

Controlling The **controlling** function evaluates an organization's performance against its objectives. Controlling assesses the success of the planning function and provides feedback for future rounds of planning.

The four basic steps in controlling are to establish performance standards, monitor actual performance, compare actual performance with established standards, and make corrections if necessary. Under the provisions of the Sarbanes-Oxley Act, for example, CEOs and CFOs must monitor the performance of the firm's accounting staff more closely than has typically been done in the past. They must personally attest to the truth of financial reports filed with the Securities and Exchange Commission.

> **Q** Answer the **Concept Check** questions.

> **WP LS** Go to your WileyPLUS Learning Space course for video episodes, examples, art, tables, Concept Checks, practice, and resources that will help you succeed in this course.

HUMAN RESOURCE MANAGEMENT FROM RECRUITMENT TO LABOR RELATIONS

8

Human Resources: The People Behind the People

Like a professional sports team, a company is only as good as its workers. If people come to work each day to do their very best, serve their customers, and help their firm compete, it's very likely that company will be a success. The best companies value their employees as much as they value customers—without workers, there would be no goods or services to offer customers. Management at such companies know that hiring good workers is vital to their overall success. Achieving the highest level of job satisfaction and dedication among employees is the goal of **human resource management**, which attracts, develops, and retains the employees who can perform the activities necessary to accomplish organizational objectives.

Q Answer the **Concept Check** questions.

Recruitment and Selection

Nowhere is the role of HR more important than in recruiting and selecting workers for a company. To ensure that candidates bring the necessary skills to the job or have the desire and ability to learn them, most firms implement the recruitment and selection process shown in ▣ **Figure 8.1**.

Before seeking candidates for a position, a manager must first determine what tasks are to be done and the best way to accomplish those tasks. This step often leads to a discussion within top management on how staff is currently deployed. For example, do any projects or businesses in the organization have a surplus of workers? Or does the firm have employees on furlough or not working full-time? Senior management is responsible for making sure current employees are working at capacity and at maximum productivity. Even then, a hiring manager must determine whether the company should hire additional employees. Outsourcing the work to an outside firm, using temporary staff, or engaging independent contractors to do the work may be better solutions. Clearly, managers have many choices when it comes to staffing their operations.

Finding Qualified Candidates

After analyzing the situation, if a manager wants to hire a new employee, he or she needs to think about the type of person to target. This process often begins with the hiring manager generating a document listing the **job requirements**—the minimum skills, education, and experience a candidate needs for the position. Additionally, the hiring manager must think about the salary or wages and benefits required to attract the appropriate candidate. Hiring managers also guide HR to the likely sources of such individuals. Whether the position calls for a highly technical individual (such as a web programmer) or an entry-level college graduate, the hiring manager plays an important role in identifying, interviewing, and selecting new employees. In all likelihood, the hiring manager will be working with the new employee, so making the right hiring decision is critical not only to their own success but also to that of their organization.

Besides the traditional methods of recruiting—such as college job fairs, personal referrals, and want ads—most companies now rely on their websites for job applicants. A firm's website might contain a career section with general employment information and a listing of open positions. Applicants are often able to submit a résumé and apply for an open position

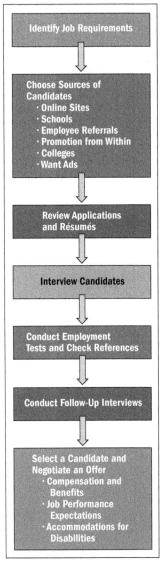

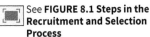
See **FIGURE 8.1 Steps in the Recruitment and Selection Process**

online. Internet recruiting is such a quick, efficient, and inexpensive way to reach a large pool of job seekers that the vast majority of companies currently use the Internet, including social networking sites, to fill job openings. This is also the best way for firms to reach new graduates and current workers. Using social media sites such as LinkedIn or Facebook allows firms to communicate directly with candidates and streamline the selection process.

Interviewing

Probably no conversation is more important or more stressful than a job interview. The interview is a chance for a manager to get to know a candidate, to see how he or she responds to questions, and to assess the candidate's "fit" within the organization. For job seekers, the interview is an opportunity to see an organization up close, perhaps meet their prospective manager, and better understand the job requirements. Finding the right fit is important for both the organization and the candidate.

Interviews often start with a manager asking a candidate to "Tell me about yourself" or asking "How did you happen to learn about this opening?" Questions like these help break the ice, put candidates at ease, and allow them to speak with confidence about something they know. As the interview progresses, the interviewer will ask more detailed questions, often based on a candidate's résumé or experience. These types of questions help the interviewer assess whether the candidate has the right skill set, work experience, or on-the-job behaviors that the organization has determined the position needs. For example, suppose the firm wanted an information technology professional whose experience included a major software launch. The interviewer might say to the candidate, "Tell me about a time when you had to implement a companywide software changeover." Interviews often conclude with questions like, "What contribution would you envision making to ABC Company?" "What would you regard as your greatest accomplishment?" or "What questions do you have for me?" Good candidates will have anticipated a broad range of interview questions and practiced answers to them, demonstrating that they are the right fit for the position and the organization.

After the interviews, a hiring manager will often meet with the HR manager to discuss the candidates. Some will be immediately eliminated as they lacked some of the requirements, they appeared unprepared for the interview, or were not a good fit for the organization. The remaining candidates are typically ranked, and the top three or four selected for a next round of interviewing, possibly with other members of the management team, prospective colleagues, or senior employees. The HR manager will then begin checking references, verifying past employment, and confirming that the candidates have the degrees and certificates that they are claiming on their application. Managers might also use Google to research the candidate to see what else they might learn about the individual. For certain positions, some organizations perform a background check of the top candidates. Once this process is completed, the HR manager and the hiring manager will meet and review the information. At this point, the top candidate is selected and the HR manager will contact the individual to offer him or her a position. Pay, benefits, and work responsibilities are discussed and placed in an offer letter. If the terms are acceptable, the candidate typically signs and returns a copy of the offer letter, and the start date is determined.

Legal Aspects of Hiring Employees

When hiring employees, every firm must follow state and federal employment laws. Title VII of the Civil Rights Act of 1964 prohibits employers from discriminating against applicants based on their race, religion, color, gender, or national origin. The Americans with Disabilities Act of 1990 prohibits employers from discriminating against applicants with disabilities. The Civil Rights Act created the *Equal Employment Opportunity Commission (EEOC)* to investigate discrimination complaints. The Uniform Employee Selection Guidelines were adopted by the EEOC in 1978 to further clarify ways in which employers must ensure that their employees will be hired and managed without discrimination.[1] The EEOC also helps employers set up *affirmative action programs* to increase job opportunities for women, minorities, people with disabilities, and other protected groups. The Civil Rights Act of 1991 expanded the alternatives available to victims of employment discrimination by including the right to a jury trial, punitive damages, and damages for emotional distress. At the same time, opponents to such laws have launched initiatives to restrict affirmative action standards and protect employers against unnecessary litigation.

Q Answer the **Concept Check** questions.

Orientation, Training, and Evaluation

Once hired, employees need to know what is expected of them and how well they are performing. Companies provide this information through orientation, training, and evaluation. New hires may complete an orientation program administered jointly by HR and the department in which they will work. During orientation, employees learn about company policies regarding their rights and benefits. They might receive an employee manual that includes the company's code of ethics and code of conduct. And they'll usually receive some form of training.

Training Programs

Training is a good investment for both employers and employees. Training helps workers build their skills and knowledge, preparing them for new job opportunities within the company. It also gives employers a better chance of retaining long-term, loyal, high-performing workers. Companies of all sizes take creative approaches to training. Information technology giant Cisco, one of *Fortune*'s "100 Best Companies to Work For," provides employees with an online learning and development community that offers access to educational materials, workshops, and stretch activities, which employees can rate after using.[2]

- *On-the-job training,* a popular teaching method, prepares employees for job duties by allowing them to perform tasks under the guidance of experienced employees. A variation of on-the-job training is apprenticeship training, in which an employee learns a job by serving for a time as an assistant to a trained worker. To bridge the gap between what students learn in the classroom and what companies require, BMW's plant in Spartanburg, South Carolina, works with students from nearby technical colleges who train and study 25 hours a week at the manufacturing facility while earning two-year degrees.[3]
- *Classroom and computer-based training* offer another option. Many firms are replacing classroom training with computer-based training programs, which can significantly reduce costs. Computer-based training offers consistent presentations along with videos that can simulate the work environment. Employees can learn at their own pace without having to sign up for a class. Through online training programs, employees can engage in interactive learning—they might conference with a mentor or instructor located elsewhere or they might participate in a simulation requiring them to make decisions related to their work.

Performance Appraisals

Feedback about performance is the best way for a company—and its employees—to improve. Most firms use an annual **performance appraisal** to evaluate an employee's job performance and provide feedback about it. A performance appraisal can include assessments of everything from attendance to goals met. Based on this evaluation, a manager will make decisions about compensation, promotion, additional training needs, transfers, or even termination. Performance appraisals are common, but not everyone agrees about their usefulness.

Some management experts argue that a performance review is skewed in favor of a single manager's subjective opinion—whether it's positive or negative—and that most employees are afraid to speak honestly to their managers during a performance review. If a performance review is to be at all effective, it should meet the following criteria:

- Establish clear, measurable, agreed-upon objectives
- Be linked to organizational goals
- Take place in the form of a two-way conversation
- Consist of frequent meetings with meaningful feedback[4]

Q Answer the **Concept Check** questions.

Compensation

Compensation—how much employees are paid in money and benefits—is one of the most highly charged issues that HR managers face. The amount employees are paid, along with whatever benefits they receive, has a tremendous influence on where they live, their lifestyle, and how they spend their leisure time. Compensation also affects job satisfaction. Balancing compensation for employees at all job levels can be a challenge for human resource managers.

The terms *wages* and *salary* are often used interchangeably, but they actually are different. A **wage** is based on an hourly pay rate or the amount of work accomplished. Typical wage earners are factory workers, construction workers, auto mechanics, retail salespeople, and restaurant servers. A **salary** is calculated periodically, such as weekly or monthly. Salaried employees receive a set amount of pay that does not fluctuate with the number of hours they work: wage earners may receive overtime pay, and salaried workers do not. Office personnel, executives, and professional employees usually receive salaries.

Most firms base their compensation policies on the following factors:

- What competing companies are paying
- Government regulation
- Cost of living
- Company profits
- An employee's productivity

Many firms try to balance rewarding workers with maintaining profits by linking more of an employee's pay to superior performance. Firms try to motivate employees to excel by offering some type of incentive compensation in addition to salaries or wages. ◼ **Figure 8.2** lists four common types of incentive compensation programs:

- Profit sharing, which awards bonuses based on company profits
- Gainsharing, a company's sharing of the financial value of productivity gains, cost savings, or quality improvements with its workers
- Lump-sum bonuses and stock options, which provide one-time cash payments and the right to purchase company stock based on performance
- Pay for knowledge, which distributes wage or salary increases as employees learn new job tasks

Profit Sharing	Gainsharing
Bonus based on company profits	Bonus based on productivity gains, cost savings, or quality improvements
Bonus	**Pay for Knowledge**
One-time cash payment or option to buy shares of company stock based on performance	Salary increase based on learning new job tasks

See **FIGURE 8.2 Four Forms of Incentive Compensation**

Employee Benefits

In addition to wages and salaries, firms provide benefits to employees and their families as part of their compensation. **Employee benefits**—such as vacation, retirement plans, profit-sharing, health insurance, gym memberships, child and elder care, and tuition reimbursement—are sometimes offered by the employer. Benefits represent a large component of an employee's total compensation. Although wages and salaries account for around 70 percent of the typical employee's compensation, the other 30 percent takes the form of employee benefits.[5] ◼ **Table 8.1** shows the breakdown of an average worker's benefits as compared to wages or salary.

See **TABLE 8.1: What are average costs for employee compensation?**

Some benefits are required by law. U.S. firms are required to make Social Security and Medicare contributions, as well as payments to state unemployment insurance and workers' compensation programs, which protect workers in case of job-related injuries or illnesses. The Family and Medical Leave Act of 1993 requires covered employers to offer up to 12 weeks of unpaid, job-protected leave to eligible employees. Firms voluntarily provide other employee benefits, such as child care and health insurance, to help them attract and retain employees. Some states, such as California, New Jersey, and Washington, have laws mandating paid family leave.

In the past, companies have paid the greater share of the cost of health care benefits, with employees paying a much smaller share. However, as health care costs rise, employers are passing along premium increases to employees. Many companies now offer incentives for workers to live healthier lives. Gym memberships, nutrition programs, wellness visits to the doctor, and smoking-cessation classes are all examples of these incentives. At Qualcomm, a global mobile technologies firm, employee benefits include unlimited sick days, on-site gyms, tuition assistance, and work-life balance programs like job sharing, compressed work-weeks, and telecommuting. In addition, Qualcomm provides a generous company match on its retirement savings plan and pays 100 percent of the monthly health insurance premium for full-time employees.[6]

Retirement plans make up a portion of employee benefits. Some companies have reduced the contributions they make to workers' *401(k) plans*—retirement savings plans to which employees can make pretax contributions. Some firms have cut back on cash contributions to the plans and contribute company stock instead. However, others provide a high level of funding. Conoco Phillips, a Houston oil and natural gas producer, topped a recent *Bloomberg* list as having the best 401k plan, with a matching formula that contributes 9 percent of annual salaries for employees who save as little as 1 percent of their pay.[7]

Flexible Benefits

In response to increasing diversity in the workplace, firms look for creative ways to structure their benefit plans to the needs of employees. One approach offers *flexible benefits,* also called a cafeteria plan. Under this system, employees have a choice of benefits, including different types of medical insurance, dental and vision plans, and life and disability insurance. Typically, each employee receives a set allowance (called flex dollars or credits) to pay for benefits, depending on his or her needs. One working spouse, for example, might choose medical coverage for the entire family while the other spouse uses benefit dollars to elect other types of coverage. Contributions to cafeteria accounts can be made by both the employee and employer. Cafeteria plans also offer tax benefits to both employees and employers.

Another way of increasing the flexibility of employee benefits involves time off from work. Instead of establishing set numbers of holidays, vacation days, and sick days, some employers give each employee a bank of *paid time off (PTO)*. Employees use days from their PTO account without having to explain why they need the time. The greatest advantage of PTO is the freedom it gives workers to make their own choices; the greatest disadvantage is that it is an expensive benefit for employers.

Flexible Work

Some firms are moving toward the option of *flexible work plans,* which are benefits that allow employees to adjust their working hours or places of work according to their needs. Flexible work plan options include flextime, compressed workweeks, job sharing, and home-based work (telecommuting). These benefit programs have reduced employee turnover and absenteeism and boosted productivity and job satisfaction. Flexible work has become critical in attracting and keeping talented human resources.

- *Flextime* allows employees to set their own work hours within certain parameters. Rather than mandating that all employees work, say, from 8:00 a.m. to 5:00 p.m., a manager might stipulate that everyone works between the core hours of 10:00 a.m. and 3:00 p.m. Outside the core hours, employees could choose to start and end early or start and end late.

- Some companies offer a *compressed workweek*, which allows employees to work longer hours on fewer days. Employees might work four 10-hour days and then have three days off each week.

- A *job sharing program* allows two or more employees to divide the tasks of one job. This plan appeals to a growing number of people—such as students, working parents, and people of all ages who want to devote time to personal interests—who prefer to work part-time rather than full-time. Job sharing requires a lot of cooperation and communication between the partners, but an employer can benefit from the talents of both people.

- Home-based work programs allow employees to become *telecommuters,* performing their jobs from home via the Internet, voice and video conferencing, and mobile devices.

> **Q** Answer the **Concept Check** questions.

Employee Separation

Employee separation is a broad term covering the loss of an employee for any reason, voluntary or involuntary. Voluntary separation includes workers who resign to take a job at another firm or start a business. Involuntary separation includes downsizing, outsourcing, and dismissal.

Voluntary and Involuntary Turnover

Turnover occurs when an employee leaves a job. Voluntary turnover occurs when the employee resigns—perhaps to take another job that pays better, start a new business, or retire. The human resource manager might conduct an exit interview with the employee to learn why he or she is leaving; this conversation can provide valuable information to a firm. An employee might decide to leave because of lack of career opportunities. Learning this, the human resource manager might offer ongoing training. Sometimes employees accept jobs at other firms because they fear upcoming layoffs. In this case, the human resource manager might be able to allay fears about job security.

Involuntary turnover occurs when employees are terminated because of poor job performance or unethical behavior. No matter how necessary a termination may be, it is never easy for the manager or the employee. The employee may react with anger or tears; co-workers may take sides. Managers should remain calm and professional and must be educated in employment laws. Protests against wrongful dismissal are often involved in complaints filed by the EEOC or by lawsuits brought by fired employees. Involuntary turnover also occurs when firms are forced to eliminate jobs as a cost-cutting measure, as in the case of downsizing or outsourcing.

Downsizing

As the economy tightens, companies are often faced with the hard choice of terminating employees in order to cut costs or streamline the organization. **Downsizing** is the process of reducing the number of employees within a firm by eliminating jobs. Downsizing can be accomplished through early retirement plans or voluntary severance programs.

Outsourcing

Firms also shrink themselves into leaner organizations by **outsourcing**. Outsourcing involves transferring jobs from inside a firm to outside the firm. Jobs that are typically outsourced include office maintenance, deliveries, food service, and security. However, other job functions can be outsourced as well, including manufacturing, design, information technology, and accounting. In general, in order to save expenses and remain flexible, many companies try to outsource functions that are not part of their core business.

 Answer the **Concept Check** questions.

Motivating Employees

Everyone wants to enjoy going to work. Smart employers know that and look for ways to motivate workers to commit to their company's goals and perform their best. Motivation starts with high employee morale—a positive attitude toward the job. Each year, *Fortune* announces its list of the "100 Best Companies to Work For." The most recent top ten are listed in **Table 8.2**. Based on these rankings, it's reasonable to believe that employees at these firms tend to have higher morale because they feel valued and empowered.

See **TABLE 8.2: Can you name the top ten companies on FORTUNE's "100 Best Companies to Work For" List?**

High morale generally results from good management, including an understanding of human needs and an effort to satisfy those needs in ways that move the company forward. Low employee morale, on the other hand, usually signals a poor relationship between managers and employees and often results in absenteeism, voluntary turnover, and a lack of motivation.

Generally speaking, managers use rewards and punishments to motivate employees. Extrinsic rewards are external to the work itself, such as pay, fringe benefits, and praise. Intrinsic rewards are feelings related to performing the job, such as feeling proud about meeting a deadline or achieving a sales goal. Punishment involves a negative consequence for such behavior as being late, skipping staff meetings, or treating a customer poorly.

There are several theories of motivation, all of which relate back to the basic process of motivation itself, which involves the recognition of a need, the move toward meeting that need, and the satisfaction of that need. For instance, if you are hungry you might be motivated to make yourself a peanut butter sandwich. Once you have eaten the sandwich, the need is satisfied and you are no longer hungry. **Figure 8.3** illustrates the process of motivation.

See **FIGURE 8.3 The Process of Motivation**

Maslow's Hierarchy of Needs Theory

The studies of psychologist Abraham H. Maslow suggest how managers can motivate employees. **Maslow's hierarchy of needs** has become a widely accepted list of human needs based on these important assumptions:

- People's needs depend on what they already possess.
- A satisfied need is not a motivator; only needs that remain unsatisfied can influence behavior.
- People's needs are arranged in a hierarchy of importance; once they satisfy one need, at least partially, another emerges and demands satisfaction.

In his theory, Maslow proposed that all people have basic needs such as hunger and protection that they must satisfy before they can consider higher-order needs such as social relationships or self-worth. He identified five types of needs:

1. *Physiological needs* include food, shelter, and clothing. On the job, employers satisfy these needs by paying salaries and wages and providing a temperature-controlled workspace.
2. *Safety needs* refer to desires for physical and economic protection. Companies satisfy these needs with benefits like health insurance and meeting safety standards in the workplace.
3. *Social (belongingness) needs* refer to people's desire to be accepted by family, friends, and co-workers. Managers might satisfy these needs through teamwork and group lunches.
4. *Esteem needs* have to do with people's desire to feel valued and recognized by others. Managers can meet these needs through special awards or privileges.
5. *Self-actualization needs* drive people to seek fulfillment of their dreams and capabilities. Employers can satisfy these needs by offering challenging or creative projects, along with opportunities for education and advancement.[8]

According to Maslow, people must satisfy the lower-order needs in the hierarchy, specifically their physiological and safety needs, before they are motivated to satisfy higher-order needs such as social, esteem, and self-actualization.

Other Motivational Theories

Equity theory is concerned with an individual's perception of fair and equitable treatment. In their work, employees first consider their effort and then their rewards. Next, employees compare their results against those of their co-workers. As shown in Figure 8.3, if employees feel they are under-rewarded for their effort in comparison with others doing similar work, equity theory suggests they will be motivated to decrease their effort. Conversely, if employees feel they are over-rewarded, they will feel guilty and put more effort into their job to restore equity and reduce guilt.

Goal-setting theory says that people will be motivated to the extent to which they accept specific, challenging goals and receive feedback that indicates their progress toward goal achievement. The basic components of goal-setting theory are goal specificity, goal difficulty, goal acceptance, and performance feedback.

More than 60 years ago, Peter Drucker introduced a goal-setting technique called **management by objectives (MBO)** in his book, *The Practice of Management*. MBO is a systematic approach that allows managers to focus on attainable goals and to achieve the best results based on the organization's resources. MBO helps motivate individuals by aligning their objectives with the goals of the organization, increasing overall organizational performance. MBO clearly outlines people's tasks, goals, and contributions to the company.

Managers' Attitudes and Motivation

A manager's attitude toward his or her employees greatly influences their motivation. Maslow's theory, described earlier, has helped managers understand that employees have a range of needs beyond their paychecks. Psychologist Douglas McGregor, a student of Maslow, studied motivation from the perspective of how managers view employees.

After observing managers' interactions with employees, McGregor created two basic labels for the assumptions that different managers make about their workers' behavior and how these assumptions affect management styles:

- *Theory X* assumes that employees dislike work and try to avoid it whenever possible, so management must coerce them to do their jobs. Theory X managers believe that the average worker prefers to receive instructions, avoids responsibility, takes little initiative, and views money and job security as the only valid motivators—Maslow's lower order of needs.

- *Theory Y* assumes that the typical person actually likes work and will seek and accept greater responsibility. Theory Y managers assume that most people can think of creative ways to solve work-related problems and should be given the opportunity to participate in decision making. Unlike the traditional management philosophy that relies on external control and constant supervision, Theory Y emphasizes self-control and self-direction—Maslow's higher order of needs.

Another perspective on management, proposed by management professor William Ouchi, has been labeled *Theory Z*. Organizations structured on Theory Z concepts attempt to blend the best of American and Japanese management practices. This approach views worker involvement as the key to increased productivity for the company and improved quality of work life for employees. Many U.S. firms have adopted the participative management style used in Japanese firms by asking workers for suggestions to improve their jobs and then giving them the authority to implement proposed changes.

Q Answer the **Concept Check** questions.

Labor–Management Relations

The U.S. workplace is far different from what it was a century ago, when child labor, unsafe working conditions, and a 72-hour workweek were common. The development of labor unions, labor legislation, and the collective bargaining process have contributed to the changed environment. Today's HR managers must be educated in labor–management relations, the settling of disputes, and the competitive tactics of unions and management.

Development of Labor Unions

A **labor union** is a group of workers who have banded together to achieve common goals in the areas of wages, hours, and working conditions. The organized efforts of Philadelphia printers in 1786 resulted in the first U.S. agreed-upon wage—$1 a day. One hundred years later, New York City streetcar conductors were able to negotiate a reduction in their workday from 17 to 12 hours.

Labor unions can be found at the local, national, and international levels. A *local union* represents union members in a specific area, such as a single community, while a *national union* is a labor organization consisting of numerous local chapters. An *international union* is a national union with membership outside the United States, usually in Canada. About 14.6 million U.S. workers—just over 11 percent of the nation's full-time workforce—belong to labor unions.[9] Although only about 6.6 percent of workers in the private sector are unionized, more than one-third of government workers belong to unions. The largest union in the United States is the 3 million member National Education Association (NEA), representing public school teachers and other support personnel. Other large unions include the 2 million members of the Service Employees International Union (SEIU), the 1.6 million members of the American Federation of State, County & Municipal Employees, the 1.4 million members of the International Brotherhood of Teamsters, the 1.3 million members of the United Food and Commercial Workers, and the 390,000 members of the United Automobile, Aerospace and Agricultural Implement Workers of America.[10]

Labor Legislation

Over the past century, some major pieces of labor legislation have been enacted, including the following:

- The *National Labor Relations Act of 1935 (Wagner Act)* legalized collective bargaining and required employers to negotiate with elected representatives of their employees. It established the National Labor Relations Board (NLRB) to supervise union elections and prohibit unfair labor practices such as firing workers for joining unions, refusing to hire union sympathizers, threatening to close if workers unionize, interfering with or dominating the administration of a union, and refusing to bargain with a union.

- The *Fair Labor Standards Act of 1938* set the first federal minimum wage (25 cents an hour) and a maximum basic workweek for certain industries. It also outlawed child labor.

- The *Taft-Hartley Act of 1947 (Labor–Management Relations Act)* limited unions' power by banning such practices as coercing employees to join unions; coercing employers to discriminate against employees who are not union members; discriminating against nonunion employees; picketing or conducting secondary boycotts or strikes for illegal purposes; and excessive initiation fees.

- The *Landrum-Griffin Act of 1959 (Labor–Management Reporting and Disclosure Act)* amended the Taft-Hartley Act to promote honesty and democracy in running unions' internal affairs. The law requires unions to set up a constitution and bylaws and to hold regularly scheduled elections of union officers by secret ballot. It set forth a bill of rights for union members and required unions to submit certain financial reports to the U.S. Secretary of Labor.

The Collective Bargaining Process

Labor unions work to increase job security for their members and to improve wages, hours, and working conditions. These goals are achieved primarily through **collective bargaining**, the process of negotiation between management and union representatives.

Union contracts, which typically cover a two- or three-year period, are often the result of weeks or months of discussion, disagreement, compromise, and eventual agreement. Once agreement is reached, union members must vote to accept or reject the contract. If the contract is rejected, union representatives may resume the bargaining process with management representatives, or union members may strike to obtain their demands.

Settling Labor–Management Disputes

Strikes make the headlines, but most labor–management negotiations result in a signed contract without a strike. If a dispute arises, it is usually settled through a mechanism such as a grievance procedure, mediation, or arbitration. Any of these alternatives is quicker and less expensive than a strike.

The union contract serves as a guide to relations between the firm's management and its employees. The rights of each party are stated in the agreement. But no contract, regardless of how detailed, will eliminate the possibility of disagreement. Such differences can be the beginning of a *grievance,* a complaint by a single employee or by the entire union that management is violating some portion of the contract. Almost all union contracts require these complaints to be submitted through a formal grievance procedure similar to the one shown in ▣ **Figure 8.4**. A grievance might involve a dispute about pay, working hours, or the workplace itself. The grievance procedure usually begins with an employee's supervisor and then moves up the company's hierarchy. If the highest level of management can't settle the grievance, it is submitted to an outside party for mediation or arbitration.

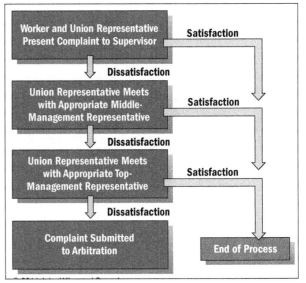

See **FIGURE 8.4 Steps in the Grievance Procedure**

Mediation is the process of settling labor–management disputes through an impartial third party. Although the mediator does not make the final decision, he or she hears the whole story and makes objective recommendations. If the dispute remains unresolved, the two parties can turn to *arbitration*—bringing in an outside arbitrator who renders a legally binding decision. The arbitrator must be acceptable both to the union and to management, and his or her decision is final. Most union negotiations go to arbitration if union and management representatives fail to reach a contract agreement.

Both unions and management use tactics to make their views known and to win support. Generally, unions are concerned with issues such as pay, job security, and benefits. Unions generally want to improve compensation and security for their members. They are also concerned about the overall health of the business and will make concessions if they feel that they need to in order for the company to continue to operate. Managers think about many of the same issues but are primarily concerned with the competitiveness of their business. Financial performance is the most important element because if the business cannot thrive, there will be no money to pay anyone. Usually, labor and management can come to some understanding and through a process of negotiation arrive at a contract acceptable to both parties. However, if there is an impasse in negotiations the union and management may need to resort to other means to get their needs met.

The Competitive Tactics of Unions

Unions chiefly use three tactics—strikes, picketing, and boycotts—to press for what they want:

- The *strike,* or walkout, is one of a union's most effective tools. It involves a temporary work stoppage by workers until a dispute has been settled or a contract signed. A strike generally seeks to disrupt business as usual, calling attention to workers' needs and union demands. Strikes can last for days or weeks and can be costly to both sides. In addition, strikes are often damaging to the very people the union is trying to help—for example, students lose valuable class time when teachers go on strike. Surrounding businesses may suffer, too. If striking workers aren't eating at their usual lunch haunts, those businesses will lose profits. Strikes seem to be on the decline, however. Over the past five years, there were, on average, 13 major work stoppages per year, half the number that took place in the 1990s.[11]
- *Picketing* consists of workers marching in a public protest against their employer. As long as picketing does not involve violence or intimidation, it is protected under the U.S. Constitution as freedom of speech. Picketing may accompany a strike, or it may be a protest against alleged unfair labor practices.
- A *boycott* is an organized attempt to keep the public from purchasing a firm's goods or services. Some unions have been quite successful in organizing boycotts, and some unions even fine members who defy a boycott.

The Competitive Tactics of Management

Management also has tactics for competing with organized labor when negotiations break down. In the past, it has used the lockout—a management "strike" to put pressure on union members by closing the firm. More commonly, however, organizations try to recruit strikebreakers (in highly visible fields such as professional sports) or transfer supervisors and other nonunion employees to continue operations during strikes.

In extreme cases, management might go so far as to close the plant and outsource the work to another company or even shut down the operation entirely and file for bankruptcy, such as what happened with Hostess Brands, bakers of the iconic Twinkie and other snack cakes. After failing to reach an agreement with the union, Hostess filed for bankruptcy. Private equity groups Apollo Global Management and Metropolis & Co.—now doing business as Hostess Brands—paid $410 million to buy the Hostess and Dolly Madison snack cake lines as well as five plants as part of the company's liquidation process. Soon after, the new owners relaunched the iconic products and recently announced they were planning to put the company up for sale again.[12]

The Future of Labor Unions

Union membership and influence grew through most of the 20th century by giving industrial workers a voice in decisions about their wages, benefits, and working conditions. However, as the United States, western Europe, and Japan have shifted from manufacturing economies to information and service economies, union membership and influence have declined. In a recent year, about 11.1 percent of wage and salary workers belonged to a union, down from 11.3 percent the year before. Subsets of that group have remained steady: 6.6 percent of private sector workers belong to a union.[13]

How can labor unions change to maintain their relevance? They can be more flexible and adapt to a global economy and diverse workforce. They can respond to the growing need for environmentally responsible business and manufacturing processes. Unions can establish collaborative relationships with human resource managers and other managers. And they can recognize the potential for prosperity for all—management and union workers included.

Q Answer the **Concept Check** questions.

WP LS Go to your WileyPLUS Learning Space course for video episodes, examples, art, tables, Concept Checks, practice, and resources that will help you success in this course.

Reading for
TOP PERFORMANCE THROUGH EMPOWERMENT, TEAMWORK, AND COMMUNICATION

WP LS Go to your WileyPLUS Learning Space course for video episodes, examples, art, tables, Concept Checks, practice, and resources that will help you succeed in this course.

Empowering Employees

An important component of effective management is the **empowerment** of employees. Managers empower employees by giving them authority and responsibility to make decisions about their work. Empowerment seeks to tap the brainpower of all workers to find improved ways of doing their jobs, better serving customers, and achieving organizational goals. It also motivates workers by adding challenges to their jobs and giving them a feeling of ownership. Managers empower employees by sharing company information and decision-making authority and by rewarding them for their performance—as well as the company's.

Sharing Information and Decision-Making Authority

One of the most effective methods of empowering employees is to keep them informed about the company's financial performance. Companies such as KIND Healthy Snacks, a New York–based maker of whole nut and fruit bars, believes that a transparent work environment is one where employees are kept informed and taught to think like owners. It's up to leaders to mentor their teams to develop this type of thinking and to consistently demonstrate how employees can make decisions as an owner in real time. The company's senior vice president of marketing believes that the benefits of this type of work environment are endless and lead to employee loyalty and trust and a flat organizational structure. When a company's employees begin to question the authenticity of company results and information, this can greatly affect the growth of the company's brand. While some decisions will continue to be made at the top, transparency about why and how decisions are made and listening to employee feedback allow for all team members to feel a part of, and more invested in, company results. Using information technology to empower employees does carry some risks, such as proprietary company information reaching competitors. KIND Healthy Snacks knows that setting up systems to share information and providing training to allow employees to understand that information is integral to its core values—a work environment in which team dynamics and decisions genuinely reflect the company's brand.[1]

The second way in which companies empower employees is to give them broad authority to make workplace decisions that implement a firm's vision and its competitive strategy. Even among non-management staff, empowerment extends to decisions and activities traditionally handled by managers. Employees might be responsible for such tasks as purchasing supplies, making hiring decisions, scheduling production or work hours, overseeing the safety program, and granting pay increases.

Linking Rewards to Company Performance

Whether they work in a small team or a large organization or are individual contributors, aligning employees' motivation and performance with that of the company is critical to success of both. Two widely used ways that companies provide workers with a sense of ownership are employee stock ownership plans and stock options. **Table 9.1** compares these two methods of employee ownership.

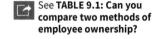 See **TABLE 9.1: Can you compare two methods of employee ownership?**

Employee Stock Ownership Plans

Over 14 million workers participate in 8,926 *employee stock ownership plans (ESOPs)* worth more than $994 billion.[2] These plans benefit employees by giving them ownership stakes in their companies, leading to potential profits as the value of their firm increases. Under ESOPs, the employer buys shares of company stock on behalf of its employees as a retirement benefit. The accounts continue to grow in value tax-free, and when employees leave the company they can cash in their shares. Employees are motivated to work harder and smarter than they would without ESOPs because, as part owners, they share in their firm's financial success. Of companies that offer ESOPs, more than 76 percent of those surveyed report an increase in employee productivity.[3]

As a retirement plan, an ESOP must comply with government regulations designed to protect pension benefits. Because ESOPs can be expensive to set up, they are more common in larger firms than in smaller ones. Public companies with ESOPs average around 14,000 employees, and private companies average about 1,500 employees.[4] One danger with ESOPs is that if the majority of an employee's retirement funds are in company stock and the value falls dramatically, the employee—like other investors— will be financially harmed.[5]

Stock Options

Another popular way for companies to share ownership with their employees is through the use of *stock options*—the right to buy a specified amount of company stock at a given price within a given time period. In contrast to an ESOP, a stock option gives employees a chance to own the stock themselves if they exercise their options by completing the stock purchase. If an employee receives an option on 100 shares at $10 per share and the stock price goes up to $20, the employee can exercise the option to buy those 100 shares at $10 each, sell them at the market price of $20, and pocket the difference. If the stock price never goes above the option price, the employee isn't required to exercise the option.[6]

Although options were once limited to senior executives and members of the board of directors, some companies now grant stock options to employees at all levels. Federal labor laws allow stock options to be granted to both hourly and salaried employees. An estimated 9 million employees in thousands of companies hold stock options.[7] About one-third of all stock options issued by U.S. corporations go to the top five executives at each firm. Much of the remainder goes to other executives and managers, who make up only about 2 percent of the U.S. workforce. Yet there is solid evidence that stock options motivate regular employees to perform better. Some argue that to be most effective as motivators, stock options need to be granted to a broad base of employees.

Stock options have turned hundreds of employees at firms such as Home Depot, Microsoft, and Google into millionaires and billionaires. But such success is no guarantee, especially when stock prices drop during an economic downturn. As with ESOPs, employees face risks when they rely on a single company's stock to provide for them.

Q Answer the **Concept Check** questions.

Five Types of Teams

According to a saying attributed to Aristotle, "The whole is greater than the sum of its parts." And so it is with employees—individually they may be "just" workers, but collectively they do amazing things: build new products, launch companies, and create whole new industries. To accomplish these tasks, a manager often creates a **team**—a group of people with certain skills who are committed to a common purpose, approach, and set of performance goals. All team members hold themselves mutually responsible and accountable for accomplishing their objectives.

Teams are widely used in business and in many not-for-profit organizations such as hospitals and government agencies. Teams are one of the most frequently discussed topics in employee training programs because teams require that people learn how to work effectively together. Many firms emphasize the importance of teams during their hiring processes, asking job applicants about their previous experiences as team members. Why? Because companies want to hire people who can work well with other people and pool their talents and ideas to achieve more together than they could achieve working alone. ▣ **Figure 9.1** outlines five basic types of teams: work teams, problem-solving teams, self-managed teams, cross-functional teams, and virtual teams.

About two-thirds of U.S. firms currently use **work teams**, which are relatively permanent groups of employees. In this approach, people with complementary skills perform the

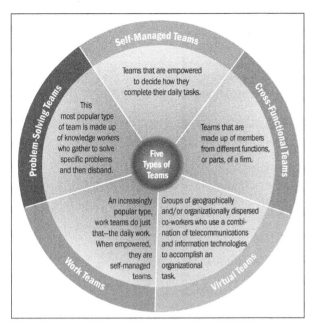

See **FIGURE 9.1 Five Types of Teams**

day-to-day work of the organization. A work team might include all the workers involved in assembling and packaging a product—it could be anything from cupcakes to cars. Most of Walmart's major vendors maintain offices near Walmart headquarters in Bentonville, Arkansas. Typically, each vendor office operates as a work team, with the head of the vendor office often holding the title of "team leader."

In contrast to a work team, a **problem-solving team** is a temporary combination of workers who gather to solve a specific problem and then disband. This team differs from a work team in important ways, though. Work teams are permanent units designed to handle any business problem that arises, but problem-solving teams pursue specific missions. When consumer products giant Johnson & Johnson discovered that 200,000 bottles of liquid Motrin for infants might contain small particles of plastic, the company immediately issued a product recall. The company then created supply chain and quality work teams to implement a single streamlined supply chain, shifting its focus to earlier detection of potential problems. More than $100 million has been spent to upgrade plant equipment at one of the company's facilities where the problems originated. In addition, an outside consulting firm was brought in to evaluate procedures and systems on an ongoing basis.[8]

Typically, when a problem is solved, a problem-solving team disbands, but in some cases, it may develop a more permanent role within the firm.

A work team empowered with the authority to decide how its members complete their daily tasks is called a **self-managed team**. A self-managed team works most effectively when it combines employees with a range of skills and functions. Members are cross-trained to perform each other's jobs as needed. Distributing decision-making authority in this way can free members to concentrate on satisfying customers.

Whole Foods Market has a structure based on self-managed work teams. Company managers decided that Whole Foods could be most innovative if employees made decisions themselves. Every employee is part of a team, and each store has about ten teams handling separate functions, such as groceries, bakery, and customer service. Each team handles responsibilities related to setting goals, hiring and training employees, scheduling team members, and purchasing merchandise. Teams meet at least monthly to review goals and performance, solve problems, and explore new ideas. Whole Foods awards bonuses based on the teams' performance relative to their goals.[9]

A team made up of members from different functions, such as production, marketing, and finance, is called a **cross-functional team**. Most often, cross-functional teams work on specific problems or projects, but they can also serve as permanent work team arrangements. The value of cross-functional teams comes from their ability to bring different perspectives—as well as different types of expertise—to a work effort. Communication is key to the success of cross-functional teams.

A **virtual team** is a group of geographically or organizationally dispersed co-workers who use a combination of telecommunications and information technologies to accomplish an organizational task. Because of the availability of e-mail, videoconferencing, and group-communication software, members of virtual teams rarely meet face to face. Their principal advantage is their flexibility. Team members can work with each other regardless of physical location, time zone, or organizational affiliation. Virtual teams whose members are scattered across the globe can be difficult to manage, but firms that are committed to them believe the benefits outweigh the drawbacks.

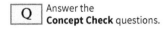 Answer the **Concept Check** questions.

Stages of Team Development

Teams typically progress through five stages of development: forming, storming, norming, performing, and adjourning. Although not every team passes through each of these stages, those that do usually perform better. These stages are summarized in ▣ **Figure 9.2**.

Stage 1: Forming

Forming is an orientation period during which team members get to know each other and find out what behaviors are acceptable to the group. Team members begin with curiosity about expectations of them and whether they will fit in with the group. An effective team leader provides time for members to become acquainted.

Stage 2: Storming

The personalities of team members begin to emerge during the storming stage, as members clarify their roles and expectations. Conflicts may arise as people disagree over the team's mission and jockey for position and control of the group. Subgroups may form based on common interests or concerns. At this stage, the team leader must encourage everyone to participate, allowing members to work through their uncertainties and conflicts. Teams must move beyond this stage to achieve real productivity.

Stage 3: Norming

During the norming stage, members resolve differences, accept each other, and reach broad agreement about the roles of the team leader and other participants. This stage is usually brief, and the team leader should use it to emphasize the team's unity and the importance of its objectives.

See **FIGURE 9.2 Stages of Team Development**

Stage 4: Performing

While performing, members focus on solving problems and accomplishing tasks. They interact frequently and handle conflicts in constructive ways. The team leader encourages contributions from all members. He or she should attempt to get any nonparticipating team members involved.

Stage 5: Adjourning

The team adjourns after members have completed the assigned task or solved the problem. During this phase, the focus is on wrapping up and summarizing the team's experiences and accomplishments. The team leader may recognize the team's accomplishments with a celebration, perhaps distributing plaques or awards.

Q Answer the **Concept Check** questions.

Team Cohesiveness and Norms

A team tends to maximize productivity when it becomes a highly cohesive unit. **Team cohesiveness** is the extent to which members feel attracted to the team and motivated to remain part of it. This cohesiveness typically increases when members interact frequently, share common attitudes and goals, and enjoy being together. Cohesive groups have a better chance of retaining their members than those that are less cohesive. As a result, cohesive groups typically experience lower turnover. In addition, team cohesiveness promotes cooperative behavior, generosity, and a willingness on the part of team members to help each other. When team cohesiveness is high, team members are more motivated to contribute to the team because they want the approval of other team members. Not surprisingly, studies have clearly established that cohesive teams quickly achieve high levels of performance and consistently perform better.

Team-building retreats are one way to encourage cohesiveness and improve satisfaction and retention. Firms that specialize in conducting these retreats offer a wide range of options.

A **team norm** is a standard of conduct shared by team members that guides their behavior. Norms are not formal written guidelines; they are informal standards that identify key values and clarify team members' expectations. In highly productive teams, norms contribute to constructive work and the accomplishment of team goals.

Team norms can be simple such as a group's expectations for working hours (staying late) or employee dress (casual Fridays). Or they can be involved and complex such as a member's

Q | Answer the
Concept Check questions.

willingness to accept a group's decision after a decision has been made. In either case, members who follow the norms are more likely to be seen as a valuable part of the team, whereas members who do not embrace the team norms may be seen as less productive. As will be seen in the next section, when team conflicts arise, they often occur because one or more members of the team are not adhering to the team's norms.

Team Conflict

Conflict occurs when one person's or a group's needs do not match those of another, and attempts may be made to block the opposing side's intentions or goals. Conflict and disagreement are inevitable in most teams. But this shouldn't surprise anyone. People who work together sometimes disagree about what and how things are done. What causes conflict in teams? Although almost anything can lead to conflict—casual remarks that unintentionally offend a team member or fighting over scarce resources—the primary cause of team conflict is disagreement over goals and priorities. Other common causes of team conflict include disagreements over task-related issues, interpersonal incompatibilities, simple fatigue, and team diversity.

Strong teams are diverse in their members' experience, ability, and background. And though diversity brings stimulation, challenge, and energy, it can also lead to conflict. The manager must create an environment in which differences are appreciated and a team of diverse individuals can work productively together. Diversity awareness training programs can reduce conflict by bringing these differences out in the open and identifying the unique talents of diverse individuals.

Although most people think conflict should be avoided, management experts note that conflict can actually enhance team performance. The key to dealing with conflict is making sure the team experiences the right kind of conflict. **Cognitive conflict** focuses on problem-related differences of opinion; reconciling these differences strongly improves team performance. With cognitive conflict, team members disagree because their different experiences and expertise lead them to different views of the problem and its solutions. Cognitive conflict is also characterized by a willingness to examine, compare, and reconcile differences to produce the best-possible solution.

By contrast, **affective conflict** refers to the emotional reactions that can occur when disagreements become personal rather than professional, and these differences strongly decrease team performance. Because affective conflict often results in hostility, anger, resentment, distrust, cynicism, and apathy, it can make people uncomfortable, cause them to withdraw, decrease their commitment to a team, lower the satisfaction of team members, and decrease team cohesiveness. Unlike cognitive conflict, affective conflict undermines team performance by preventing teams from engaging in activities that are critical to team effectiveness.

What can managers do to manage team conflict—and even make it work for them? Perhaps the team leader's most important contribution to conflict resolution can be facilitating good communication so that teammates respect each other and are free to disagree with each other. Ongoing, effective communication ensures that team members perceive each other accurately, understand what is expected of them, and obtain the information they need. Taking this step further, organizations should evaluate situations or conditions in the workplace that might be causing conflict. Solving a single conflict isn't helpful if there are problems systemic to the team or to the company. Team-building exercises, listening exercises, and role-playing can help employees learn to become better team members.[10]

Q | Answer the
Concept Check questions.

The Importance of Effective Communication

No matter how well the rest of an organization operates, few businesses can succeed without effective **communication**, the meaningful exchange of information through messages. American Giant, a South Carolina–based maker of sweatshirts and other apparel, experienced miscommunications with its Indian fabric suppliers that caused manufacturing issues, shipment delays, and increased costs. After unsuccessful attempts to get fabric made in India according to its specifications, the company decided to bring manufacturing back to the United States.[11]

Managers spend about 80 percent of their time—6 hours and 24 minutes of every 8-hour day—in direct communication with others, whether on the telephone, in meetings, via e-mail, or in individual conversations. Company recruiters consistently rate effective communication, such as listening, conversing, and giving feedback, as the most important skill they look for when hiring new employees.

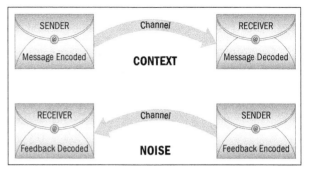

The Process of Communication

Every communication follows a step-by-step process that involves interactions among six elements: sender, message, channel, audience, feedback, and context. This process is illustrated in ▣ **Figure 9.3**.

See **FIGURE 9.3 The Communication Process**

In the first step, the *sender* composes the *message* and sends it through a communication carrier, or *channel*. Encoding a message means that the sender crafts its meaning in understandable terms and in a form that allows transmission through a chosen channel. The sender can communicate a particular message through many different channels, including face-to-face conversations, phone calls, and e-mail or texting. A promotional message to the firm's customers may be communicated through such forms as radio and television ads, billboards, magazines and newspapers, sales presentations, and social media such as Facebook and Twitter. The *audience* consists of the person or persons who receive the message. In decoding, the receiver of the message interprets its meaning. *Feedback* from the audience—in response to the sender's communication—helps the sender determine whether the audience has correctly interpreted the intended meaning of the message.

Every communication takes place in some sort of situational or cultural context. The *context* can exert a powerful influence on how well the process works. A conversation between two people in a quiet office, for example, may be a very different experience from the same conversation held at a noisy party. And words have different meanings in different cultures. For example, an American who orders chips in a British tavern will receive French fries.

Anthropologists classify cultures as *low context* or *high context*. Communication in low-context cultures such as Switzerland, Austria, Germany, and the United States tends to rely on explicit written and verbal messages. In contrast, communication in high-context cultures—such as those of Japan, Latin America, and India—depends not only on the message itself but also on the conditions that surround it, including nonverbal cues, past and present experiences, and personal relationships among the parties. Westerners must carefully temper their low-context style to the expectations of colleagues and clients from high-context countries. Although Americans tend to favor direct interactions and want to "get down to business" soon after shaking hands or sitting down to a business dinner, businesspeople in Mexico and Asian countries prefer to become acquainted before discussing details. When conducting business in these cultures, wise visitors allow time for relaxed meals during which business-related topics are avoided.

Senders must pay attention to audience feedback, even requesting it if none is forthcoming, because this response clarifies whether the communication has conveyed the intended message. Feedback can indicate whether the receiver heard the message and was able to decode it accurately. Even when the receiver tries to understand, the communication may fail if the message contained jargon or ambiguous words.

Noise during the communication process is any type of interference that affects the transmission of messages and feedback. Noise can result from simple physical factors, such as poor reception of a cell phone message or static that drowns out a radio commercial. It can also be caused by more complex differences in people's attitudes and perceptions. Consequently, even when people are exposed to the same communications, they can end up with very different perceptions and understandings because of communication noise.

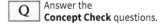

Answer the **Concept Check** questions.

Basic Forms of Communication

Managers and co-workers communicate in many different ways—by making a phone call, sending an e-mail, holding a staff meeting, or chatting in the hallway. They also communicate

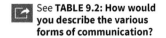

See **TABLE 9.2: How would you describe the various forms of communication?**

with facial expressions, gestures, and other body language. Subtle variations can significantly influence the reception of a message. As 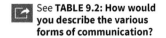 **Table 9.2** points out, communication takes various forms: oral and written, formal and informal, and nonverbal.

Oral Communication

Managers spend much time engaged in oral communication, both in person and on the phone. Some people prefer to communicate this way, believing that oral channels convey messages more accurately. Face-to-face oral communication allows people to combine words with such cues as facial expressions and tone of voice. Oral communication over the telephone lacks visual cues, but it does allow people to hear the tone of voice and creates an opportunity to provide immediate feedback by asking questions or restating the message. Because of its immediacy, oral communication has drawbacks. If one person is agitated or nervous during a conversation, noise enters the communication process. A hurried manager might brush off an employee who has an important message to deliver. A frustrated employee might feel compelled to fire a harsh retort at an unsupportive supervisor instead of thinking before responding.

In any medium, a vital component of oral communication is **listening**—receiving a message and interpreting its genuine meaning by accurately grasping the facts and feelings conveyed. Although listening may be the most important communication skill, most of us don't use it enough—or as well as we should.

Listening may seem easy because the listener appears to make no effort. But the average person talks at a rate of roughly 150 words per minute, while the brain can handle up to 400 words per minute. This gap can lead to listener boredom, inattention, and misinterpretation. In fact, immediately after listening to a message, the average person can recall only half of it. After several days, the proportion of a message that a listener can recall falls to 25 percent or less.

Certain types of listening behaviors are common in both business and personal interactions:

- *Cynical or defensive listening.* Occurs when the receiver of a message feels the sender is trying to gain some advantage from the communication.
- *Offensive listening.* Receiver tries to catch the speaker in a mistake or contradiction.
- *Polite listening.* Receiver listens to be polite rather than to contribute to communication. Polite listeners are usually inattentive and spend their time rehearsing what they want to say when the speaker finishes.
- *Active listening.* Receiver is involved with the information and shows empathy for the speaker's situation. In both business and personal life, active listening is the basis for effective communication.

Learning how to be an active listener is an especially important goal for business leaders because effective communication is essential to their role. Listening is hard work, but it pays off with increased learning, better interpersonal relationships, and greater influence.

Written Communication

Channels for written communication include reports, letters, memos, online discussion boards and social media, e-mails, and text messages. Many of these channels permit only delayed feedback and create a record of the message. It is important for the sender of a written communication to prepare the message carefully and review it to avoid misunderstandings—particularly before pressing that "send" button.

Effective written communication reflects its audience, the channel carrying the message, and the appropriate degree of formality. When writing a formal business document such as a complex marketing research report, a manager must plan in advance and carefully construct the document. The process of writing a formal document involves planning, research, organization, composition and design, and revision. Written communication via e-mail may call for a less-formal writing style, including short sentences, phrases, and lists.

E-mail is an effective communication channel for delivering straightforward messages and information. But e-mail's perceived effectiveness also leads to one of its biggest drawbacks: too much e-mail! Many workers find their valuable time being consumed with e-mail. To relieve this burden and leave more time for performing the most important aspects of the job, some companies are looking into ways to reduce the time employees spend sending and reading e-mail. To fulfill this need, some firms provide e-mail management services. Boston-based SaneBox provides customized e-mail solutions for firms that struggle to keep up with the volume of e-mail they receive and the time it takes to operate an in-house server.[12]

Security and retention present other e-mail concerns. Because e-mail messages are often informal, senders occasionally forget they're creating a written record. Even if the recipient deletes an e-mail message, other copies exist on company e-mail servers. Such e-mails can be used as evidence in lawsuits or disciplinary actions.

Formal Communication

A *formal communication channel* carries messages that flow within the chain-of-command structure defined by an organization. The most familiar channel, downward communication, carries messages from someone senior in the organization to subordinates. Managers may communicate downward by sending employees e-mail messages, presiding at department meetings, distributing policy manuals, posting notices on bulletin boards, and reporting news in company newsletters. The most important factor in formal communication is to be open and honest. "Spinning" bad news to make it look better almost always backfires. In a work environment characterized by open communication, employees feel free to express opinions, offer suggestions, and even voice complaints. Research has shown that open communication has the following seven characteristics:

1. *Employees are valued.* Employees are happier and more motivated when they feel they are valued and their opinions are heard.
2. *A high level of trust exists.* Telling the truth maintains a high level of trust, forming a foundation for open communication and employee motivation and retention.
3. *Conflict is invited and resolved positively.* Without conflict, innovation and creativity are stifled.
4. *Creative dissent is welcomed.* By expressing unique ideas, employees feel they have contributed to the organization and improved performance.
5. *Employee input is solicited.* The key to any organization's success is input from employees, which establishes a sense of involvement and improves working relations.
6. *Employees are well informed.* Employees are kept informed about what is happening within the organization.
7. *Feedback is ongoing.* Both positive and negative feedback are ongoing and are provided in a manner that builds relationships rather than assigns blame.[13]

Many firms also define formal channels for upward communications, encouraging communication from employees to supervisors and upward to leadership. Some examples of upward communication channels are employee surveys, suggestion boxes, and systems that allow employees to propose ideas for new products or voice complaints. Upward communication is also necessary for managers to evaluate the effectiveness of downward communication. ▣ **Figure 9.4** illustrates the forms of organizational communication, both formal and informal.

See **FIGURE 9.4 Formal and Informal Channels of Communication**

Informal Communication

Informal communication channels carry messages outside formally authorized channels within an organization's hierarchy. A familiar example of an informal channel is the **grapevine**, an internal channel that carries information from unofficial sources. All organizations, large or small, have grapevines. Grapevines disseminate information with speed and economy and are surprisingly reliable. But company communications must be managed effectively so that the grapevine is not the main source of information.

When properly nurtured, the grapevine can help managers get a feel for employee morale, understand what employees are thinking about, and evaluate the effectiveness of formal communications. Managers can improve the quality of information circulating through the company grapevine by sharing what they know, even if it is preliminary or partial information. By feeding information to selected people, smart leaders can harness the power of the grapevine.

But the grapevine is also a chief carrier of gossip. And because gossip can spread misinformation quickly—particularly if it reaches the Internet—a manager should deal directly with gossip to attempt to maintain the grapevine as a legitimate source of information.

More than ever before, as organizations become more decentralized and globally dispersed, informal communication provides an important source of information, through e-mail, texting, and social media.

Nonverbal Communication

So far, this section has considered different forms of verbal communication, or communication that conveys meaning through words. Equally important is *nonverbal communication,* which transmits messages through actions and behaviors. Gestures, posture, eye contact, tone and volume of voice, and even clothing choices are all nonverbal actions that become communication cues. Nonverbal cues can have a far greater impact on communications than many people realize. In fact, an estimated 70 percent of interpersonal communication is conveyed through nonverbal cues. Top salespeople are particularly adept at reading and using these cues. For example, they practice "mirroring" a customer's gestures and body language in order to indicate agreement.[14]

Even personal space—the physical distance between people engaging in communication—can convey powerful messages.

See **FIGURE 9.5 Influence of Personal Space in Nonverbal Communication**

■ **Figure 9.5** shows a continuum of personal space and social interaction with four zones: intimate, personal, social, and public. In the United States, most business conversations occur within the social zone, roughly from 4 to 12 feet apart. If one person tries to approach closer than that, the other individual will likely feel uncomfortable or even threatened.

Interpreting nonverbal cues can be especially challenging for people with different cultural backgrounds. Concepts of appropriate personal space differ dramatically throughout most of the world. Latin Americans conduct business discussions in positions that most Americans and northern Europeans would find uncomfortably close. Americans often back away to preserve their personal space, a gesture that Latin Americans perceive as a sign of unfriendliness. To protect their personal space, some Americans separate themselves across desks or tables from their Latin American counterparts—at the risk of challenging their colleagues to maneuver around those obstacles to reduce the uncomfortable distance.

People send nonverbal messages even when they consciously try to avoid doing so. Sometimes nonverbal cues convey a person's true attitudes and thoughts, which may differ from spoken meanings. Generally, when verbal and nonverbal cues conflict, receivers of the communication tend to believe the nonverbal content. This is why firms seeking to hire people with good attitudes and a team orientation closely watch nonverbal behavior during job interviews in which job applicants participate in group sessions with other job candidates applying for the same job. If in those group interviews an applicant frowns or looks discouraged when a competing candidate gives a good answer, that nonverbal behavior suggests that this person may not be strongly team oriented.

External Communication

External communication is a meaningful exchange of information through messages transmitted between an organization and its major audiences, such as customers, suppliers, other firms, the general public, the media, and government officials. Businesses use external communication for many purposes:

- To keep their operations functioning
- To maintain their position in the marketplace

- To preserve their corporate reputation
- To build customer relationships

Using external communication, organizations provide information on such topics as product modifications and price changes. Every communication with customers—including sales presentations and advertisements—should create goodwill and contribute to customer satisfaction. Letting the public know about the firm's new initiatives for environmentally friendly processes, community projects, and other socially responsible activities is an important function of external communication.

Q Answer the **Concept Check** questions.

WP LS Go to your WileyPLUS Learning Space course for video episodes, examples, art, tables, Concept Checks, practice, and resources that will help you succeed in this course.

Reading for

PRODUCTION AND OPERATIONS MANAGEMENT

WP LS Go to your WileyPLUS Learning Space course for video episodes, examples, art, tables, Concept Checks, practice, and resources that will help you success in this course.

See **FIGURE 10.1 The Production Process: Converting Inputs to Outputs**

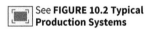

See **FIGURE 10.2 Typical Production Systems**

Q Answer the **Concept Check** questions.

Businesses can create or enhance four basic kinds of **utility:** time, place, ownership, and form. A firm's marketing operation generates time, place, and ownership utility by offering products to customers at a time and place that is convenient for the purchase. **Production** creates form utility by converting raw materials and other inputs into finished products. **Production and operations management** in a firm refers to overseeing the production process by managing people and machinery in converting materials and resources into finished goods and services (■ **Figure 10.1**).

People sometimes use the terms *production* and *manufacturing* interchangeably, but the two are actually different. Production spans both manufacturing and nonmanufacturing industries. For instance, companies that engage in fishing or mining engage in production, as do firms that provide package deliveries or lodging. Similarly, a hospital's services could be thought of as production—in this case, the number of patients seen versus the number of cars produced or the number of packages delivered. ■ **Figure 10.2** lists five examples of production systems for a variety of goods and services.

But whether the production process results in a tangible good such as a car or an intangible service such as cable television, it always converts *inputs* into *outputs*. A cabinetmaker combines wood, tools, and skill to create finished kitchen cabinets for a new home. A transit system combines buses, trains, and employees to create its output: passenger transportation. Both of these production processes create utility.

This chapter describes the process of producing goods and services, highlights the importance of production and operations management, and discusses the new technologies that are transforming the production function.

The Four Main Categories of Production Processes

Along with marketing and finance, production is a vital business activity. Without goods or services to sell, companies cannot generate money to pay their employees, lenders, and stockholders. And without profits, firms quickly fail. The production process is just as crucial in not-for-profit organizations, such as St. Jude Children's Research Hospital, because without financially profitable operations they too will fail. Effective production and operations management can lower a firm's costs of production, allowing it to respond dependably to customer demands and create sufficient cash to renew itself, providing new products to its customers. Throughout their business operations, firms must continually strive to provide high-quality goods and services. Quality is an essential element of all modern business operations. By building quality into every one of its business processes, a firm will be able to consistently meet customers' expectations and compete in their industry. The most successful firms in any industry are those that are able to provide the greatest utility to their customers.

When thinking about production, it is not surprising that an Apple iPad and a computer mouse pad are produced with very different processes. Some products, like the iPad, require a wide range of processes. Others, like the mouse pad, may require only a few. However, whether it's one process or many thousand, almost all production processes can be separated into several unique groups.

An *analytic production process* reduces a raw material to its component parts in order to extract one or more marketable products. Petroleum refining breaks down crude oil into several marketable products, including gasoline, heating oil, and aviation fuel. When corn is processed, the resulting marketable food products include animal feed and corn sweetener.

A *synthetic production process* is the reverse of an analytic process. It combines a number of raw materials or parts or transforms raw materials to produce finished products. Canon's assembly line produces a camera by assembling various parts such as a shutter or a lens cap. Other synthetic production systems make drugs, chemicals, computer chips, and canned soup.

A *continuous production process* generates finished items over a lengthy period of time. The steel industry provides a classic example. Its blast furnaces never completely shut down except for malfunctions. Petroleum refineries, chemical plants, and nuclear power facilities also practice continuous production. A shutdown can damage sensitive equipment, with extremely costly results.

An *intermittent production process* generates products in short production runs, shutting down machines frequently or changing their configurations to produce different products. Most services result from intermittent production systems. For instance, accountants, plumbers, and dentists traditionally have not attempted to standardize their services because each service provider confronts different problems that require individual approaches.

Answer the **Concept Check** questions.

Three Major Production Methods

Production activity can take place under various arrangements. *Mass production* is a system for manufacturing products in large quantities through effective combinations of employees with specialized skills, mechanization, and standardization. Mass production makes outputs (goods and services) available in large quantities at lower prices than individually crafted items would cost. Mass production is effective for creating large quantities of one item; *flexible production* is usually more cost-effective for producing smaller runs. A *customer-driven production* system evaluates customer demands in order to make the connection between products manufactured and products bought.

Mass Production

Mass production begins with the *specialization of labor,* dividing work into its simplest components so that each worker can concentrate on performing one task. By separating jobs into small tasks, managers create conditions for high productivity through *mechanization*, in which machines perform much of the work previously done by people. *Standardization* involves producing uniform, interchangeable goods and parts. Standardized parts simplify the replacement of defective or worn-out components. For instance, if your car's windshield wiper blades wear out, you can easily buy replacements at a local auto parts store such as AutoZone.

A logical extension of these principles of specialization, mechanization, and standardization led to development of the *assembly line process,* a common process in today's industries. This manufacturing method moves the product along a conveyor belt past a number of workstations, where workers perform specialized tasks such as welding, painting, installing individual parts, and tightening bolts. Henry Ford's application of this concept revolutionized auto assembly. Before the assembly line, it took Ford's workers 12 hours to assemble a Model T car. But with an assembly line, it took just 1.5 hours to make the same car.

Although mass production has important advantages, it has limitations, too. Mass production is highly efficient for producing large numbers of similar products, but it is highly inefficient when producing small batches of different items. This trade-off might tempt some companies to focus on efficient production methods rather than on making what customers really want. In addition, the labor specialization associated with mass production can lead to boring jobs because workers keep repeating the same task. To improve their competitive capabilities, many firms adopt flexible production and customer-driven production systems. These methods won't replace mass production in every case, but in many instances might lead to improved product quality and greater job satisfaction. It might also enhance the use of mass production.

Flexible Production

Flexible production can take many forms, but it generally involves using information technology to share the details of customer orders, programmable equipment to fulfill the orders, and skilled people to carry out whatever tasks are needed to fill a particular order. This system is even more beneficial when combined with lean production methods that use automation and information technology to reduce requirements for workers and inventory. Flexible production requires a lot of communication among everyone in the organization.

Customer-Driven Production

A customer-driven production system evaluates customer demands in order to make the connection between products manufactured and products bought. Many firms use this approach with great success. One method is to establish computer links between factories and retailers' scanners, using data about sales as the basis for creating short-term forecasts and designing production schedules to meet those forecasts. Another approach to customer-driven production systems is simply not to make the product until a customer orders it—whether it's a taco or a computer.

Massachusetts–based Custom Made is an online marketplace connecting buyers who want one-of-a-kind creations with a large variety of goods, including furniture and jewelry. By submitting a budget, photo, or description of what they would like to purchase, buyers connect with makers interested in producing the item. Buyers can also browse maker portfolios on the website and contact them directly.[1]

Q Answer the **Concept Check** questions.

The Strategic Decisions Made by Production and Operations Managers

Developing a production strategy often begins with a rereading of a firm's mission statement, identifying its core strengths, comparative advantages, and vision for the future. For example, an Internet retailer may decide that one of its core strengths is the management of a complex inventory system. Consequently, the organization may create an extensive warehousing system to offer customers quick, efficient product delivery (Amazon). Or a firm may decide the customer interface is its core strength, and it may then choose to rely on others to fulfill customer orders (eBay). Similarly, a firm may decide that they want to develop an extensive manufacturing capability (GE), or they may decide that they want to let others produce merchandise for them (Apple). These types of strategic choices often come down to what is known as a **make, buy, or lease decision**, choosing whether to produce a good or service in-house or purchase it from an outside supplier.

Many factors affect the make, buy, or lease decision, including the costs of leasing or purchasing parts from vendors compared with the costs of producing them in-house. The decision sometimes hinges on the availability of outside suppliers that can dependably meet a firm's standards for quality and quantity. A firm might not yet have the technology to produce certain components or materials, the technology might be too costly, or the firm may be concerned about maintaining control over its intellectual property (patents and copyrights).

The Location Decision

Once the basic strategy is established, one of the next decisions is where to locate an output facility. This decision often hinges on well-understood factors such as the cost of construction and the availability of utilities, transportation, and workers (as shown in 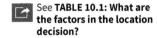 **Table 10.1**). Transportation factors include proximity to markets and raw materials and the availability of alternative modes for transporting both inputs and outputs. Automobile assembly plants are located near major rail lines. Inputs—such as engines, plastics, and metal parts—

 See **TABLE 10.1: What are the factors in the location decision?**

arrive by rail, and the finished vehicles are shipped out by rail. Shopping malls are often located next to major streets and freeways in suburban areas because most customers arrive by car.

Physical variables involve such issues as weather, water supplies, available energy, and options for disposing of hazardous waste. Theme parks, such as Walt Disney World, are often located in warm climates so they can be open and attract visitors year-round. A manufacturing business that wants to locate near a community must prepare an *environmental impact study* that analyzes how a proposed plant would affect the quality of life in the surrounding area. Regulatory agencies typically require these studies to cover topics such as the impact on transportation facilities; energy requirements; water and sewage treatment needs; natural plant life and wildlife; and water, air, and noise pollution.

Human factors in the location decision include an area's labor supply, local regulations, taxes, and living conditions. Management considers local labor costs as well as the availability of qualified workers. Software makers and other computer-related firms concentrate in areas with the technical talent they need, including Boston, California's Silicon Valley, and Austin, Texas. By contrast, some labor-intensive industries have located plants in rural areas with readily available labor pools and limited high-wage alternatives. And some firms with headquarters in the United States and other industrialized countries have moved production off-shore in search of low wages.

A continuing trend in location strategy is bringing production facilities closer to the markets where the goods will be sold. One reason for this is reduced time and cost for shipping. Another reason is a closer cultural affinity between the parent company and supplier (in cases where production remains overseas). Global snack food company Mondelez International, maker of such products as Oreo cookies, Cadbury candy, and Trident chewing gum, recently invested $190 million as part of its ongoing supply chain plan, which will address growth demands in emerging markets like India, as well as improving productivity and reducing costs.[2]

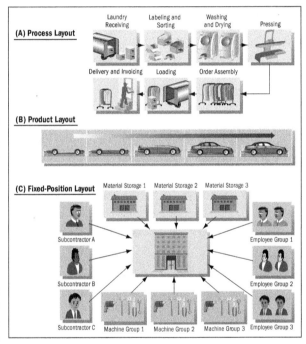

Determining the Facility Layout

Once decisions are made as to the basic design of the production process and location, production management's task is determining the best layout for the facility. An efficient facility layout can reduce material handling, decrease costs, and improve product flow through the facility. This decision requires managers to consider all phases of production and the necessary inputs at each step. ■ **Figure 10.3** shows three common layout designs: process, product, and fixed-position layouts.

See **FIGURE 10.3 Basic Facility Layouts**

A *process layout* groups machinery and equipment according to their functions. The work in process moves around the plant to reach different workstations. A process layout often facilitates production of a variety of nonstandard items in relatively small batches. Its purpose is to process goods and services that have a variety of functions. For instance, a typical machine shop generally has separate departments where machines are grouped by functions such as grinding, drilling, pressing, and lathing. Process layouts accommodate a variety of production functions and use general-purpose equipment that can be less costly to purchase and maintain than specialized equipment. Similarly, a service firm should arrange its facilities to enhance the interactions between customers and its services. If you think of patients as inputs, a hospital implements a form of the process layout. Banks, libraries, dental offices, and hair salons also use process layouts.

A *product layout*, also referred to as an assembly line, sets up production equipment along a product-flow line, and the work in process moves along this line past workstations. This type of layout efficiently produces large numbers of similar items, but it may prove inflexible and able to accommodate only a few product variations. Although product layouts date back at least to the Model T assembly line, companies are refining this approach with modern touches. Many auto manufacturers continue to use a product layout, but robots perform many of the activities that humans once performed. Automation overcomes one of the major drawbacks of this system—unlike humans, robots don't get bored doing a dull, repetitive job.

A *fixed-position layout* places the product in one spot, and workers, materials, and equipment come to it. This approach suits production of very large, bulky, heavy, or fragile products. For example, a bridge cannot be built on an assembly line. Fixed-position layouts dominate several industries including construction, shipbuilding, aircraft and aerospace, and oil drilling, to name a few. In all of these industries, the nature of the product generally dictates a fixed-position layout.

Selection of Suppliers

Once a company decides what inputs to purchase, it must choose the best vendors for its needs. To make this choice, production managers compare the quality, prices, dependability of delivery, and services offered by competing companies. Different suppliers may offer virtually identical quality levels and prices, so the final decision often rests on factors such as the firm's experience with each supplier, speed of delivery, warranties on purchases, and other services.

For a major purchase, negotiations between the purchaser and potential vendors may stretch over several weeks or even months, and the buying decision may rest with a number of colleagues who must say yes before the final decision is made. The choice of a supplier for an industrial drill press, for example, may require a joint decision by the production, engineering, purchasing, and quality-control departments. These departments often must reconcile their different views to settle on a purchasing decision.

The Internet has given buyers powerful tools for finding and comparing suppliers. Buyers can log on to business exchanges to compare specifications, prices, and availability. Ariba, now a division of German software maker SAP, provides cloud-based applications to the world's largest business-to-business community of more than 1.7 million businesses. This allows companies to collaborate with a global network of suppliers and partners valued at more than $700 billion in commerce.[3]

Approach to Inventory Control

Production and operations managers' responsibility for **inventory control** requires them to balance the need to keep stock on hand to meet demand against the costs of carrying inventory. Among the expenses involved in storing inventory are warehousing costs, taxes, insurance, and maintenance. Firms waste money if they hold more inventory than they need. On the other hand, having too little inventory on hand may result in a shortage of raw materials, parts, or goods for sale that could lead to delays and unhappy customers.

A **just-in-time (JIT) system** implements a broad management philosophy that reaches beyond the narrow activity of inventory control to influence the entire system of production and operations management. A JIT system seeks to eliminate anything that does not add value in operations activities by providing the right part at the right place at just the right time—right before it is needed in production.

Production using JIT shifts much of the responsibility for carrying inventory to vendors, which operate on forecasts and keep stock on hand to respond to manufacturers' needs. This concept is known as *vendor-managed inventory*. Suppliers that cannot keep enough high-quality parts on hand may be assessed steep penalties by purchasers. Another risk of using JIT systems is what happens if manufacturers underestimate demand for a product. Strong demand will begin to overtax JIT systems, as suppliers and their customers struggle to keep up with orders with no inventory cushion to tide them over.

Besides efficiency, effective inventory control requires careful planning to ensure the firm has all the inputs it needs to make its products. How do production and operations managers coordinate all of this information? They rely on **materials requirement planning (MRP)**, a computer-based production planning system that ensures a firm has all the parts and materials it needs to produce its output at the right time and place and in the right amounts.

Production managers use MRP programs to create schedules that identify the specific parts and materials required to produce an item. These schedules specify the exact quantities needed and the dates on which to order those quantities from suppliers so that they are delivered at the correct time in the production cycle. A small company might get by without an MRP system. If a firm makes a simple product with few components, a telephone call may ensure overnight delivery of crucial parts. However, for a complex product like a high-definition TV or commercial aircraft, a more sophisticated system is required.

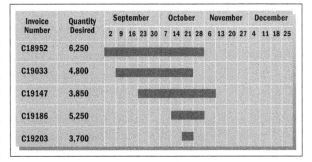 Answer the **Concept Check** questions.

Steps in the Production Control Process

While senior production executives set the strategy for a production operation, it is often the mid-level managers creating an operations plan that gets the facility "up and running." As a key component of an operations plan, **production control** creates a well-defined set of procedures for coordinating people, materials, and machinery to provide maximum production efficiency.

Suppose a watch factory must produce 80,000 watches during October. Production control managers break down this total into a daily production assignment of 4,000 watches for each of the month's 20 working days. Next, they determine the number of workers, raw materials, parts, and machines the plant needs to meet the production schedule. Similarly, a manager in a service business such as a restaurant must estimate how many dinners the kitchen will serve each day and then determine how many people are needed to prepare and serve the food, as well as what food to purchase. Production managers are responsible for all aspects of the production process, and careful planning, scheduling, routing, and monitoring are critical to their success.

Planning Details

In manufacturing, a production manager often starts with a *Bill of Materials (BOM),* a document that lists all the parts and materials needed to create the product. By comparing information about needed parts and materials with the firm's inventory data, purchasing staff can identify necessary purchases. Production managers will also identify the equipment, supplies, and labor required to build the product. Building more of a product, where the product design, manufacturing process, and production equipment exist, may be relatively straightforward. However, when a company is considering a new product (as Apple did with the iPad), it will spend considerable time and effort understanding the costs and the *lead times* of the new production processes, equipment, materials, and worker skills. Establishing the costs and times for production is an important part of a production manager's work, and often a company's success or failure is built on getting these details right.

Scheduling

In the *scheduling* phase of production control, managers develop timetables that specify how long each operation in the production process takes and when workers should perform it. Efficient scheduling ensures that production will meet delivery schedules and make efficient use of resources.

Whether the product is complex or simple to produce and whether it is a tangible good or a service, scheduling is important. A pencil is simpler to produce than a computer, but each production process has scheduling requirements. A stylist may take 25 minutes to complete each haircut with just one or two tools, whereas every day a hospital has to schedule procedures and treatments ranging from X-rays to surgery to follow-up appointments.

Production managers use a number of analytical methods for scheduling. One of the oldest methods, the *Gantt chart*, tracks projected and actual work progress over time. Gantt charts like the one in ■ **Figure 10.4** remain popular because they show at a glance the status of a particular project. However, they are most effective for scheduling relatively simple projects.

Invoice Number	Quantity Desired	September					October				November				December			
		2	9	16	23	30	7	14	21	28	6	13	20	27	4	11	18	25
C18952	6,250																	
C19033	4,800																	
C19147	3,850																	
C19186	5,250																	
C19203	3,700																	

See **FIGURE 10.4 Sample Gantt Chart**

A complex project might require a *PERT (program evaluation and review technique)* chart, which seeks to minimize delays by coordinating all aspects of the production process. First developed for the military, PERT has been modified for industry. The simplified PERT

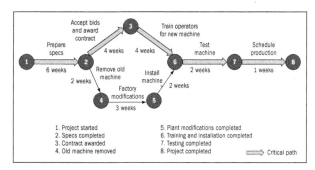

See **FIGURE 10.5 PERT Diagram for the Purchase and Installation of a New Robot**

diagram in ▣ **Figure 10.5** summarizes the schedule for purchasing and installing a new robot in a factory. The heavy, gold line indicates the *critical path*—the sequence of operations that requires the longest time for completion. In this case, the project cannot be completed in fewer than 17 weeks.

In practice, a PERT network may consist of thousands of events and may cover months of time. Complex computer programs help production managers develop such a network and find the critical path among the maze of events and activities. The construction of a huge office building requires complex production planning of this nature.

Routing and Dispatching

Moving an item through the production process is called *routing*. In general, routing determines the path or sequence of work throughout the facility, specifying who will perform the work at what location. Routing choices depend on two factors: the nature of the good or service and the facility layouts (discussed earlier in the chapter)—product, process, fixed position, or customer oriented. *Dispatching* is the phase of production control in which management instructs operators when to do the work. The dispatcher (often an automated system) authorizes performance, provides instructions, and sets priorities. For example, FedEx trucks are routed and then dispatched based on a complicated formula of package pick-up time, location, and type of shipment. Minimizing cost, maximizing employee productivity, and creating a high level of customer satisfaction are key goals of the FedEx operations.

Metrics and Measures

Measuring output is an important part of a production manager's responsibilities. The first step in implementing financial controls is to create a *budget* for the expected cost of the good or service. Budget elements include labor, materials, and overhead as well as test and inspection costs. Once the budget is established, the production manager can use the budget to determine whether the process is in financial control. Cost *variances* are the differences between the actual cost and the budgeted costs, with positive cost variances indicating that a process has higher costs than budgeted and negative cost variances showing a process costing less than budgeted. Operational controls are items such as throughput, yield, number of reworked parts, and production staffing level. Obviously, maintaining strict control over all these elements will allow the production manager to achieve their production targets.

Automation

Many manufacturers have freed workers from boring, sometimes dangerous jobs by replacing them with automated systems. A *robot* is a reprogrammable machine capable of performing a variety of tasks that require the repeated manipulation of materials and tools. Robots can repeat the same tasks many times without varying their movements. Many factories use robots today to stack their output on pallets and shrink-wrap them for shipping. Other types of automated systems include those that inspect, transport, and measure products. Inspection technology, for example, allows production managers to continuously track a process, including those that measure a product's length, width, weight, fill level, and the like. Automated systems extend well beyond individual robots and measurement stations. The whole assembly line can be automated with many robotic systems linked together. The end results of these efforts are production processes with lower costs, high yields, faster throughput, and better quality.

Computer-Aided Design and Manufacturing

Of all the technologies used in the *Star Trek* series, probably none is as interesting as the transporter. "Beam me up, Scotty" became one of the more memorable lines from the television show and movies. Being able to decompose a solid, transport it through space, and reconstruct it perfectly would be an extraordinary technical accomplishment. For now, "beaming" Captain Kirk or anyone "up" is clearly in the realm of science fiction. However, the rapid development of imaging, printing, and material technology has allowed "beaming" of a sort to take place. Today what is "beamed" is not the object itself but rather the information that describes the object. Teleportation in this way starts with a digital map of an object. Whether this map is made in a computer program such as AutoCAD or from images of the object, a geometric representation of the object is created in a digital format and stored in a computer memory. This information composed solely of 1's and 0's describes an object's size, shape, color, and material composition. When uploaded onto a 3D printer, the image becomes real.

Chuck Hull developed many of the key technologies for this process, which he went on to name photo stereolithography. His process used a liquid compound called photo resist (a material that hardens when exposed to light). By illuminating the photo resist with carefully directed beams of light, he was able to produce solid objects from the liquid photo resist. The company Hull founded, 3D Systems Inc., brought this technology to market.[4]

Today's 3D printers use a wide variety of processes and materials to create solid objects. And instead of costing many tens of thousands of dollars, desktop versions can be purchased for a few thousand dollars. While the object itself is not transported, the information used to describe the object can be "beamed" around the world and even into space.

What makes this technology possible is the combination of **computer-aided design (CAD)** software and **computer-aided manufacturing (CAM)** processes. Using these technologies, engineers can design components as well as entire products faster and with fewer mistakes that they could achieve using traditional systems. Software such as AutoCAD or TurboCAD allows designers to create entire products in the computer, specifying the physical dimensions, materials finishes, and mechanical properties. In the realm of architecture, AutoCAD is often the first and only drafting program used to render a building, creating wall, window, door, and structural elements as well as the mechanical and electrical fixtures. The customer gets a chance to see the building, including the ability to "fly" through the rooms long before it is built. When created in this fashion, engineers can make any changes required in the computer, saving both cost and time.

The process of CAM picks up where CAD systems leave off. When using CAM, engineers first develop a plan for creating the product. For example, if a metal part is required, the engineer would specify the size and shape of the block of metal from which the part will be fabricated. Then, the engineer would determine which parts of a block are to be cut away and which are to remain.

Programmable tools such as milling machines, lathes, laser cutters, and water jets are then chosen to perform these steps based on the amount of material to be removed and the configuration of the final product. Electronic files with this information are created and transmitted to the processing equipment. Automated systems take over from there with operators standing by to load and unload finished product. In the production of integrated circuits, no humans are involved, and the entire CAM process is handled by automated equipment. CAD and CAM technologies are used together in most modern production facilities, saving time and money and creating more precise products.

Q Answer the **Concept Check** questions.

The Importance of Quality Control

As it relates to the production of goods and services, **quality** is defined as being free of deficiencies. Quality matters because fixing, replacing, or redesigning deficient products or services is costly. If Seagate makes a defective computer hard drive, it has to either fix the drive or replace it to keep a customer happy. If American Airlines books too many passengers for a flight, it has to offer vouchers worth several hundred dollars to encourage passengers to give up their seats and take a later flight. As such, quality defines virtually all of a firm's processes from the way it designs products, delivers services, and handles customer complaints.

For most companies, the costs of poor quality can amount to 20 percent of sales revenue, if not more. Some typical costs of poor quality include downtime, repair costs, rework, and employee turnover. Poor quality can also result in lost sales and a tarnished image, something companies want to avoid. Lululemon, the Vancouver, Canada–based athletic apparel company, experienced quality issues with some of its yoga pants, which consumers complained were too sheer. Product recalls cost Lululemon millions of dollars, and the company suffered bad publicity when the situation was not handled promptly.[5]

Statistical Process Control

Quality control involves measuring output against established quality standards. Firms need such checks to spot defective products and to avoid delivering inferior shipments to customers. Standards should be set high enough to meet customer expectations. A 90 or 95 percent success rate might seem to be a good number, but consider what your phone service or ATM network would be like if it worked only 90 percent of the time. You would feel frustrated and inconvenienced and would probably switch your account to another phone service or ATM network provider.

Because the typical factory can spend up to half its operating budget identifying and fixing mistakes, a company cannot rely solely on inspections to achieve its quality goals. Instead, quality-driven production managers identify all processes involved in producing goods and services and work to maximize their efficiency. The causes of problems in the processes must be found and eliminated. If a company concentrates its efforts on better designs of products and processes with clear quality targets, it can ensure virtually defect-free production.

Statistical Process Control (SPC) is one method that companies use to evaluate a product or process quality. This method requires knowledge of the capabilities of the process and the requirement for the output. The process is then designed to achieve the desired result with data collected on the process measurements. With these data, production managers can create charts showing the process performance over time and allow corrections in the process before it creates out-of-tolerance parts.

Benchmarking

One process that companies use to ensure that they produce high-quality products from the start is **benchmarking**—determining how well other companies perform business functions or tasks. In other words, benchmarking is the process of determining other firms' standards and best practices. Automobile companies routinely purchase each other's cars and then take them apart to examine and compare the design, components, and materials used to make even the smallest part. They then make improvements to match or exceed the quality found in their competitors' cars.

Companies may use many different benchmarks, depending on their objectives. For instance, some organizations that want to make more money may compare their operating profits or expenses to those of other firms. Retailers concerned with productivity may want to benchmark sales per square foot. It's important when benchmarking for a firm to establish what it wants to accomplish, what it wants to measure, and which company can provide the most useful benchmarking information. A firm might choose a direct competitor for benchmarking, or it might select a company in an entirely different industry—but one that has processes the firm wants to study and emulate.

ISO Standards

The International Organization for Standardization (ISO, as it is often called) is an organization whose mission is to develop and promote international standards for business, government, and society to facilitate global trade and cooperation.

Operating since 1947, ISO is a network of national standards bodies from 162 countries. Its mission is to develop and promote international standards to facilitate global trade and cooperation. ISO has developed voluntary standards for everything from the format of banking and telephone cards to freight containers to paper sizes to metric screw threads. The U.S. member body of ISO is the American National Standards Institute.

The ISO 9000 family of standards gave requirements and guidance for quality management to help organizations ensure that their goods and services achieve customer satisfaction and also provide a framework for continual improvement. The ISO 14000 family of standards for environmental management helps organizations ensure that their operations cause minimal harm to the environment and achieve continual improvement of their environmental performance.

Both ISO 9001:2008 and ISO 14001:2004 can be used for certification, which means that the organization's management system (the way it manages its processes) is independently audited by a certification body (also known in North America as a registration body, or registrar) and confirmed as conforming to the requirements of the standard. The organization is then issued an ISO 9001:2008 or an ISO 14001:2004 certificate.

It should be noted that certification is not a requirement of either standard, which can be implemented solely for the benefits it provides the organization and its customers. However, many organizations opt to seek certification because of the perception that an independent audit adds confidence in its abilities. Business partners, customers, suppliers, and consumers may prefer to deal with or buy products from a certified organization. Certifications have to be periodically renewed through accompanying audits.

Though ISO develops standards, it does not itself carry out auditing and certification activities. This is done independently by hundreds of certification bodies around the world. The certificates they issue carry their own logo but not ISO's because the latter does not approve or control their activities.[6]

Q Answer the **Concept Check** questions.

WP LS Go to your WileyPLUS Learning Space course for video episodes, examples, art, tables, Concept Checks, practice, and resources that will help you success in this course.

Reading for
CUSTOMER-DRIVEN MARKETING

WP LS Go to your WileyPLUS Learning Space course for video episodes, examples, art, tables, Concept Checks, practice, and resources that will help you success in this course.

What is Marketing?

Every organization—from profit-seeking firms such as Jimmy John's and Zappos to not-for-profits such as the Make-a-Wish Foundation and the American Cancer Society—must serve customer needs to succeed. Perhaps the retail pioneer J. C. Penney best expressed this priority when he told his store managers, "Either you or your replacement will greet the customer within the first 60 seconds."

According to the American Marketing Association Board of Directors, **marketing** is "the activity, set of institutions, and processes for creating, communicating, delivering, and exchanging offerings that have value for customers, clients, partners, and society at large."[1] In addition to selling goods and services, marketing techniques help people advocate ideas or viewpoints and educate others. The American Heart Association has an online heart attack risk calculator and prevention guideline tools for consumers. Such tools help educate the general public about this widespread condition by listing its risk factors and common symptoms while describing the work of the association.[2]

To be a marketing professional means to understand a consumer's hopes, dreams, desires, and fears better than they do themselves and to create goods and services that will satisfy those needs. The best marketers not only give consumers what they want but even anticipate consumers' needs before those needs surface. Ideally, they can get a jump on the competition by creating a link in consumers' minds between the new need and the fulfillment of that need by the marketers' products. Examples of this approach include:

- NetJets offers fractional jet ownership to executives who want the luxury and flexibility of private ownership without the cost of owning their own plane.
- Airbnb is an online vacation rental site where people can list or lease spare rooms, apartments, homes, and other accommodations around the world.[3]

As these examples also illustrate, marketing is more than just developing exciting new products. It is a systematic process that begins with discovering unmet customer needs, researching the potential market; producing a good or service capable of satisfying the targeted customers; and promoting, pricing, and distributing that good or service. Throughout the entire marketing process, a successful organization focuses on building customer relationships.

Consider the simple act of purchasing a cup of coffee. Your purchase decision begins with the thought that a cup of coffee will satisfy a need you have, whether it be something warm to drink, to see your favorite barista, or to fulfill a morning ritual. Meeting this need (or any need, for that matter) requires that you identify a willing partner to the transaction. In the case of a cup of coffee, the other party may be a convenience store clerk, a vending machine, or a Seattle's Best server. When two or more parties benefit from trading things of value, they have entered into an **exchange process**.

On the surface, the exchange seems simple—some money changes hands, and you receive your cup of coffee. But the exchange process is more complex than that. It could not occur if you didn't feel the need for a cup of coffee or if the convenience store or vending machine were not available. You wouldn't choose Seattle's Best Coffee unless you were aware of the brand. Marketing plays a role in all aspects of this transaction.

How Marketing Creates Utility

The ability of a good or service to satisfy the wants and needs of customers is called **utility**. A company's production function creates *form utility* by converting raw materials, components, and other inputs from less valuable forms to more valuable finished goods and services. In the case of a cup of coffee, the beans, water, sugar, and cream (which together are worth only a few cents) are transformed into hot coffee (worth many times as much). In addition to form utility, the marketing function also creates time, place, and ownership utility.

- *Time utility* is created by making a good or service available when customers want to purchase it.
- *Place utility* is created by making a product available in a location convenient for customers.
- *Ownership utility* refers to an orderly transfer of goods and services from the seller to the buyer.

 Answer the **Concept Check** questions.

Evolution of the Marketing Concept

Marketing has always been a part of business, from the earliest village traders to large 21st century organizations producing and selling complex goods and services. Over time, however, marketing activities evolved through the five eras shown in 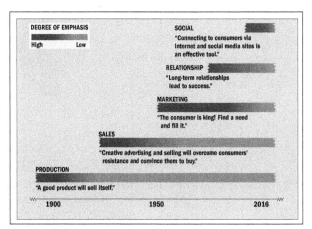**Figure 11.1**: the production, sales, marketing, and relationship eras, and now the social era. Note that these eras parallel some of the time periods discussed in Chapter 1.

For centuries, organizations operating in the *production era* stressed efficiency in producing quality products. Their philosophy could be summed up by the remark, "A good product will sell itself." Although this production orientation continued into the 20th century, it gradually gave way to the *sales era,* in which businesses assumed that consumers would buy as a result of their energetic sales efforts. Organizations didn't fully recognize the importance of their customers until the *marketing era* of the 1950s, when they began to adopt a consumer orientation.

See **FIGURE 11.1 Five Eras in the History of Marketing**

The emergence of the marketing era can be explained best by the shift from a *seller's market,* one with a shortage of goods and services, to a *buyer's market,* one with an abundance of goods and services. During the 1950s, the United States became a strong buyer's market, forcing companies to satisfy customers rather than just producing and selling goods and services. The marketing era continues today with companies focused on understanding their customers' needs and creating goods and services to meet these needs.

Recently, this focus has intensified, leading to the emergence of the *relationship era* in the 1990s and the *social era* of today. In the relationship era, companies emphasized customer satisfaction and building long-term business relationships. Today, the social era continues to grow exponentially, thanks to the Internet and social media sites like Facebook, Twitter, and LinkedIn. Companies routinely use mobile, social media, and the web as a way of marketing their goods and services to consumers.

Emergence of the Marketing Concept

The marketing era can also be identified with the term **marketing concept**, which refers to a companywide customer orientation with the objective of achieving long-run success. The basic idea of the marketing concept is that marketplace success begins with the customer. Successful firms analyze their customers' needs and then work backward to offer products that fulfill them. Exceptional firms are those that do a better job of understanding and meeting their customers' needs than their competitors. Apple, Nike, Budweiser, and GEICO are examples of firms that do an outstanding job marketing their products.

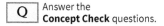 Answer the **Concept Check** questions.

Consumer Behavior

In the marketing era, all businesses, large or small, work diligently to provide the goods and services that satisfy their customers' needs. But who exactly are these customers? What are their needs? Where do they purchase and how do they use these products? The answers to these and many other questions are critical to a firm's understanding of their customers and the larger market for their products.

Both personal and interpersonal factors influence the way buyers behave. Personal influences on **consumer behavior** include individual needs and motives, perceptions, attitudes, learned experiences, and self-concept. For instance, to-day people are constantly looking for ways to save time, so firms do everything they can to provide goods and services designed for convenience. However, when it comes to products such as dinner foods, consumers want convenience, but they also want to enjoy the flavor of a home-cooked meal and spend quality time with their families. So companies offer frozen meals in family-size portions, and supermarkets offer freshly prepared take-out meals.

Sometimes external events influence consumer behavior. One study suggests that as a result of the recent recession, consumers may have permanently altered their buying and spending behavior. Industry analysts believe the increasing importance and growth of private label brands and consumers' focus on product value will continue. Manufacturers and retailers—especially small businesses—will need to create new marketing strategies in response to these ongoing challenges.[4]

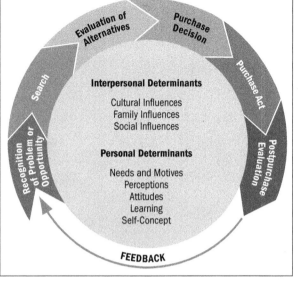

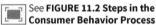

See **FIGURE 11.2 Steps in the Consumer Behavior Process**

Steps in the Consumer Behavior Process

In general, consumer decision making follows the sequential process outlined in ▣ **Figure 11.2**, with interpersonal and personal influences affecting every step. The process begins when the consumer recognizes a problem or opportunity. If someone needs a new pair of shoes, that need becomes a problem to solve. If you receive a promotion at work and a 20 percent salary increase, that change may also become a purchase opportunity.

To solve the problem or take advantage of the opportunity, consumers seek information about their intended purchase and evaluate alternatives, such as available brands. The goal is to find the best response to the problem or opportunity. Eventually, consumers reach a decision and complete the transaction. Later, they evaluate the experience by making a post-purchase evaluation. Feelings about the experience serve as feedback that will influence future purchase decisions. The various steps in the sequence are affected by both interpersonal and personal factors.

Q Answer the **Concept Check** questions.

Marketing Research

In addition to studying individual consumers, a firm can also investigate the larger market for their products. Whether it is conducted by the owner of a small business or by the marketing department of a Fortune 500 company, marketing research is more than just collecting data. **Marketing research** is the process of collecting and evaluating information to help marketers make effective decisions. Researchers must decide how to collect data, interpret the results, convert the data into decision-oriented information, and communicate those results to managers for use in decision making. This research links business decision makers to the marketplace by providing data about potential target markets that help them design—as in the case of GEICO Insurance—effective marketing approaches.

The technological advances over the last 20 years—the Internet, social media, mobile devices, and the like—have given rise to what's been called **big data**, information collected in massive amounts and at unprecedented speeds from both traditional and digital sources. These advances have made it possible for businesses to gather and analyze information from customers, visitors to company websites, social media sites, and more. Big data has the potential to increase revenue, create new business and marketing strategies, and build market share for companies large and small. The greatest challenge for marketers, however, is the ability to manage and analyze all of this data. According to IBM, more than 2.5 *quintillion* bytes of data are created worldwide every day.[5]

Obtaining Market Data

To get a complete picture of their markets, researchers need both internal and external data. Firms generate *internal data* within their organizations. Financial records provide a tremendous amount of useful information, such as changes in unpaid bills; inventory levels; sales generated by different categories of customers or product lines; profitability of particular divisions; or comparisons of sales by territories, salespeople, customers, or product lines.

Researchers gather *external data* from outside sources, including previously published data. Trade associations publish reports on activities in particular industries. Advertising agencies collect information on the audiences reached by various media. National marketing research firms offer information through subscription services. Some of these professional research firms specialize in specific markets, such as teens or ethnic groups. This information helps companies make decisions about developing or modifying products.

Secondary data, or previously published data, are low cost and easy to obtain. Federal, state, and local government publications are excellent data sources, and most are available online. The most frequently used government statistics include census data, which contain the population's age, gender, education level, household size and composition, occupation, employment status, and income. Even private research firms such as TRU (formerly Teenage Research Unlimited), which studies the purchasing habits of teens, provide some free information on their websites. This information helps firms evaluate consumers' buying behavior, anticipate possible changes in the marketplace, and identify new markets.

Even though secondary data are a quick and inexpensive resource, marketing researchers sometimes discover that this information isn't specific or current enough for their needs. If so, researchers may conclude that they must collect *primary data*—data collected firsthand through such methods as observation and surveys.

Simply observing customers cannot provide some types of information. A researcher might observe a customer buying a red sweater but have no idea why the purchase was made—or for whom. When researchers need information about consumers' attitudes, opinions, and motives, they need to ask the consumers themselves. They may conduct surveys by telephone, in person, online, or in focus groups.

A *focus group* gathers 8 to 12 people in a room or over the Internet to discuss a particular topic. A focus group can generate new ideas, address consumers' needs, and even point out flaws in existing products. Campbell Soup Company held nationwide focus groups in which respondents reviewed ingredients from two soups. Two of three focus group participants overwhelmingly chose the Campbell's brand.[6] Marketing researchers continue to take advantage of social media such as Facebook, Twitter, Pinterest, Tumblr, Instagram, and blogs, as well as mobile marketing.

Advanced Research Techniques

Once a company has built a database, marketers must be able to analyze the data and use the information it provides. **Data mining**, part of the broader field of **business intelligence**, is the task of using computer-based technology to evaluate data in a database and identify useful trends. These trends or patterns may suggest predictive models of real-world business activities. Accurate data mining can help researchers forecast sales levels and pinpoint sales prospects.

Companies such as TowerData collect publicly available personal information from social-networking sites like Facebook, Twitter, and other forums. They then sell this information to entities such as airlines and credit card companies that regard those individuals as potential customers. Such information can include everything from your blogging or posting habits to your credit rating. Among the issues arising from data mining are ownership of web user data, the targeting capabilities of the web, government supervision—and, of course, privacy.

Q Answer the **Concept Check** questions.

Market Segmentation

As a firm begins to develop a picture of its customers' needs, companies will often attempt to form their customers into groups called market segments. This is an important process, as companies can be much more efficient with their product design, production process, and promotional activities if they are targeting similar customers. Simply put, **market segmentation** is the process of dividing a market into homogeneous groups by isolating the traits that distinguish a certain group of customers from the overall market.

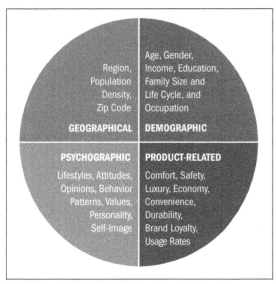

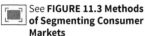
See **FIGURE 11.3 Methods of Segmenting Consumer Markets**

Firms have been segmenting markets since people first began selling products. Tailors made some clothing items for men and others for women. Tea was imported from India for tea drinkers in England and in other European countries. In addition to the segments based on demographic (gender, for example) and geographical (location) segmentation, today's marketers also define customer groups based on psychographic criteria—lifestyle and values—as well as product-related distinctions. ■ **Figure 11.3** illustrates the segmentation methods for consumer markets.

Geographic Segmentation

The oldest segmentation method is **geographic segmentation**—dividing a market into homogeneous groups on the basis of their locations. Geographic location does not guarantee that consumers in a certain region will all buy the same kinds of products, but it does provide some indication of needs. For instance, suburbanites buy more lawn care products than do central-city dwellers. Consumers who live in northern states, where winter is more severe, are more likely to buy ice scrapers, snow shovels, and snow blowers than those who live in warmer climates. Marketers also look at the size of the population of an area, as well as who lives there.

Demographic Segmentation

By far the most common method of market segmentation, **demographic segmentation**, distinguishes markets on the basis of various demographic or socioeconomic characteristics.

Common demographic measures include gender, income, age, occupation, household size, stage in the family life cycle, education, and racial or ethnic group. The U.S. Census Bureau is one of the best sources of demographic information for the domestic market. ■ **Figure 11.4** lists some of the measures used in demographic segmentation.

Gender is one of the simplest demographic segments and follows the basic premise that shopping and buying patterns are different between men and women.

With a rapidly aging population, age is perhaps the most volatile factor in demographic segmentation in the United States. Of

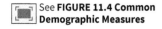
See **FIGURE 11.4 Common Demographic Measures**

the 325-plus million people projected to live in the United States over the next few years, almost 87 million will be age 55 or older.[7] Working from these statistics, marketers in the travel and leisure, retirement, and investments industries work hard to attract the attention of these Baby Boomers—people born between 1946 and 1964. Active-adult housing communities are one result of these efforts.

Young adults are another rapidly growing market. The entire scope of Generation Y—those born between 1976 and 1997—encompasses about 113 million Americans, a little more than one-third of the total U.S. population. Often called Millennials, these consumers are tech-savvy shoppers who are more likely than their Baby Boomer parents to use digital and mobile technologies to guide their purchase decisions.[8]

Psychographic Segmentation

Although demographic classifications such as age, gender, and income are relatively easy to identify and measure, researchers also need to define **psychographic segmentation** categories. Often marketing research firms conduct extensive studies of consumers and then share their psychographic data with clients. In addition, businesses look to studies done by sociologists and psychologists to help them understand their customers.

For instance, while children may fall into one age group and their parents in another, they also live certain lifestyles together. Recent marketing research reveals that today's parents are willing and able to spend more on goods and services for their children than parents were a generation or two ago. Current estimates suggest that middle income parents who had a baby last year will spend nearly $300,000 over the next 17 years while higher income families will spend close to $500,000 per child—and these amounts do not include the cost of a college education.[9] Psychographic information of this sort may give a company's management confidence that their proposed exclusive preschool or high-priced children's shoes might now be successful.

Product-Related Segmentation

Using **product-related segmentation**, sellers can divide a consumer market into groups based on buyers' relationships to the good or service. The three most popular approaches to product-related segmentation are based on benefits sought, usage rates, and brand loyalty levels.

Segmenting by *benefits sought* focuses on the attributes that people seek in a good or service and the benefits they expect to receive from it. As more firms respond to consumer demand for eco-friendly products, marketers find ways to emphasize the benefits of these products. Home-goods retailer IKEA follows strict guidelines for sourcing its solid-wood furniture products. For example, the worldwide company does not accept any illegally felled wood. IKEA's own forest specialists trace batches of timber to their origins to ensure that the lumber is properly documented and certified by the Forest Stewardship Council. In addition, these specialists work with suppliers to promote more sustainably managed forests worldwide. IKEA uses its website and signage in its stores to educate consumers about its wood-source policies.[10]

Consumer markets can also be segmented according to the amounts of a product that people buy and use. Segmentation by *product usage rate* usually defines such categories as light, medium, and heavy users. According to what is commonly referred to as the "80/20 principle," roughly 80 percent of a product's revenues come from only 20 percent of its buyers. Companies can now pinpoint which of their customers are the heaviest users—and even the most profitable customers—and direct their greatest marketing efforts toward those customers.

Marketers also segment users by *brand loyalty*—the degree to which consumers recognize, prefer, and insist on a particular brand. They then attempt to tie loyal customers to a good or service by giving away premiums, which can be anything from a logo-emblazoned T-shirt to a pair of free tickets to a concert or sports event.

Q | Answer the **Concept Check** questions.

Steps in Building a Marketing Strategy

Once a firm has a good understanding about likely customer behavior, the market in which it will operate, and how customers might group together, it transforms this information into a *marketing strategy*. Decision makers in any successful organization, for-profit or not-for-profit, follow a two-step process to develop their strategy. First, they study and analyze potential target markets, choosing those likely to yield the greatest profit, give them long-term growth potential, and provide defensible positions relative to their competitors. Second, they create a series of goods or services that will satisfy the chosen market.

A marketing plan is a key component of a firm's overall business plan. The marketing plan outlines its marketing strategy and includes information about the target market, sales and revenue goals, the marketing budget, and the timing for implementing the elements of the marketing mix.

Selecting Target Markets

Markets can be classified by type of product. **Consumer products (B2C)**—often known as business-to-consumer products—are goods and services, such as an SUV, tomato sauce, or a haircut, that are purchased by end users. **Business products (B2B)**—or business-to-business products—are goods and services purchased to be used, either directly or indirectly, in the production of other goods for resale. Some products can fit either classification, depending on who buys them and why. For example, your neighbors may buy a global positioning system (GPS) for their next road trip, or General Motors buys GPS systems by the thousands for installation on its assembly lines.

An organization's **target market** is the group of potential customers toward whom it directs its marketing efforts. Customer needs and wants vary considerably, and no single organization has the resources to satisfy everyone. *Popular Science* is geared toward readers who are interested in science and technology, whereas *Bon Appétit* is aimed at readers who are interested in fine food and cooking.

Decisions about marketing involve strategies for four areas of marketing activity: product, distribution, promotion, and pricing. A firm's **marketing mix** blends the four strategies to fit the needs and preferences of a specific target market. Marketing success depends not on the four individual strategies but on their unique combination.

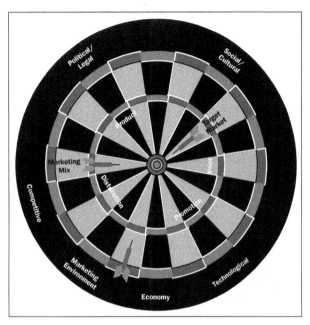

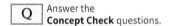 See **FIGURE 11.5 Target Market and Marketing Mix within the Marketing Environment**

Q Answer the **Concept Check** questions.

- *Product strategy* involves more than just designing a good or service with needed attributes. It also includes decisions about package design, brand names, trademarks, warranties, product image, new product development, and customer service. Think about your favorite pair of jeans. Do you like them because they fit the best, or do other attributes—such as styling and overall image—also contribute to your brand preference?
- *Distribution strategy* ensures that customers receive their purchases in the proper quantities at the right times and locations.
- *Promotional strategy* effectively blends advertising, personal selling, sales promotion, and public relations to achieve its goals of informing, persuading, and influencing purchase decisions.
- *Pricing strategy* involves one of the most difficult areas of marketing decision making: setting prices for a good or service. Pricing is sometimes subject to government regulation and considerable public scrutiny. It also represents a powerful competitive weapon and frequently produces responses by industry competitors who match price changes to avoid losing customers. Think about your jeans again. Would you continue to purchase them if they were priced either much higher or much lower?

Figure 11.5 shows the relationships among the target market, the marketing mix variables, and the marketing environment.

Relationship Marketing

The past decade has brought rapid change to most industries, as consumers have become better informed and more demanding purchasers by comparing competing goods and services. They expect, even demand, new benefits from product offerings, making it harder for firms to gain a competitive advantage based on product features alone.

In these competitive times, businesses need to find new ways of relating to customers if they hope to maintain long-term success. Businesses are developing strategies and tactics that draw them into tighter connections with their customers, suppliers, and even employees. As a result, many firms are turning their attention to the issues of relationship marketing. **Relationship marketing** goes beyond making the sale. It develops and maintains long-term, cost-effective exchange relationships with such partners as individual customers, suppliers, and employees. Its ultimate goal: customer satisfaction.

Managing relationships instead of simply completing transactions often leads to creative partnerships. However, customers enter into relationships with firms only if they are assured that the relationship will somehow benefit them. As the intensity of commitment increases, so does the likelihood of a business continuing a long-term relationship with its customers.

Businesses are building relationships by partnering with customers, suppliers, and other businesses. Timberland, maker of footwear and clothing, creates many partnerships that foster long-term relationships. The firm partners with not-for-profit organizations such as City Year and the Planet Water Foundation to complete service projects for communities and the environment. Through its Serv-a-palooza, hundreds of Timberland employees engage in volunteer tasks in their communities. Those opportunities even extend to customers who have expressed an interest in participating in programs in their own regions. To volunteer for a food drive or help restore a marsh, log on to the Timberland website to see what's available. All of these activities help build relationships with customers, communities, and other organizations.[11]

Benefits of Relationship Marketing

Relationship marketing helps all parties involved. In addition to providing mutual protection against competitors, businesses that forge solid links with vendors and customers are often rewarded with lower costs and higher profits than they would generate on their own. Long-term agreements with a few high-quality suppliers frequently reduce a firm's production costs. Unlike one-time sales, these ongoing relationships encourage suppliers to offer customers preferential treatment, quickly adjusting shipments to accommodate changes in orders and correcting any quality problems that might arise.

Good relationships with customers can be vital strategic weapons for a firm. By identifying current purchasers and maintaining positive relationships with them, organizations can efficiently target their best customers. Studying current customers' buying habits and preferences can help marketers identify potential new customers and establish ongoing contact with them. Attracting a new customer can cost five times as much as keeping an existing one. Not only are marketing costs lower with existing customers, they usually buy more, require less service, refer other customers, and provide valuable feedback. Together, these elements contribute to a higher **lifetime value of a customer**—the revenues and intangible benefits (referrals and customer feedback) from the customer over the life of the relationship, minus the amount the company must spend to acquire and serve that customer. Keeping that customer may occasionally require some extra effort, especially if the customer has become upset or dissatisfied with a good or service.

Businesses also benefit from strong relationships with other companies. Purchasers who repeatedly buy from one business may find they save time and gain service quality as the business learns their specific needs. Some relationship-oriented companies also customize items based on customer preferences. Because many businesses reward loyal customers with discounts or bonuses, some buyers may even find they save money by developing long-term relationships.

Alliances with other firms to serve the same customers also can be rewarding. The partners combine their capabilities and resources to accomplish goals that they could not reach on their own. In addition, alliances with other firms may help businesses develop the skills and experiences they need to successfully enter new markets or improve service to current customers.

Tools for Nurturing Customer Relationships

Although relationship marketing has important benefits for both customers and businesses, most relationship-oriented businesses quickly discover that some customers generate more profitable business than others. Assume 20 percent of a firm's customers account for roughly 80 percent of its sales and profits—the 80/20 principle mentioned earlier in the chapter—a customer in that category undoubtedly has a higher lifetime value than one who buys only once or twice or who makes small purchases.

While businesses shouldn't ignore any customer, they need to allocate their marketing resources wisely. A firm may choose to customize goods or services for high-value customers while working to increase repeat sales of stock products to less valuable customers. Differentiating between these two groups also helps marketers focus on each in an effort to increase their commitment.

Frequency Marketing and Affinity Marketing Programs

Marketers try to build and protect customer relationships with **frequency marketing** programs. Such programs reward frequent customers with cash, rebates, merchandise, or other premiums. Frequency programs have grown more sophisticated over the years, offering more personalization and customization than in the past. Airlines, hotel groups, restaurants, and many retailers, including supermarkets, offer frequency programs. For example, vacationers who book a certain number of nights at a Caribbean resort may earn airfare or dining credits for their trip.

Affinity programs build emotional links with customers. In an **affinity program**, an organization solicits involvement by individuals who share common interests and activities.

Affinity programs are common in the credit card industry. For instance, a person can sign up for a credit card emblazoned with the logo of his or her college, favorite charity, or a sports team.

One-on-One Marketing

The ability to customize products and rapidly deliver goods and services has become increasingly dependent on technology such as computer-aided design and manufacturing (CAD/CAM). The Internet offers a way for businesses to connect with customers in a direct and intimate manner. Companies can take orders for customized products, gather data about buyers, and predict what items a customer might want in the future. Computer databases provide strong support for effective relationship marketing. Marketers can maintain databases on customer tastes, price range preferences, and lifestyles, and they can quickly obtain names and other information about promising prospects.

Amazon.com greets each online customer with a list of suggested products he or she might like to purchase. Many online retailers send their customers e-mails about upcoming sales, new products, and special events.

Small and large companies often rely on *customer relationship management* software technology that helps them gather, sort, and interpret data about customers. Software firms develop this software to help businesses build and manage their relationships with customers. QueueBuster is one such product. The software offers a caller the choice of receiving an automated return call at a convenient time instead of waiting on hold for the next available representative. After implementing the software to support its central reservations team, the Apex Hotel chain minimized the number of dropped customer calls and increased customer-service levels. This simple solution to customers' frustration not only helped build customer loyalty and improve employee morale but also helped save Apex Hotels from losing business.[12]

Q | Answer the **Concept Check** questions.

> **WP LS** Go to your WileyPLUS Learning Space course for video episodes, examples, art, tables, Concept Checks, practice, and resources that will help you success in this course.

Reading for
PRODUCT AND DISTRIBUTION STRATEGIES

12

WP LS Go to your WileyPLUS Learning Space course for video episodes, examples, art, tables, Concept Checks, practice, and resources that will help you success in this course.

Products and Services

Most people respond to the question "What is a product?" by listing its physical features. In contrast, marketers take a broader view. To them, a **product** is a bundle of physical, service, and symbolic characteristics designed to satisfy consumer wants. The chief executive officer of a major tool manufacturer once startled his stockholders with this statement: "Last year our customers bought over 1 million quarter-inch drill bits, and none of them wanted to buy the product. They all wanted quarter-inch holes." Product strategy involves considerably more than just producing a good or service; instead, it focuses on benefits. The marketing conception of a product includes decisions about package design, brand name, trademarks, warranties, product image, new product development, and customer service.

Classifying Consumer Goods and Services

The classification that marketers typically use for products that consumers buy for their own use and enjoyment and not for resale is based on consumer buying habits. *Convenience products* are items the consumer seeks to purchase frequently, immediately, and with little effort. Items stocked in gas station mini-markets, vending machines, and local newsstands are usually convenience products—for example, newspapers, snacks, candy, coffee, and bread. *Shopping products* are those typically purchased only after the buyer has compared competing products in competing stores. A person intent on buying a new sofa or dining room table may visit many stores, examine perhaps dozens of pieces of furniture, and spend days making the final decision. *Specialty products* are those that a purchaser is willing to make a special effort to obtain. The purchaser is already familiar with the item and considers it to have no reasonable substitute. The nearest Lexus dealer may be 75 miles away, but if you have decided you want one, you will make the trip.

The interrelationship of marketing mix factors is shown in 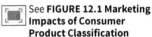 **Figure 12.1**. By knowing the appropriate classification for a specific product, the marketing decision maker knows quite a bit about how to adapt the other mix variables to create a profitable, customer-driven marketing strategy.

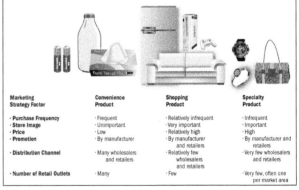

Marketing Strategy Factor	Convenience Product	Shopping Product	Specialty Product
· Purchase Frequency	· Frequent	· Relatively infrequent	· Infrequent
· Store Image	· Unimportant	· Very important	· Important
· Price	· Low	· Relatively high	· High
· Promotion	· By manufacturer	· By manufacturer and retailers	· By manufacturer and retailers
· Distribution Channel	· Many wholesalers and retailers	· Relatively few wholesalers and retailers	· Very few wholesalers and retailers
· Number of Retail Outlets	· Many	· Few	· Very few, often one per market area

See **FIGURE 12.1 Marketing Impacts of Consumer Product Classification**

Classifying Business Goods

Business products are goods and services used in operating an organization. They can be as simple as paper towels and coffee filters for the break room to machinery, tools, raw materials, components, and buildings. Consumer products are classified by buying habits, and business products are classified based on how they are used and by their basic characteristics. Products that are long-lived and relatively expensive are called *capital items.* Less costly products that are consumed within a year are referred to as *expense items.*

Classifying Services

Services can be classified as intended for the consumer market or the business market. Child- and elder-care centers and auto detail shops provide services for consumers; the Pinkerton security patrols at a local factory and Kelly Services' temporary office workers are examples of business services. In some cases, a service can accommodate both consumer and business markets. For example, ServiceMaster may clean the upholstery in a home or spruce up the painting system and robots in a manufacturing plant.

Like tangible goods, services can also be considered "convenience," "shopping," or "specialty," depending on customers' buying patterns. However, services are distinguished from goods in several ways. First, unlike goods, services are intangible. In addition, they are perishable because firms cannot stockpile them in inventory. Services are also difficult to standardize because they must meet individual customers' needs. Finally, from a buyer's perspective, the service provider *is* the service; the two are inseparable in the buyer's mind.

Product Lines and Product Mix

Few firms operate with a single product. If their initial entry is successful, they often try to increase their profit and growth chances by adding new offerings. A company's **product line** is a group of related products marked by physical similarities or intended for a similar market. A **product mix** is the assortment of product lines and individual goods and services that a firm offers to consumers and business users. The Coca-Cola Company and PepsiCo both have product lines that include old standards—Coke Classic and Diet Coke, Pepsi and Diet Pepsi.

Marketers must assess their product mix continually to ensure company growth, to satisfy changing consumer needs and wants, and to adjust to competitors' offerings. To remain competitive, marketers look for gaps in their product lines and fill them with new offerings or modified versions of existing ones. A helpful tool frequently used in making product decisions is the product life cycle.

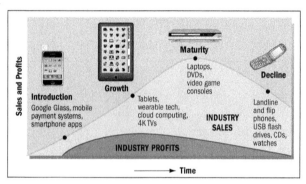

See **FIGURE 12.2 Stages in the Product Life Cycle**

Q Answer the **Concept Check** questions.

Product Life Cycle

Once a product is on the market, it typically goes through four stages known as the **product life cycle**: introduction, growth, maturity, and decline. As **Figure 12.2** shows, industry sales and profits vary depending on the life cycle stage of an item.

Product life cycles are not set in stone; not all products follow this pattern precisely, and different products may spend different periods of time in each stage. However, the concept helps marketers anticipate developments throughout the various stages of a product's life. Profits assume a predictable pattern through the stages, and promotional emphasis shifts from dispensing product information in the early stages to heavy brand promotion in the later ones.

Stages of the Product Life Cycle

In the *introduction stage,* the firm tries to stimulate demand for its new offering; inform the market about it, give free samples, and explain its features, uses, and benefits. Sales are limited in this phase, and new product development costs and extensive introductory promotions are expensive and commonly lead to losses in the introductory stage. Figure 12.2 shows an introduction phase of smoothly increasing sales, but this is not always the case. Sometimes an introduction begins well but quickly runs out of steam as product pricing or production issues restrict the number of buyers. Plasma televisions, Apple's Maps app, and Google Buzz are all examples of products that didn't quite make it through the introduction stages as planned.

During the *growth stage,* sales climb quickly as new customers join early users who now are repurchasing the item. Word-of-mouth referrals and continued advertising and other special promotions by the firm induce others to make trial purchases. At this point, the company begins to earn profits on the new product. This success may encourage competitors to enter the field with similar offerings, and if a number of new competitors come into the market, price competition develops. After its initial success with the Kindle, Amazon faced competition from Barnes & Noble's Nook. After Amazon rushed to launch its Kindle for the iPad, Barnes & Noble countered with its Nook Color. Since then, the tablet market has become increasingly crowded, with the iPad still leading the sector with more than 26 percent of the global market share.[1]

In the *maturity stage,* industry sales at first increase but eventually reach a saturation level at which further expansion is difficult. Competition also intensifies, increasing product availability. Firms concentrate market share, trying to capture their competitors' customers, often by dropping prices to increase the appeal of their product. Manufacturers of mature products look to product line extension to redesign their products to appeal to smaller and smaller groups of customers. Soft drink and beer producers are constantly bringing out new products: low calorie, no-calorie, colored, uncolored, flavors, and more. Smart phones are in the maturity stage: competitors compete not only on price but also on features, such as operating systems, screen size, weight, battery life, and the like. Sales volume fades late in the maturity stage, and weaker competitors may leave the market.

Sales continue to fall in the *decline stage.* Profits decline and may become losses as further price cutting occurs in the reduced overall market for the item. Competitors gradually exit, making some profits possible for the remaining firms in the shrinking market. The decline stage usually is caused by a product innovation or a shift in consumer preferences. Sometimes technology change can hasten the decline stage for a product. For example, DVD players have been replaced by other technologies, including online streaming of content.

Stages in New Product Development

So, what does it take to develop a successful new product? Most of today's newly developed items are aimed at satisfying specific consumer demands. New product development is becoming increasingly efficient and cost effective because marketers use a systematic approach to developing new products. As 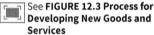 **Figure 12.3** shows, the new product development process has six stages. Each stage requires a "go/no-go" decision by management before the idea can move to a subsequent stage. Significant investments of time and money are involved in products as they go through each development stage—sometimes only to be rejected at one of the final stages. For this reason, the sooner decision makers can identify a marginal product and drop it from further consideration, the less time and money will be wasted.

The starting point in the new product development process is generating ideas. Ideas come from many sources, including customer suggestions, suppliers, employees, research scientists, marketing research, inventors outside the firm, and competitors' products. The most successful ideas are directly related to satisfying customer needs. California-based Future Motion has created Onewheel, a self-balancing, single-wheel skateboard with speeds of up to 12 miles per hour. Using self-balancing technology, leaning forward speeds up the skateboard and leaning back slows it down. Features include a rechargeable lithium battery and iPhone and Android apps to monitor speed, acceleration, and range.[2]

In the second stage, screening eliminates ideas that do not mesh with overall company objectives or that cannot be developed, given the company's resources. Some firms hold open discussions of new product ideas with specialists who work in different functional areas in the organization.

Further screening occurs during the concept development and business analysis phase. The analysis involves assessing the new product's potential sales, profits, growth rate, and competitive strengths and determining whether it fits with the company's product, distribution, and promotional resources. *Concept testing*—marketing research designed to solicit initial consumer reaction to new product ideas—may be used at this stage. For example, potential consumers might be asked about proposed brand names and other methods of product identification. *Focus groups* are sessions in which consumers meet with marketers to discuss what they like or dislike about current products and perhaps test or sample a new offering to provide some immediate feedback.

Next, an actual product is developed, subjected to a series of tests, and revised. Functioning prototypes or detailed descriptions of the product may be created. These

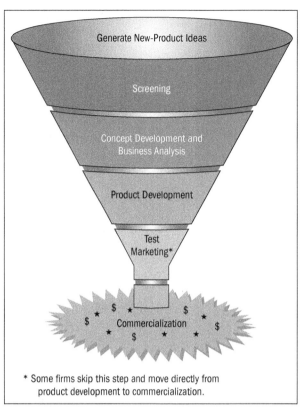

Generate New-Product Ideas

Screening

Concept Development and Business Analysis

Product Development

Test Marketing*

Commercialization

* Some firms skip this step and move directly from product development to commercialization.

See **FIGURE 12.3 Process for Developing New Goods and Services** designs are the joint responsibility of the firm's development staff and its marketers, who provide feedback on consumer reactions to the proposed product design, color, and other physical features.

Sometimes prototypes do not meet the stated requirements. In search of a quick-drying camouflage uniform for tropical environments, the U.S. Marines are back to the drawing board after testing four prototypes at the jungle warfare training center in Okinawa, Japan. Although the uniforms provide ample protection and durability, they need to dry in 20 minutes rather than the usual 40 minutes.[3]

Test marketing introduces a new product supported by a complete marketing campaign to a selected city or TV coverage area. Marketers look for a location with a manageable size, where residents match their target market's demographic profile, to test their product. During the test-marketing stage, the item is sold in a limited area while the company examines both consumer responses to the new offering and the marketing effort used to support it. Test-market results can help managers determine the product's likely performance in a full-scale introduction. Some firms skip test marketing, however, because of concerns that the test could reveal their strategies to the competition. Also, the expense of doing limited production runs of complex products such as a new auto or refrigerator is sometimes so high that marketers skip the test-marketing stage and move directly to the next stage.

In the final stage, commercialization, the product is made available in the marketplace. Sometimes this stage is referred to as a product launch. Considerable planning goes into this stage because the firm's distribution, promotion, and pricing strategies must all be geared to support the new product offering. Mercedes-Benz recently announced plans to launch 30 new models over the next several years as part of an ongoing effort to revitalize its product lines. The S600 is the first Mercedes to have a jet fighter–inspired display for the driver that includes navigation instructions, vehicle speed, and cruise control settings. The car also has a touchpad controller for the onboard "infotainment" system, which functions like a smart phone or tablet.[4]

> **Q** Answer the **Concept Check** questions.

Product Identification

A major aspect of developing a successful new product involves methods for identifying a product and distinguishing it from competing offerings. Both tangible goods and intangible services are identified by brands, brand names, and trademarks. A **brand** is a name, term, sign, symbol, design, or some combination that identifies the products of one firm and differentiates them from competitors' offerings. Tropicana, Pepsi, and Gatorade are all made by PepsiCo, but a unique combination of name, symbol, and package design distinguishes each brand from the others.

A **brand name** is that part of the brand consisting of words or letters included in a name used to identify and distinguish the firm's offerings from those of competitors. The brand name is the part of the brand that can be vocalized. Many brand names, such as Coca-Cola, McDonald's, American Express, Google, and Nike, are famous around the world. Likewise, the "golden arches" brand mark of McDonald's also is widely recognized.

A **trademark** is a brand that has been given legal protection. The protection is granted solely to the brand's owner. Trademark protection includes not only the brand name but also design logos, slogans, packaging elements, and product features such as color and shape. A well-designed trademark, such as the Nike "swoosh," can make a difference in how positively consumers perceive a brand.

Brand Categories, Loyalty, and Equity

A brand offered and promoted by a manufacturer is known as a *manufacturer's* (or *national*) *brand*. Examples are Tide, Cheerios, Windex, North Face, and Nike. But not all brand names belong to manufacturers; some are the property of retailers or distributors. A *private* (or *store*) *brand* identifies a product that is not linked to the manufacturer but instead carries a wholesaler's or retailer's label. Sears's Craftsman tools and Walmart's Ol' Roy dog food are examples.

Marketers measure brand loyalty in three stages: brand recognition, brand preference, and brand insistence. *Brand recognition* is brand acceptance strong enough that the consumer is aware of the brand but not strong enough to cause a preference over other brands. *Brand preference* occurs when a consumer chooses one firm's brand over a competitor's if the favored brand is available. *Brand insistence* is the ultimate degree of brand loyalty, in which the consumer will look for it at another outlet, special-order it from a dealer, order by mail, or search the Internet for it.

Brand loyalty is at the heart of **brand equity**, the added value that a respected and successful name gives to a product. This value results from a combination of factors, including awareness, loyalty, and perceived quality, as well as any feelings or images the customer associates with the brand. High brand equity offers financial advantages to a firm because the product commands a relatively large market share and sometimes reduces price sensitivity, generating higher profits. ■ **Figure 12.4** shows the world's ten most valuable brands and their estimated worth.

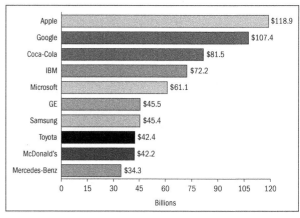

See **FIGURE 12.4 The World's Ten Most Valuable Brands (sales in billions)**

Source: Company website, "Interbrand's 15th Annual Best Global Brands Report," http://interbrand.com, accessed March 26, 2015.

Packages and Labels

Packaging and labels are important in product identification. They also play an important role in a firm's overall product strategy. Packaging affects the durability, image, and convenience of an item and is the biggest cost in many consumer products. Due to a growing demand to produce smaller, more environmentally friendly packages, box manufacturers and chemical companies are now working harder to create packaging that uses less material, is made from renewable sources, and is recyclable.

Choosing the right package is especially crucial in international marketing because marketers must be aware of such factors as language variations and cultural preferences. Package size can vary according to a country's purchasing patterns and market conditions. In countries with small refrigerators, people may want to buy their beverages one at a time rather than in six-packs. Package weight is another important issue because shipping costs are often calculated based on weight.

Labeling is an integral part of the packaging process. In the United States, federal law requires companies to provide enough information on labels to allow consumers to make value comparisons among competing products. In the case of food packaging, labels must also provide nutrition information. Companies that ship products to other countries must comply with labeling requirements in those nations.

Another important aspect of packaging and labeling is the *Universal Product Code (UPC),* the bar code read by optical scanners that print the name of the item and the price on a receipt. For many stores, these identifiers are useful not just for packaging and labeling but also for simplifying and speeding retail transactions and for evaluating customer purchases and controlling inventory. Industry observers believe that radio-frequency identification technology—embedded chips that can broadcast their product information to receivers— may ultimately replace UPC bar codes.

A technology akin to bar codes, Quick Response (QR) codes are also used in product packaging, allowing companies to create electronic paths directly to a company's website and providing consumers with information about the product or company.

Answer the **Concept Check** questions.

Distribution Strategy

The next element of the marketing mix, **distribution**, deals with the marketing activities and institutions involved in getting the right good or service to the firm's customers. Distribution decisions involve modes of transportation, warehousing, inventory control, order processing, and selection of marketing channels. Marketing channels typically are made up of intermediaries such as retailers and wholesalers that move a product from producer to final purchaser.

The two major components of an organization's distribution are distribution channels and physical distribution. **Distribution channels** are the paths that products—and legal ownership of them—follow from producer to consumer or business user. They are the means by which all organizations distribute their goods and services. **Physical distribution** is the

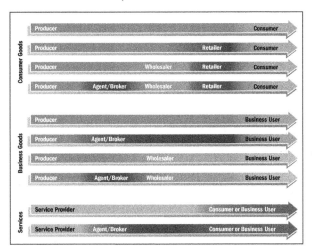

Consumer Goods:
- Producer → Consumer
- Producer → Retailer → Consumer
- Producer → Wholesaler → Retailer → Consumer
- Producer → Agent/Broker → Wholesaler → Retailer → Consumer

Business Goods:
- Producer → Business User
- Producer → Agent/Broker → Business User
- Producer → Wholesaler → Business User
- Producer → Agent/Broker → Wholesaler → Business User

Services:
- Service Provider → Consumer or Business User
- Service Provider → Agent/Broker → Consumer or Business User

See **FIGURE 12.5 Alternative Distribution Channels**

Q Answer the **Concept Check** questions.

actual movement of products from producer to consumers or business users. Physical distribution covers a broad range of activities, including customer service, transportation, inventory control, materials handling, order processing, and warehousing.

Distribution Channels

In their first decision for distribution channel selection, marketers choose which type of channel will best meet both their firm's marketing objectives and customers' needs. As shown in **Figure 12.5**, marketers can choose either a *direct distribution channel*, which carries goods directly from producer to consumer or business user, or distribution channels that involve several different marketing intermediaries. A *marketing intermediary* (also called a *middleman*) is a business firm that moves goods between producers and consumers or business users. Marketing intermediaries perform various functions that help the distribution channel operate smoothly, such as buying, selling, storing, and transporting products; sorting and grading bulky items; and providing information to other channel members. The two main categories of marketing intermediaries are wholesalers and retailers.

- **Direct Distribution** The shortest and simplest means of connecting producers and customers is direct contact between the two parties. Consumers who buy fresh fruits and vegetables at rural roadside stands or farmers markets use direct distribution, as do services ranging from banking and 10-minute oil changes to ear piercing and Mary Kay Cosmetics.
- **Using Marketing Intermediaries** Although direct channels allow simple and straightforward connections between producers and their customers, the list of channel alternatives in Figure 12.5 suggests that direct distribution is not the best choice in every instance. Some products sell in small quantities for relatively low prices to thousands of widely scattered consumers. Makers of such products cannot cost effectively contact each of their customers, so they distribute products through specialized intermediaries called *wholesalers* and *retailers*.

Wholesaling

How do retailers get the products that fill their shelves? A **wholesaler** is the distribution channel member that sells primarily to retailers, other wholesalers, or business users. For instance, Sysco is a wholesaler that buys food products from producers and then resells them to restaurants, hotels, and other institutions across North America.

Wholesaling is a crucial part of the distribution channel for many products, particularly consumer goods and business supplies. Wholesaling intermediaries can be classified on the basis of ownership; some are owned by manufacturers, some are owned by retailers, and others are independently owned. The United States has about 434,000 wholesalers, three-quarters of which have fewer than 20 employees.[5]

Manufacturer-Owned Wholesaling Intermediaries

A manufacturer may decide to distribute goods directly through company-owned facilities to control distribution or customer service. Firms operate two main types of manufacturer-owned wholesaling intermediaries: sales branches and sales offices.

A *sales branch* stocks the products it distributes and fills orders from its inventory. It also provides offices for sales representatives. Sales branches are common in the chemical, petroleum products, motor vehicle, and machine and equipment industries.

A *sales office* is exactly what its name implies: an office for a producer's salespeople. Manufacturers set up sales offices in various regions to support local selling efforts and improve customer service. Some kitchen and bath fixture manufacturers maintain showrooms to display their products. Builders and designers can visit these showrooms to see how the items would look in place. Unlike sales branches, however, sales offices do not store any inventory. When a customer orders from a showroom or other sales office, the merchandise is delivered from a separate warehouse.

110

Independent Wholesaling Intermediaries

An independent wholesaling intermediary is a business that represents a number of different manufacturers and makes sales calls on retailers, manufacturers, and other business accounts. Independent wholesalers are classified as either merchant wholesalers or agents and brokers, depending on whether they take title to the products they handle.

A *merchant wholesaler,* like apparel wholesaler WholesaleSarong.com, is an independently owned wholesaling intermediary that takes title to the goods it handles. Within this category, a *full-function merchant wholesaler* provides a complete assortment of services for retailers or industrial buyers, such as warehousing, shipping, and even financing. A subtype of full-function merchant is a *rack jobber,* such as Choice Books, which handles distribution of inspirational books to retail stores. This type of firm stocks, displays, and services particular retail products, such as calendars, books, and note cards, in drug stores and gift shops. Usually, the retailer receives a commission based on actual sales as payment for providing merchandise space to a rack jobber.

A *limited-function merchant wholesaler* also takes legal title to the products it handles, but it provides fewer services to the retailers to which it sells. Some limited-function merchant wholesalers only warehouse products but do not offer delivery service. Others warehouse and deliver products but provide no financing. One type of limited-function merchant wholesaler is a *drop shipper* such as Kate Aspen, a wholesaler of wedding favors. Drop shippers also operate in such industries as coal and lumber, characterized by bulky products for which no single producer can provide a complete assortment. They give access to many related goods by contacting numerous producers and negotiating the best possible prices. Cost considerations call for producers to ship such products directly to the drop shipper's customers.

Another category of independent wholesaling intermediaries consists of *agents* and *brokers.* They may or may not take possession of the goods they handle, but they never take title, working mainly to bring buyers and sellers together. Stockbrokers and real estate agents perform functions similar to those of agents and brokers, but at the retail level. They do not take title to the sellers' property; instead, they create time and ownership utility for both buyer and seller by helping carry out transactions.

A *manufacturers' rep* acts as an independent sales force by representing the manufacturers of related but noncompeting products. This agent intermediary, sometimes referred to as a *manufacturers' agent,* receives commissions based on a percentage of sales.

Retailer-Owned Cooperatives and Buying Offices

Retailers sometimes band together to form their own wholesaling organizations. Such organizations can take the form of either a buying group or a cooperative. Participating retailers set up the new operation to reduce costs or to provide some special service that is not readily available in the marketplace. To achieve cost savings through quantity purchases, independent retailers may form a buying group that negotiates bulk sales with manufacturers. Ace Hardware is a retailer-owned cooperative. The independent owners of its more than 4,600 stores have access to bulk merchandise purchases that save them—and their customers—money.[6] In a cooperative, an independent group of retailers may decide to band together to share functions such as shipping or warehousing.

Q Answer the **Concept Check** questions.

Retailing

The **retailer** is the distribution channel member that sells goods and services to individuals for their own use rather than for resale. Consumers usually buy their food, clothing, shampoo, furniture, and appliances from some type of retailer. The supermarket where you buy your groceries may have bought some of its items from a wholesaler such as Unified Grocers and then resold them to you. Retailers are a critical element—the so-called "last three feet"—in the distribution channel. Because retailers are often the only channel member that deals directly with consumers, manufacturers rely heavily on them to get their products into the hands of consumers. Retailers can be classified in two categories: nonstore and store.

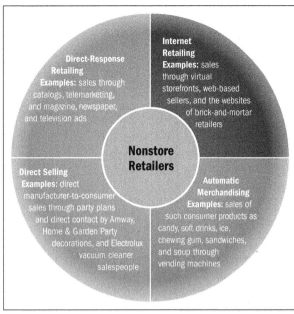

Nonstore Retailers

As 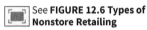 **Figure 12.6** shows, nonstore retailing includes four forms: direct-response retailing, Internet retailing, automatic merchandising, and direct selling. *Direct-response retailing* reaches prospective customers through catalogs, telemarketing, and even magazine, newspaper, and television ads. *Internet retailing,* another form of nonstore retailing, has grown rapidly. Tens of thousands of retailers have set up shop online, with sales growing at a rate of more than 15 percent a year (as compared to total retail sales growing at about 3.8 percent per year). Today, online sales account for about 6.5 percent of total retail sales.[7]

Automatic merchandising provides retailing convenience through vending machines. *Direct selling* includes direct-to-consumer sales by Pampered Chef kitchen consultants and salespeople for Silpada sterling silver jewelry through party-plan selling methods. Both are forms of direct selling.

Store Retailers

In-store sales still outpace nonstore retailing methods like direct-response retailing and Internet selling. Store retailers range in size from tiny newsstands to multi-story department stores and multi-acre warehouse-like retailers such as Sam's Club. **Table 12.1** lists different types of store retailers.

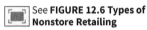 See **FIGURE 12.6 Types of Nonstore Retailing**

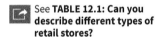 See **TABLE 12.1: Can you describe different types of retail stores?**

Choosing a Location

A good location often marks the difference between success and failure in retailing. The location decision depends on the retailer's size, financial resources, product offerings, competition, and, of course, its target market. Traffic patterns, parking, the visibility of the store's signage, and the location of complementary stores also influence the choice of a retail location.

A *planned shopping center* is a group of retail stores planned, coordinated, and marketed as a unit to shoppers in a geographical trade area. By providing convenient locations with free parking, shopping centers have replaced downtown shopping in many urban areas. But time-pressed consumers are increasingly looking for more efficient ways to shop, including catalogs, Internet retailers, and one-stop shopping at large free-standing stores such as Walmart Supercenters. To lure more customers, shopping centers are recasting themselves as entertainment destinations, with movie theaters, restaurants, art displays, carousel rides, and musical entertainment. The giant Mall of America in Bloomington, Minnesota, features a seven-acre amusement park and an aquarium.

Large regional malls have witnessed a shift in shopping center traffic to smaller strip centers, name-brand outlet centers, and *lifestyle centers,* open-air complexes containing retailers that often focus on specific shopper segments and product interests.[8]

Creating a Store Atmosphere

A successful retailer closely aligns its merchandising, pricing, and promotion strategies with *store atmospherics,* the physical characteristics of a store and its amenities, to influence consumers' perceptions of the shopping experience. Atmospherics begin with the store's exterior, which may use eye-catching architectural elements and signage to attract customer attention and interest. Interior atmospheric elements include store layout, merchandise presentation, lighting, color, sound, and cleanliness. A high-end store such as Nordstrom, for instance, features high ceilings in selling areas that spotlight tasteful and meticulously cared-for displays of carefully chosen items of obvious quality. Dick's Sporting Goods, on the other hand, carries an ever-changing array of moderately priced clothing and gear in its warehouse-like settings furnished with industrial-style display hardware.

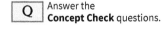 Answer the **Concept Check** questions.

Distribution Channel Decisions and Logistics

A firm's choice of distribution channels creates the final link in the **supply chain**, the complete sequence of suppliers that contribute to creating a good or service and delivering it to business users and final consumers. The supply chain begins when the raw materials used in production are delivered to the producer and continues with the actual production activities that create finished goods. Finally, the finished goods move through the producer's distribution channels to end customers.

The process of coordinating the flow of goods, services, and information among members of the supply chain is called **logistics**. The term originally referred to strategic movements of military troops and supplies. Today, however, it describes all of the business activities involved in the supply chain, with the ultimate goal of getting finished goods to customers.

Physical Distribution

A major focus of logistics management—identified earlier in the chapter as one of the two basic dimensions of distribution strategy—is *physical distribution,* the activities aimed at efficiently moving finished goods from the production line to the consumer or business buyer. As **Figure 12.7** shows, physical distribution is a broad concept that includes transportation and numerous other elements that help link buyers and sellers. An effectively managed physical distribution system can increase customer satisfaction by ensuring reliable movements of products through the supply chain.

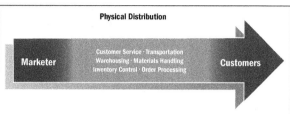

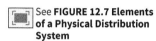

See **FIGURE 12.7 Elements of a Physical Distribution System**

The form of transportation used to ship products depends primarily on the kind of product, the distance involved, and the cost. The logistics manager can choose from a number of companies and modes of transportation. As **Table 12.2** shows, the five major transport modes are—in order of total expenditures—trucks (with about 75 percent of total expenditures), railroads (approximately 12 percent), water carriers (6 percent), air freight (4 percent), and pipelines (3 percent). The faster methods typically cost more than the slower ones. Speed, reliable delivery, shipment frequency, location availability, handling flexibility, and cost are all important considerations when choosing the most appropriate mode of transportation.

See **TABLE 12.2: What are the five major transport modes?**

About 26.4 million trucks operate in the United States, carrying most finished goods all or part of the way to the consumer. Nearly 3 million of these are tractor trailers.[9] But railroads, which compete with many truck routes, despite their recent loss of market share, are a major mode of transportation. The 565 freight railroads in the United States operate across nearly 140,000 miles of track and employ more than 180,000 people.[10]

Warehousing is the physical distribution activity that involves the storage of products. *Materials handling* is moving items within factories, warehouses, transportation terminals, and stores. *Inventory control* involves managing inventory costs, such as storage facilities, insurance, taxes, and handling. The physical distribution activity of *order processing* includes preparing orders for shipment and receiving orders when shipments arrive.

Radio-frequency identification (RFID) technology relies on a computer chip implanted somewhere on a product or its packaging that emits a low-frequency radio signal identifying the item. The radio signal doesn't require a line of sight to register on the store's computers the way a bar code does, so a handheld RFID reader can scan crates and cartons before they are unloaded. Because the chip can store information about the product's progress through the distribution channel, retailers can efficiently manage inventories, maintain stock levels, reduce losses, track stolen goods, and cut costs.

The wide use of electronic data interchange (EDI) and the constant pressure on suppliers to improve their response time have led to *vendor-managed inventory*, in which the producer and the retailer agree that the producer (or the wholesaler) will determine how much of a product a buyer needs and automatically ship new supplies when needed.

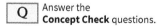

Answer the **Concept Check** questions.

WP LS Go to your WileyPLUS Learning Space course for video episodes, examples, art, tables, Concept Checks, practice, and resources that will help you success in this course.

13

Reading for
PROMOTION AND PRICING STRATEGIES

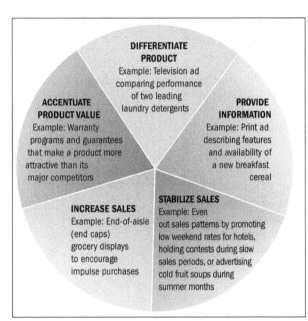

DIFFERENTIATE PRODUCT
Example: Television ad comparing performance of two leading laundry detergents

PROVIDE INFORMATION
Example: Print ad describing features and availability of a new breakfast cereal

ACCENTUATE PRODUCT VALUE
Example: Warranty programs and guarantees that make a product more attractive than its major competitors

INCREASE SALES
Example: End-of-aisle (end caps) grocery displays to encourage impulse purchases

STABILIZE SALES
Example: Even out sales patterns by promoting low weekend rates for hotels, holding contests during slow sales periods, or advertising cold fruit soups during summer months

See **FIGURE 13.1 Five Major Promotional Objectives**

Integrated Marketing Communications

Marketers choose from among many promotional options to communicate with potential customers. Each marketing message a buyer receives—whether through a television or radio commercial, a newspaper or magazine ad, a website, a direct-mail flyer, or a sales call—reflects the product, place, person, cause, or organization promoted in the content. Through **integrated marketing communications (IMC)**, marketers coordinate all promotional activities—media advertising, direct mail, personal selling, sales promotion, and public relations—to produce a unified, customer-focused promotional strategy. This coordination is designed to avoid confusing the consumer and to focus positive attention on the promotional message.

Promotional Objectives

Promotional objectives vary by organization. Some use **promotion** to expand their markets; others, to defend their current position. As **Figure 13.1** illustrates, common objectives include providing information, differentiating a product, increasing sales, stabilizing sales, and accentuating a product's value.

- **Provide Information** A major portion of U.S. advertising is information oriented. Credit card ads provide information about benefits and rates. Ads for hair care products include information about benefits such as shine and volume. Ads for breakfast cereals often contain nutritional information. TV advertising for prescription drugs, a $3 billion industry, is sometimes criticized for relying on emotional appeals rather than providing information about the causes, risk factors, and especially the prevention of disease.[1]

- **Differentiate a Product** Promotion can differentiate a firm's offerings from the competition. Applying a concept called **positioning**, marketers attempt to establish their products in the minds of customers. The idea is to communicate to buyers meaningful distinctions about the attributes, price, quality, or use of a good or service.

- **Increase Sales** Increasing sales volume is the most common objective of a promotional strategy. Luxury automakers like Cadillac, Lexus, Infiniti, and Mercedes-Benz are trying to lure younger customers by creating smaller, more performance-oriented car models. In its first year of sales, Mercedes sold more than 14,000 CLA-class cars—with one in five purchasers in their 20s—significantly younger than the majority of the brand's typical customers.[2]

- **Stabilize Sales** Firms can stabilize sales during slack periods through sales contests that motivate salespeople with such prizes as vacations, TVs, smart phones, and cash to those who meet certain goals. Companies attempt to stimulate sales during the off-season by distributing sales promotion materials such as calendars, pens, and notepads to customers. Jiffy Lube puts that little sticker on your windshield to remind you when to schedule your car's next oil change; regular visits help stabilize Jiffy Lube sales. A stable sales pattern brings several advantages. It evens out the production cycle, reduces some management and production costs, and simplifies financial, purchasing, and marketing planning. An effective promotional strategy can contribute to these goals.

- **Accentuate the Product's Value** Explaining the hidden benefits of ownership can enhance a product's value. Carmakers offer long-term warranty programs; life insurance companies promote certain policies as investments. The creation of brand awareness and brand loyalty also enhances a product's image and increases its desirability. Advertising with luxurious images supports the reputation of premium brands like Jaguar, Tiffany, and Rolex.

Pushing and Pulling Strategies

Before developing its promotional plan, a firm's marketers need to consider two general promotional strategies: a pushing strategy or a pulling strategy. A **pushing strategy** relies on personal selling to market an item to wholesalers and retailers in a company's distribution channels. So companies promote the product to members of the marketing channel, not to end users. Sales personnel explain to marketing intermediaries why they should carry particular merchandise, usually supported by offers of special discounts and promotional materials. All of these strategies are designed to motivate wholesalers and retailers to "push" the good or service to their own customers.

A **pulling strategy** attempts to promote a product by generating consumer demand for it, traditionally through advertising and sales promotions and more recently through Internet searches, social media, video-sharing sites, blogs, and other business directory/review services. From these sources, potential buyers develop favorable impressions of the product and then request that suppliers—retailers or local distributors—carry the product, thereby "pulling" it through the distribution channel.

The Promotional Mix

Once the objectives and strategy are set, marketers create a **promotional mix** that blends various facets of promotion into a cohesive plan. This mix consists of two broad components—personal and nonpersonal selling. Marketers combine elements of both personal and nonpersonal selling to effectively communicate their message to targeted customers.

Each component in the promotional mix has its own advantages and disadvantages, as described in 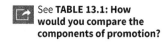 **Table 13.1**.

 See **TABLE 13.1: How would you compare the components of promotion?**

 Answer the **Concept Check** questions.

Different Types of Advertising

According to one survey, consumers receive from 3,000 to 20,000 marketing messages each day, many of them in the form of advertising.[3] Advertising is the most visible form of nonpersonal promotion—and the most effective for many firms. **Advertising** is paid nonpersonal communication usually targeted at large numbers of potential buyers. Although Americans often regard advertising as a typically American function, it is a global activity. In a recent report, the spending on global advertising is expected to continue to grow and reach $545 billion as the global economy gets stronger. The report also indicated that spending for online advertising will overtake spending on print advertising in just a few years.[4]

Advertising expenditures vary among industries, companies, and media. The top five categories for global advertisers are consumer goods, entertainment, industry and services, media, and automotive. The categories recently showing the greatest percentage change were telecommunications and consumer goods. Because advertising expenditures are so great and because consumers around the world are bombarded with messages, advertisers need to be increasingly creative and efficient at attracting consumers' attention.[5]

Types of Advertising

The two basic types of ads are product and institutional advertisements. **Product advertising** consists of messages designed to sell a particular good or service. Advertisements for Chobani Greek Yogurt, Apple iPads, and Capital One credit cards are examples of product advertising. One relatively recent form of product advertising is the practice of **product placement**. A growing number of marketers pay placement fees to have their products showcased in various media, ranging from newspapers and magazines to television and movies.

Institutional advertising involves messages that promote concepts, ideas, philosophies, or goodwill for industries, companies, organizations, or government entities. Each year, the Juvenile Diabetes Research Foundation promotes its "Walk for the Cure" fund-raising event, and your college may place advertisements in local papers or news shows to promote its activities.

A form of institutional advertising that is growing in importance, **cause advertising**, promotes a specific viewpoint on a public issue as a way to influence public opinion and the legislative process about issues such as literacy, hunger and poverty, and alternative energy sources.

Advertising and the Product Life Cycle

Both product and institutional advertising fall into one of three categories based on whether the ads are intended to inform, persuade, or remind.

- **Informative advertising** builds initial demand for a product in the introductory phase of the product life cycle. Highly publicized new product entries attract the interest of potential buyers who seek information about the advantages of the new products over existing ones, warranties provided, prices, and places that offer the new products.

- **Persuasive advertising** attempts to improve the competitive status of a product, institution, or concept, usually in the late growth and maturity stages of the product life cycle. One of the most popular types of persuasive product advertising, *comparative advertising,* compares products directly with their competitors—either by name or by inference.

- **Reminder-oriented advertising** often appears in the late maturity or decline stages of the product life cycle to maintain awareness of the importance and usefulness of a product, concept, or institution.

Advertising Media

Marketers must choose how to allocate their advertising budget among various media. All media offer advantages and disadvantages. Cost is an important consideration in media selection, but marketers must also choose the media best suited for communicating their message. As ▦ **Figure 13.2** indicates, the three leading media outlets for advertising are television, the Internet, and newspapers.

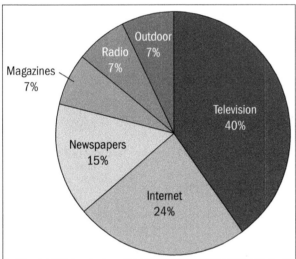

See **FIGURE 13.2 Global Advertising Spend by Medium**

Source: "Executive Summary: Advertising Expenditure Forecasts December 2014," *ZenithOptimedia,* accessed March 27, 2015, www.zenithoptimedia.com.

- **Television** Television is still one of America's leading national advertising media. Television advertising can be classified as network, national, local, or cable. The four major national networks—ABC, CBS, NBC, and Fox—broadcast almost one-fifth of all television ads. Despite a decline in audience share and growing competition from cable TV, network television remains the easiest way for advertisers to reach large numbers of viewers—10 million to 20 million with a single commercial. Automakers, fast food restaurants, and food manufacturers are heavy users of network TV advertising.

- **Internet Advertising** The digital ad market is growing faster than the rest of the advertising sector due mainly to the rising number of smart phones and tablets in use and increased social media usage. Total digital advertising, including mobile, rose to more than $35 billion in a recent year, making up almost 25 percent of all advertising revenues. Ad types include search and banner, the largest category, along with classified, rich media, video lead generation, sponsorship, and e-mail. Another example is *viral advertising*, which creates a message that is novel or entertaining enough for consumers to forward it to others, spreading like a virus. The great advantage is spreading the word online, which often relies on social media sites like Facebook, YouTube, Twitter, and Instagram.[6]

- **Newspapers** As companies shift advertising dollars to other platforms, print advertising revenues continue to fall. Although one advantage of newspaper advertising is the ease with which marketers can tailor ads to local tastes and preferences, the downside is the relatively short lifespan of daily newspapers—people usually discard them soon after reading. Most newspapers now have websites and digital pay plans for viewing content, which have offset some of the declines in advertising dollars.[7]

- **Radio** Despite the proliferation of other media, the average U.S. household owns a number of radios—including those in cars—a market penetration that makes radio an important advertising medium. Advertisers like the captive audience of listeners as they commute to and from work. As a result, morning and evening drive-time shows command top ad rates. In major markets, many stations serve different demographic groups with targeted programming. Internet radio programming also offers opportunities for yet more focused targeting. Recent marketing research shows that almost half of U.S. listeners tune in to online radio.[8]

- **Magazines** Magazines include consumer publications and business trade journals. *Time, Reader's Digest,* and *Sports Illustrated* are consumer magazines, whereas *Advertising Age* and *Oil & Gas Journal* fall into the trade category. Magazines are a natural choice for targeted advertising. Media buyers study the demographics of subscribers and select magazines that attract the desired readers. American Express advertises in *Fortune* and *Bloomberg Businessweek* to reach businesspeople, while PacSun clothes and Clearasil skin medications are advertised in *Teen Vogue*. Magazine print ads have been driven by a recent shift from print editions to online editions, accessed via smart phones and tablets.

- **Direct Mail** About 90 percent of consumers receive catalogs through the mail. Approximately 12.5 billion catalogs were mailed in a recent year, and the median expenditure per consumer was $347. The huge growth in the variety of direct-mail offerings combined with the convenience they offer today's busy, time-pressed shoppers has made direct-mail advertising a multibillion-dollar business. E-mail is a low-cost form of direct marketing. Marketers can target the most interested Internet users by offering website visitors an option to register to receive e-mail. Companies like Amazon.com, Gardener's Supply, and Abercrombie & Fitch routinely send e-mails to regular customers.

- **Outdoor Advertising** In one recent year, outdoor advertising accounted for more than $7 billion in advertising revenues.[9] The majority of spending on outdoor advertising is for billboards, but spending for other types of outdoor advertising, such as signs in transit stations, stores, airports, and sports stadiums, is growing fast. Advertisers are exploring new forms of outdoor media, many of which involve technology: computerized paintings; digital billboards; "trivision," which displays three revolving images on a single billboard; and moving billboards mounted on trucks. Other innovations include ads displayed on the Goodyear blimp, using an electronic system that offers animation and video.

- **Sponsorship** One trend in promotion offers marketers the ability to integrate several elements of the promotional mix. *Sponsorship* involves providing funds for a sporting or cultural event in exchange for a direct association with the event. Sponsors benefit in two major ways: exposure to the event's audience and association with the image of the activity. NASCAR, the biggest spectator sport in the United States, thrives on sponsorships. Sponsorships can run in the tens of millions. Hendricks Motorsports, currently the wealthiest and most successful NASCAR team, has more than $125 million in sponsorships from firms such as PepsiCo, DuPont, Lowes, and Farmers Insurance Group.[10]

> Q Answer the **Concept Check** questions.

Tasks in Personal Selling

Many companies consider **personal selling**—a person-to-person promotional presentation to a potential buyer—the key to marketing effectiveness. Unless a seller matches a firm's goods or services to the needs of a particular client or customer, none of the firm's other activities produces any benefits. Today, sales and sales-related jobs employ more than 15 million U.S. workers.[11] Businesses often spend five to ten times more on personal selling than on advertising. Given the significant cost of hiring, training, benefits, and salaries, businesses are very concerned with the effectiveness of their sales personnel.

How do marketers decide whether to make personal selling the primary component of their firm's marketing mix? In general, firms are likely to emphasize personal selling rather than advertising for sales promotion under four conditions:

1. Customers are relatively few in number and are geographically concentrated.
2. The product is technically complex, involves trade-ins, or requires special handling.
3. The product carries a relatively high price.
4. The product moves through direct-distribution channels.

Selling luxury items such as the carbon fiber–constructed Porsche 918 Spyder ($1 million) or a Kuhn Bösendorfer piano ($1.2 million) would require a personal touch. Then there's the $35,000 home theater offered by Prima Cinema, which automatically sends Hollywood films to customers' home systems the same day they open in theaters. Installation, including how to use the system, would require personal selling.[12]

Personal selling can occur in several environments, each of which can involve business-to-business or business-to-consumer selling. Sales representatives who make sales calls on prospective customers at their businesses are involved in *field selling.* Companies that sell major industrial equipment typically rely heavily on field selling. *Over-the-counter selling* describes sales activities in retailing and some wholesale locations, where customers visit the seller's facility to purchase items. *Telemarketing* sales representatives make their presentations over the phone. A later section reviews telemarketing in more detail.

Sales Tasks

All sales activities involve assisting customers in some manner. Although a salesperson's work can vary significantly from one company or situation to another, it usually includes a mix of three basic tasks: order processing, creative selling, and missionary selling.

- **Order Processing** Although both field selling and telemarketing involve this activity, **order processing** is most often related to retail and wholesale firms. The salesperson identifies customer needs, points out merchandise to meet them, and processes the order. Route sales personnel process orders for such consumer goods as bread, milk, soft drinks, and snack foods. They check each store's stock, report inventory needs to the store manager, and complete the sale. Most of these jobs include at least minor order-processing functions.

- **Creative Selling** Sales representatives for most business products and some consumer items perform **creative selling**, a persuasive type of promotional presentation. Creative selling promotes a good or service whose benefits are not readily apparent or whose purchase decision requires a close analysis of alternatives. Sales of intangible products such as insurance rely heavily on creative selling, but sales of tangible goods benefit as well.

  Most retail salespeople just process orders, but many consumers are looking for more in the form of customer service, which is where creative selling comes in. Personal shoppers at upscale Topshop help customers create entire looks from three floors of clothing. They also offer customers refreshments and the option to ring up purchases at a special cash register without waiting in line.

- **Missionary Selling** Sales work also includes **missionary selling**, an indirect form of selling in which the representative promotes goodwill for a company or provides technical or operational assistance to the customer. Many businesses that sell technical equipment, such as Oracle and Fujitsu, provide systems specialists who act as consultants to customers. These salespeople work to solve problems and sometimes help their clients with questions not directly related to their employers' products.

Telemarketing

Personal selling conducted by telephone, known as **telemarketing**, provides a firm with a high return on its marketing expenditures, an immediate response, and an opportunity for personalized, two-way conversation. Many firms use telemarketing because expense or other obstacles prevent salespeople from meeting many potential customers in person. Telemarketers can use databases to target prospects based on demographic data.

Telemarketing takes two forms. A sales representative who calls you is practicing *outbound telemarketing.* And outbound telemarketers must abide by the Federal Trade Commission's 1996 Telemarketing Sales Rule. Congress enacted another law in 2003 that created the National Do Not Call registry, intended to help consumers block unwanted telemarketing calls. On the other hand, *inbound telemarketing* occurs when you call a toll-free phone number to get product information or place an order.

The Sales Process

The sales process typically follows the seven-step sequence shown in ▣ **Figure 13.3**: prospecting and qualifying, the approach, the presentation, the demonstration, handling objections, closing, and the follow-up. Remember the importance of flexibility, though; a good salesperson is not afraid to vary the sales process based on a customer's responses and needs. The process of selling to a potential customer who is unfamiliar with a company's products differs from the process of serving a long-time customer.

Prospecting, Qualifying, and Approaching

At the prospecting stage, salespeople identify potential customers. They may seek leads for prospective sales from such sources as news reports, business associates, existing customers, friends, and family. The qualifying process identifies potential customers who have the financial ability and authority to buy.

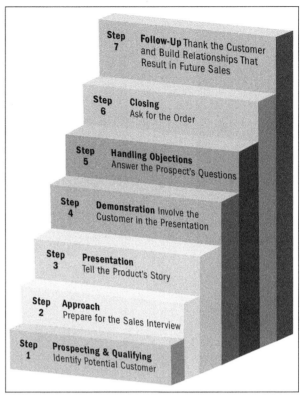

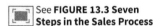
See **FIGURE 13.3 Seven Steps in the Sales Process**

Companies use different tactics to identify and qualify prospects. Some companies rely on business development teams, passing responses from direct mail along to their sales reps. Others believe in personal visits. Many firms are now using social media, which costs little or nothing, to boost sales. Online newsletters, virtual trade shows, podcasts, webinars, and blogs are good examples. Experts advise developing a clear strategy in order to be successful with social media.[13]

Successful salespeople make careful preparations, analyzing available data about a prospective customer's product lines and other pertinent information before making the initial contact. They realize the importance of a first impression in influencing a customer's future attitudes toward the seller and its products.

Presentation and Demonstration

At the presentation stage, salespeople communicate promotional messages. They may describe the major features of their products, highlight the advantages, and cite examples of satisfied consumers. A demonstration helps reinforce the message that the salesperson has been communicating—a critical step in the sales process. Department store shoppers can get a free makeover at the cosmetics counter. Anyone looking to buy a car will take it for a test drive before deciding whether to purchase it.

Handling Objections

Some salespeople fear potential customers' objections because they view the questions as criticism. But a good salesperson can use objections as an opportunity to answer questions and explain how the product will benefit the customer. Responding to a customer's objection that a product's price is too high, a salesperson might remind the individual that the product is exclusive and that a high price not only represents quality but also prevents the product from being widely available to everyone.

Closing

The critical point in the sales process—the time at which the salesperson actually asks the prospect to buy—is the closing. If the presentation effectively matches product benefits to customer needs, the closing should be a natural conclusion. If there are more bumps in the process, the salesperson can try some different techniques, such as offering alternative products, offering a special incentive for purchase, or restating the product benefits. Closing the sale—and beginning a relationship in which the customer builds loyalty to the brand or product—is the ideal outcome of this interaction. But even if the sale is not made at this time, the salesperson should regard the interaction as the beginning of a potential relationship anyway. The prospect might very well become a customer in the future.

Follow-Up

A salesperson's post-sale actions may determine whether the customer will make another purchase. Follow-up is an important part of building a long-lasting relationship. After closing, the salesperson should process the order efficiently. By calling soon after a purchase, the salesperson provides reassurance about the customer's decision to buy and creates an opportunity to correct any problems.

Q Answer the **Concept Check** questions.

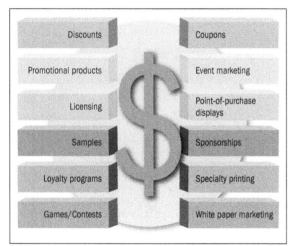

See **FIGURE 13.4 The Most Common Forms of Sales Promotion**

Sales Promotion Activities

Traditionally viewed as a supplement to a firm's sales or advertising efforts, sales promotion has emerged as an integral part of the promotional mix. **Sales promotion** consists of activities that support advertising and personal selling. **Figure 13.4** highlights the most common forms of sales promotions.

Both retailers and manufacturers use sales promotions to offer consumers extra incentives to buy. Examples include samples, coupons, contests, displays, trade shows, and dealer incentives. Beyond the short-term advantage of increased sales, sales promotions can also help marketers build brand equity and enhance customer relationships.

Consumer-Oriented Promotions

The goal of a consumer-oriented sales promotion is to get new and existing customers to try or buy products. In addition, marketers want to encourage repeat purchases by rewarding current users, increase sales of complementary products, and boost impulse purchases.

Premiums, Coupons, Rebates, and Samples

Nearly 60 percent of all sales promotion dollars are spent on *premiums*—items given free or at a reduced price with the purchase of another product. Cosmetics companies such as Clinique often offer sample kits with purchases of their products. Customers redeem *coupons* for small price discounts when they purchase the promoted products. Such offers may persuade a customer to try a new or different product. *Rebates* offer cash back to consumers who mail in required proofs of purchase. Rebates help packaged-goods manufacturers increase purchase rates, promote multiple purchases, and reward product users. A *sample* is a gift of a product distributed by mail, door to door, in a demonstration, or inside packages of another product.

Trade-Oriented Promotions

Sales promotion techniques can also contribute to campaigns directed to retailers and wholesalers. **Trade promotion** is sales promotion geared to marketing intermediaries rather than to consumers. Marketers use trade promotion to encourage retailers to stock new products, continue carrying existing ones, and promote both new and existing products effectively to consumers. Successful trade promotions offer financial incentives. They require careful timing, attention to costs, and easy implementation for intermediaries. These promotions should bring quick results and improve retail sales. Major trade promotions include point-of-purchase advertising and trade shows.

Point-of-purchase (POP) advertising consists of displays or demonstrations that promote products when and where consumers buy them, such as in retail stores. Marketing research has shown that consumers are more likely to purchase certain products when such displays are present. Sunscreen, painting supplies, and snacks are typically displayed this way.

Manufacturers and other sellers often exhibit at *trade shows* to promote goods or services to members of their distribution channels. These shows are often organized by industry trade associations and attract large numbers of exhibitors and attendees each year.

Q Answer the **Concept Check** questions.

Publicity as a Promotional Tool

A final element of the promotional mix, public relations (PR)—including publicity—supports advertising, personal selling, and sales promotion, usually by pursuing broader objectives. Through PR, companies attempt to improve their image with the public by distributing specific messages or ideas to target audiences. Cause-related promotional activities are often supported by PR and publicity campaigns. In addition, PR helps a firm establish awareness of goods and services and then builds a positive image of them.

Public relations refers to an organization's communications and relationships with its various public audiences, such as customers, vendors, news media, employees, stockholders, the government, and the general public. Many of these communication efforts serve marketing purposes. Public relations is an efficient, indirect communications channel for promoting products. It can publicize items and help create and maintain a positive image of the company.

The public relations department links a firm with the media. It provides the media with news releases and video and audio clips, as well as holding news conferences to announce new products, the formation of strategic alliances, management changes, financial results, and similar developments. Publications issued by the department include newsletters, brochures, and reports.

Publicity

The type of public relations that is tied most closely to promoting a company's products is **publicity**—nonpersonal stimulation of demand for a good, service, place, idea, event, person, or organization by unpaid placement of information in print or broadcast media. Press releases generate publicity, as does news or TV coverage. Publicity can even help find investors to grow a business. Shawn Davis appeared on the reality TV show *Shark Tank* hoping to have the show's entrepreneurs invest in his company. The investors didn't bite, but when the episode aired Davis received calls from other interested parties. He negotiated a deal and has recently grown his business to over $5 million.[14]

Not-for-profit organizations also benefit from publicity when they receive coverage of various charitable events, which raise money for research, advocacy, and other programs.

Q Answer the **Concept Check** questions.

Pricing Objectives and Strategies

Price, the last element of the marketing mix, can best be thought of as the sum of all the other parts. If a firm has a unique product, creates a world class distribution strategy, or has an inventive promotional campaign, they become a *price setter* such as Apple. On the other hand, if a firm sells an undifferentiated product, with no distribution or promotional advantages, they are most likely a *price taker*. While firms have the freedom to set their prices at any level they choose, their success will be determined by how the firm's competitors and customers react to their prices. For example, if a firm sets prices too high relative to the perceived value of the product, customers will not purchase the product and the firm will generate little revenue. Alternately, if they set their prices too low, the firm may sell all their products but not make needed profits.

In making pricing decisions, businesspeople seek to accomplish certain objectives. Pricing objectives vary from firm to firm, and many companies pursue multiple pricing objectives at the same time. Some try to improve profits by setting higher prices, while others set lower prices to attract new business. Whatever a company's objectives, determination of price generally falls into two areas, those based on external market issues and those based on a firm's production costs. The following sections detail both approaches, identifying the pricing objective and the strategies that support the objective.

Market-Based Pricing

Economic theory assumes that a market price will be set at the point at which the amount of a product demanded and the amount supplied are equal. Recall the supply and demand discussion from Chapter 3. In many lines of business, this holds true, as firms in any particular industry set their prices to match those of established leaders. In these markets, price becomes a nonissue and consumers will make their purchase decisions based on other attributes of the product or firm. Gas stations are a good example of this type of pricing. However, once a firm knows the equilibrium market price, the *competitive price*, they can choose to price their products at that price or move higher or lower to achieve specific business objectives. The following section describes pricing objectives that cause a firm to deviate from the equilibrium price.

Volume Objective

Marketers attempting to build market share may use price to achieve their goal. The **volume objective** makes pricing decisions based on market share, the percentage of a market controlled by a certain company or product. One firm may seek to achieve a 25 percent market share in a certain product category, and another may want to maintain or expand its market share for particular products.

Dollar General stores rely on volume sales to make a profit, and these types of retailers typically price products lower than their competition to build sales. The nationwide chain of stores, which sells everything from ice cube trays to holiday decorations—for a dollar each—must find ways to attract as much traffic and sell as much product as possible on a given day.

Prestige Pricing

On the other end of the spectrum, **prestige pricing** establishes a relatively high price to develop and maintain an image of quality and exclusiveness. Marketers set such objectives because they recognize the role of price in communicating an overall image for the firm and its products. People expect to pay more for a Mercedes, Christian Louboutin shoes, or a vacation on St. Barts in the Caribbean. Much of the value that consumers place on these types of products comes from the fact that they are expensive. A Rolex would not be a Rolex without a hefty price tag.

Everyday Low Pricing and Discount Pricing

Everyday low pricing (EDLP) is a strategy devoted to maintaining continuous low prices rather than relying on short-term price-cutting tactics such as coupons, rebates, and special sales. This strategy has been used successfully by retailers such as Walmart and Lowe's to consistently offer low prices to consumers; manufacturers also use EDLP to set stable prices for retailers and create the impression among consumers that they do not need to shop the "sales" to find a good deal at these stores.

Skimming Pricing

A shorter-term strategy, **skimming pricing**, sets an intentionally high price relative to the prices of competing products. The term comes from the expression "skimming the cream." This pricing strategy often works for the introduction of a distinctive good or service with little or no competition, although it can be used at other stages of the product life cycle as well. A skimming strategy can help marketers set a price that distinguishes a firm's high-end product from those of competitors. It can also help a firm recover its product development costs before competitors enter the field. This is often the case with prescription drugs.

Penetration Pricing

Another shorter-term approach and a variant of volume pricing is **penetration pricing**, a strategy that sets a low price in an effort to enter competitive markets. When using penetration pricing, businesses may price new products noticeably lower than competing offerings of competing brands. These firms may even price their products below their cost to gain market share. Once the new product achieves some market recognition through consumer trial purchases stimulated by its low price, marketers may increase the price to the level of competing products. However, stiff competition might prevent the price increase.

Cost-Based Pricing

Economic theory might lead to the best pricing decisions, but businesses may not have all the information they need to make those decisions. Additionally, many well-crafted pricing strategies end up costing a firm significant profits. So, firms almost always review their market-based strategies against their product costs using **cost-based pricing** formulas. Approaching pricing this way allows a firm to determine how much investment they will have to make to complete their strategy.

Breakeven Analysis

Businesses often conduct a **breakeven analysis** to determine the minimum sales volume a product must generate at a certain price level to cover all costs. This method involves a consideration of various costs and total revenues. *Total cost* is the sum of total variable costs and total fixed costs. *Variable costs* change with the level of production, as labor and raw materials do, while *fixed costs* such as insurance premiums and utility rates charged by water, natural gas, and electric power suppliers remain stable regardless of the production level. *Total revenue* is determined by multiplying price by the number of units sold.

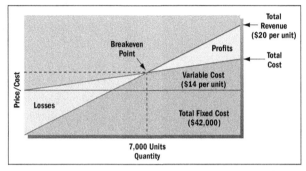

Finding the Breakeven Point

The level of sales that will generate enough revenue to cover all of the company's fixed and variable costs is called the *breakeven point*. It is the point at which total revenue just equals total costs. Sales beyond the breakeven point will generate profits; sales volume below the breakeven point will result in losses. The following formulas give the breakeven point in units and dollars:

See **FIGURE 13.5 Breakeven Analysis**

$$\text{Breakeven Point (in units)} = \frac{\text{Total fixed costs}}{\text{Contribution to fixed costs per unit}}$$

$$\text{Breakeven Point (in dollars)} = \frac{\text{Total fixed costs}}{1 - \text{Variable costs per unit/Price}}$$

A product selling for $20 with a variable cost of $14 per unit produces a $6 per-unit contribution to fixed costs. If the firm has total fixed costs of $42,000, it must sell 7,000 units to break even on the product, as shown in **Figure 13.5**. The calculation of the breakeven point in units and dollars is as follows:

$$\text{Breakeven Point (in units)} = \frac{\$42,000}{\$20 - \$14} = \frac{\$42,000}{\$6} = 7,000 \ units$$

$$\text{Breakeven Point (in dollars)} = \frac{\$42,000}{1 - \$14/\$20}$$

$$= \frac{\$42,000}{1 - 0.7} = \frac{\$42,000}{0.3} = \$140,000$$

Marketers use breakeven analysis to determine the profits or losses that would result from several different proposed prices. Because different prices produce different breakeven points, marketers could compare their calculations of required sales to break even with sales estimates from marketing research studies. This comparison can identify the best price—one that would attract enough customers to exceed the breakeven point and earn profits for the firm.

Answer the **Concept Check** questions.

WP LS Go to your WileyPLUS Learning Space course for video episodes, examples, art, tables, Concept Checks, practice, and resources that will help you success in this course.

Reading for

USING TECHNOLOGY TO MANAGE INFORMATION

Data, Information, and Information Systems

Daily, in organizations around the world, businesspeople ask themselves questions like these:

- How is our product doing in Boston compared to Phoenix? Are sales to our target market growing, declining, or staying static?
- Is the price of gas affecting our distribution costs?
- Are we winning the battle for market share?

An effective information system can help answer these and many other questions. **Data** refers to raw facts and figures that may or may not be relevant to a business decision. For example, the U.S. Census might report the average home price in a particular neighborhood. And while this information might be interesting, it is probably not very useful to someone living across the country. On the other hand, data on home prices in your own neighborhood are clearly more valuable. **Information**—the knowledge gained from processing the facts and figures of raw data about home prices—would be useful for would-be buyers and sellers of these properties. So, although businesspeople need to gather data about the demographics of a target market or the specifications of a certain product, the data are useless unless they are transformed into relevant information that can be used to make a competitive decision.

An **information system** is an organized method for collecting, storing, and communicating past, present, and projected business information. Most information systems today use computer and telecommunications technology to handle the enormous volumes of information generated by large companies. A large organization typically assigns responsibility for directing its information systems and related operations to an executive called the **chief information officer (CIO)**. Often, the CIO reports directly to the firm's chief executive officer (CEO). An effective CIO will understand and harness technology so that the company can communicate internally and externally in one seamless operation. But small companies rely just as much on information systems as do large ones, even if they do not employ a manager assigned to this area on a full-time basis.

Information systems can be tailored to assist many business functions and departments—from marketing and manufacturing to finance and accounting. They can manage the overwhelming flood of information by organizing data in a logical and accessible manner. Through the system, a company can monitor all components of its operations and business strategy, identifying problems and opportunities. Information systems gather data from inside and outside the organization, then process the data to produce information that is relevant to all aspects of the organization. Processing steps could involve storing data for later use, classifying and analyzing them, and retrieving them easily when needed.

Q Answer the **Concept Check** questions.

Components and Types of Information Systems

The definition of *information system* in the previous section does not specifically mention the use of computers or technology. In fact, information systems have been around since the beginning of civilization but, by today's standards, they were very low tech. Think about your college or university's library. At one time the library probably had card catalog files to help you find information. Those files were information systems because they stored data about books and periodicals on 3- by 5-inch index cards.

Today, however, when businesspeople think about an information system, they are most likely thinking about a **computer-based information system**. Such systems rely on computer and related technologies to store information electronically in an organized, accessible manner. So, instead of card catalogs, your college library uses a computerized information system that allows users to search through library holdings much faster and easier.

Computer-based information systems consist of four components and technologies:

- computer hardware
- computer software
- telecommunications and computer networks
- data resource management.

Computer hardware consists of machines that range from supercomputers to smart phones. It also includes the input, output, and storage devices needed to support computing machines. Software includes operating systems, such as Microsoft's Windows 8 or Linux, and applications programs, such as Adobe Acrobat or Oracle's PeopleSoft Enterprise applications. Telecommunications and computer networks encompass the hardware and software needed to provide wired or wireless voice and data communications. This includes support for external networks such as the Internet and private internal networks. Data resource management involves developing and maintaining an organization's databases so that decision makers are able to access the information they need in a timely manner.

In the case of your institution's library, the computer-based information system is generally made up of computer hardware, such as monitors and keyboards, which are linked to the library's network and a database containing information on the library's holdings. Specialized software allows users to access the database. In addition, the library's network is likely also connected to a larger private network and the Internet. This connection gives users remote access to the library's database, as well as access to other computerized databases such as LexisNexis.

Databases

The heart of any information system is its **database**, a centralized integrated collection of data resources. A company designs its databases to meet particular information processing and retrieval needs of its workforce. Businesses obtain databases in many ways. They can hire a staff person to build them on site, hire an outside source to do so, or buy packaged database programs from specialized vendors, such as Oracle, SAP, or Salesforce.com. A database serves as an electronic filing cabinet, capable of storing massive amounts of data and retrieving it within seconds.

Decision makers can also look up online data. Online systems give access to enormous amounts of government data, such as economic data from the Bureau of Labor Statistics and the Department of Commerce. One of the largest online databases is that of the U.S. Census Bureau. The census of population, conducted every ten years, collects data on more than 120 million households across the United States. Another source of free information is company websites. Interested parties can visit firms' home pages to look for information about customers, suppliers, and competitors. Trade associations and academic institutions also maintain websites with information on topics of interest.

Types of Information Systems

Many different types of information systems exist. In general, however, information systems fall into two broad categories: operational support systems and management support systems.

- An **operational support system** is designed to produce a variety of information on an organization's activities for both internal and external users. Examples of operational support systems include transaction processing systems and process control systems.
- A **transaction processing system** records and processes data from business transactions. For example, major retailers use point-of-sale systems, which link electronic cash registers to the retailer's computer centers. Sales data are transmitted from cash registers to the computer center either immediately or at regular intervals.

- A **process control system** monitors and controls physical processes. A steel mill, for instance, may have electronic sensors linked to a computer system monitoring the entire production process. The system makes necessary changes and alerts operators to potential problems.

Management Support Systems

An information system designed to provide support for effective decision making is classified as a **management support system**. Several different types of management support systems are available. A **management information system (MIS)** is designed to produce reports for managers and other personnel.

A **decision support system (DSS)** gives direct support to businesspeople during the decision-making process. For instance, a marketing manager might use a decision support system to analyze the impact on sales and profits of a product price change.

An **executive support system (ESS)** lets senior executives access the firm's primary databases, often by touching the computer screen, pointing and clicking a mouse, or using voice recognition. The typical ESS allows users to choose from many kinds of data, such as the firm's financial statements and sales figures for the company or industry. If they wish, managers can start by looking at summaries and then access more detailed information when needed.

Finally, an **expert system** is a computer program that imitates human thinking through complicated sets of "if-then" rules. The system applies human knowledge in a specific subject area to solve a problem. Expert systems are used for a variety of business purposes: determining credit limits for credit card applicants, monitoring machinery in a plant to predict potential problems or breakdowns, making mortgage loans, and determining optimal plant layouts. They are typically developed by capturing the knowledge of recognized experts in a field, whether within a business itself or outside it.

Q Answer the **Concept Check** questions.

Computer Hardware and Software

It may be hard to believe, but only a few decades ago computers were considered exotic curiosities, used only for very specialized applications and understood by only a few people. The first commercial computer, UNIVAC I, was sold to the U.S. Census Bureau in the early 1950s. It cost $1 million, took up most of a room, and could perform about 2,000 calculations per second.[1] The invention of transistors and then integrated circuits (microchips) quickly led to smaller and more powerful devices. By the 1980s, computers could routinely perform several million calculations per second. Now, computers perform billions of calculations per second, and some fit in the palm of your hand.

When the first personal computers were introduced in the late 1970s and early 1980s, the idea of a computer on every desk, or in every home, seemed farfetched. Today they have become indispensable to both businesses and households. Not only have computers become much more powerful and faster over the past 25 years, they are less expensive as well. IBM's first personal computer (PC), introduced in 1981, cost well over $5,000 fully configured. Today, the typical PC sells for between $400 and $700.

Types of Computer Hardware

Hardware consists of all tangible elements of a computer system—the input devices, the components that store and process data and perform required calculations, and the output devices that present the results to information users. Input devices allow users to enter data and commands for processing, storage, and output. The most common input devices are the keyboard and mouse. Storage and processing components consist of the hard drive as well as various other storage components, including DVD drives and flash memory devices. Flash memory devices are increasingly popular because they are small and can hold large amounts of data. Some, called thumb drives, can even fit on a keychain. To gain access to the data they hold, users just plug them into an unused USB (universal serial bus) port, standard on today's computers. Output devices, such as monitors and printers, are the hardware elements that transmit or display documents and other results of a computer system's work.

Different types of computers incorporate widely varying memory capacities and processing speeds. These differences define four broad classifications: mainframe computers, midrange systems, personal computers, and handheld devices. A mainframe computer is the largest type of computer system with the most extensive storage capacity and the fastest processing speeds. Especially powerful mainframes called *supercomputers* can handle extremely rapid, complex calculations involving thousands of variables, such as weather modeling and forecasting. One of the fastest supercomputers today is the Tianhe-2 in China, with 33,860 trillion calculations per second.[2]

Midrange systems consist of high-end network servers and other types of computers that can handle large-scale processing needs. They are less powerful than mainframe computers but more powerful than most personal computers. A **server** is a dedicated computer that provides services to other computers on a network. Many Internet-related functions at organizations are handled by servers. File servers, gaming servers, print servers, and database servers are but a few of the applications of these types of computers. They are also commonly employed in process control systems, computer-aided manufacturing (CAM), and computer-aided design (CAD).

Once the center of the digital universe, a full-scale Windows or Mac OS personal desktop computer was the way most people accessed the Internet, wrote papers, played games, organized music and photos, and more. While some believe the PC is on its way to extinction and ownership rates have declined, PCs are still popular in homes, businesses, schools, and government agencies. Tablet sales, however, have recently surpassed PC sales.[3]

Desktop computers were once the standard PC seen in offices and homes. And while millions of people still use desktop computers, laptop computers (including notebooks and netbooks) have surpassed desktop units in sales. The increasing popularity of these computers can be explained by smaller, lighter, more powerful computing, and by their improved displays, faster processing speeds, ability to handle more complex graphics, larger storage capacities, and more durable designs. Business owners, managers, salespeople, and students all benefit from laptops' portability and instantaneous access to information. In the next few years, analysts predict that more than half of the smart connected devices sold will be tablets, followed by laptops and desk computers.

Handheld devices such as smart phones are even smaller. The most popular smart phones today are powered by Google's Android and Apple's iOS mobile operating systems. Smart phones like the iPhone and Samsung's Galaxy essentially combine a mobile phone with more advanced computing capabilities than their predecessor, the basic cell phone.

Tablets and e-readers are taking market share from laptops. According to Pew Research Center's Internet and American Life Project, more than 42 percent of U.S. adults now own a tablet.[4] In addition to Apple's iPad, which is the top-selling tablet, there are a proliferation of tablet models on the market, including those from Samsung, Google, Amazon, and Sony. E-readers such as Amazon's line of Kindle products continue to expand their market share. About 32 percent of U.S. adults own an e-reader. A hybrid device called a phablet is a cross between a smart phone and a tablet, with a screen larger than a smart phone but smaller than a tablet.

In addition to smart phones, specialized handheld devices are used in a variety of businesses for different applications. Some restaurants, for example, have small wireless devices that allow servers to swipe a credit card and print out a receipt right at the customer's table. Drivers for UPS and FedEx use special handheld scanning devices to track package deliveries and accept delivery signatures. The driver scans each package as it is delivered, and the information is transmitted to the delivery firm's network. Within a few seconds, using an Internet connection, a sender can obtain the delivery information and even see a facsimile of the recipient's signature.

Computer Software

Software includes all of the programs, routines, and computer languages that control a computer and tell it how to operate. The software that controls the basic workings of a computer system is its *operating system*. More than 80 percent of personal computers use a version of Microsoft's popular Windows operating system. Personal computers made by Apple use the Mac operating system. The Android and iPhone models have their own operating systems. Other operating systems include Unix, which runs on many midrange computer systems, and Linux, which runs on both PCs and midrange systems.

See **TABLE 14.1: Can you describe some common types of application software?**

 Answer the **Concept Check** questions.

A program that performs the specific tasks that the user wants to carry out—such as writing a letter or looking up data—is called *application software*. Examples of application software include Adobe Acrobat, Microsoft PowerPoint, and Quicken. **Table 14.1** lists the major categories of application software. Most application programs are currently stored on individual computers. However, most application software has become web based, with the programs themselves stored on Internet-connected, cloud-based servers.

Computer Networks

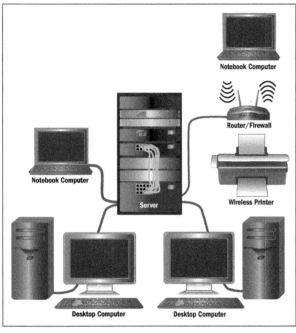

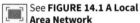 See **FIGURE 14.1 A Local Area Network**

As mentioned earlier, virtually all computers today are linked to networks. In fact, if your computer has Internet access, you're linked to a network. Local area networks and wide area networks allow businesses to communicate, transmit and print documents, and share data. These networks, however, require businesses to install special equipment and connections between office sites. But Internet technology has also been applied to internal company communications and business tasks, tapping a ready-made network. Among these Internet-based applications are intranets, virtual private networks (VPNs), and voice over Internet protocol (VoIP). Each has contributed to the effectiveness and speed of business processes, so we discuss them next.

Local Area Networks and Wide Area Networks

Most organizations connect their offices and buildings by creating a **local area network (LAN)**, a computer network that connects machines within limited areas, such as a building or several nearby buildings. LANs are useful because they link computers and allow them to share printers, documents, and information and provide access to the Internet. **Figure 14.1** shows what a small business computer network might look like.

A **wide area network (WAN)** ties larger geographical regions together by using telephone lines and microwave and satellite transmission. One familiar WAN is long-distance telephone service. Companies such as AT&T and Verizon provide WAN services to businesses and consumers. Firms also use WANs to conduct their own operations. Typically, companies link their own network systems to outside communications equipment and services for transmission across long distances.

Wireless Local Networks

A wireless network allows computers, printers, and other devices to be connected without the hassle of stringing cables in traditional office settings. The current standard for wireless networks is called Wi-Fi. **Wi-Fi**—short for *wireless fidelity*—is a wireless network that connects various devices and allows them to communicate with one another through radio waves. Any PC with a Wi-Fi receptor can connect with the Internet at so-called hot spots—locations with a wireless router and a high-speed Internet modem. Hundreds of thousands of hot spots exist worldwide today, in such places as airports, libraries, and coffee shops.

Many believe that the successor to Wi-Fi will be *Wi-Max*. Unlike Wi-Fi's relatively limited geographic coverage area—generally around 300 feet—a single Wi-Max access point can provide coverage over many miles. In addition, cell phone service providers, such as Sprint and AT&T, offer broadband network cards for notebook PCs. These devices allow users to access the provider's mobile broadband network from virtually any location where cell phone reception is available.

Intranets

A broad approach to sharing information in an organization is to establish a company network patterned after the Internet. Such a network is called an **intranet**. Intranets are similar to the Internet, but they limit access to employees or other authorized users. An intranet blocks outsiders without valid passwords from entering its network by incorporating both software and hardware known as a **firewall**. Firewalls limit data transfers to certain locations and log system use so that managers can identify attempts to log on with invalid passwords and other threats to a system's security. Highly sophisticated systems immediately alert administrators about suspicious activities and permit authorized personnel to use smart cards to connect from remote terminals.

Intranets solve the problem of linking different types of computers. Like the Internet, intranets can integrate computers running all kinds of operating systems. In addition, intranets are relatively easy and inexpensive to set up because most businesses already have some of the required hardware and software.

Virtual Private Networks

To gain increased security for Internet communications, companies often turn to a **virtual private network (VPN)**, a secure connection between two points on the Internet. VPNs use firewalls and programs that encapsulate data to make them more secure during transit. Loosely defined, a VPN can include a range of networking technologies, from secure Internet connections to private networks from service providers like IBM. A VPN is cheaper for a company to use than leasing several of its own lines. It can also take months to install a leased line in some parts of the world, but a new user can be added to a VPN in a day. Because a VPN uses the Internet, it can be wired, wireless, or a combination of the two.

Advanced Systems Group (ASG) is a provider of data storage and management services. As the company expanded and opened branch offices, its own security became a concern. ASG turned to Check Point, which created a secure VPN connecting ASG's home office and its branch offices. The VPN allows ASG to add new sites and new remote users automatically.[5]

VoIP

VoIP—which stands for *Voice over Internet Protocol*—is an alternative to traditional telecommunication services. The VoIP service is not connected to a traditional phone jack but rather to a personal computer with any type of broadband connection. Special software transmits phone conversations over the Internet rather than through telephone lines. A VoIP user dials the phone as usual and can make and receive calls to and from those with traditional telephone connections (landline or wireless).

A growing number of consumers and businesses have embraced VoIP, mainly due to its cost savings and extra features. As technology continues to advance, demand for the service has increased. Several wireless companies, including AT&T and Verizon, permit VoIP on smart phones. Google integrates its Google Voice over VoIP. The various VoIP providers are working together with the goal of creating VoIP standards that would, among other things, permit seamless roaming worldwide.[6]

Q | Answer the **Concept Check** questions.

Security and Ethical Issues Affecting Information Systems

Numerous security and ethical issues affect information systems. As information systems become increasingly important business assets, they also become progressively harder and more expensive to replace. Damage to information systems or theft of data can have disastrous consequences. When computers are connected to a network, a problem at any individual computer can affect the entire network. Two of the major security threats are cybercrime and so-called malware.

Cybercrime

Computers provide efficient ways for employees to share information, but they may also allow people with more malicious intentions to access information. Or they may allow pranksters—who have no motive other than to see whether they can hack into a system—to gain access to private information. Common cybercrimes involve stealing or altering data in several ways:

• Employees or outsiders may change or invent data to produce inaccurate or misleading information.

- Employees or outsiders may modify computer programs to create false information or illegal transactions or to insert viruses.
- Unauthorized people can access computer systems for their own benefit or knowledge or just to see if they can get in.

Information system administrators implement two basic protections against computer crime: they try to prevent access to their systems by unauthorized users and the viewing of data by unauthorized system users. The simplest method of preventing access requires authorized users to enter passwords. The company may also install firewalls, described earlier. To prevent system users from reading sensitive information, the company may use encryption software, which encodes, or scrambles, messages. To read encrypted messages, users must use an electronic key to convert them to regular text. But as fast as software developers invent new and more elaborate protective measures, hackers seem to break through their defenses. Thus, security is an ongoing battle.

Consumers with credit cards are particularly at risk from hackers. Home Depot said hackers got into its system and compromised more than 56 million credit card accounts as well as 53 million customer e-mail addresses. It is important for payment-processing companies used by major credit card companies to put protections in place so that consumer information remains safe.[7]

As the size of computer hardware diminishes, it becomes increasingly vulnerable to theft. Handheld devices, for instance, can easily vanish with a pickpocket or purse snatcher. Many notebook computers and handheld devices contain special security software or passwords that make it difficult for a thief or any unauthorized person to access the data stored in the computer's memory.

Computer Viruses, Worms, Trojan Horses, and Spyware

Viruses, worms, Trojan horses, and spyware, collectively referred to as **malware**, are malicious software programs designed to infect computer systems. These programs can destroy data, steal sensitive information, and even render information systems inoperable. Recently, malware was discovered in advertisements on major sites such as Yahoo, Firefox, and Google as well as the *New York Times* and WhitePages.com. Malware attacks cost consumers and businesses billions of dollars annually. And malware is proliferating: according to a recent estimate, companies are spending nearly $500 billion annually to deal with malware-related cyber-attacks.[8]

Computer **viruses** are programs that secretly attach themselves to other programs (called *hosts*) and change them or destroy data. Viruses can be programmed to become active immediately or to remain dormant for a period of time, after which the infections suddenly activate themselves and cause problems. A virus can reproduce by copying itself onto other programs stored in the same drive. It spreads as users install infected software on their systems or exchange files with others, usually by exchanging e-mail, accessing electronic bulletin boards, trading disks, or downloading programs or data from unknown sources on the Internet.

A **worm** is a small piece of software that exploits a security hole in a network to replicate itself. A copy of the worm scans the network for another machine that has a specific security hole. It copies itself to the new machine using the security hole and then starts replicating from there as well. Unlike viruses, worms don't need host programs to damage computer systems.

A **botnet** is a network of PCs that have been infected with one or more data-stealing viruses. Computer criminals tie the infected computers into a network, often without the owners being aware of it, and sell the botnet on the black market. They or others use the botnet to commit identity theft, sell fake pharmaceuticals, buy blocks of concert tickets for scalping, and attack the Internet itself.

A **Trojan horse** is a program that claims to do one thing but in reality does something else, usually something malicious. For example, a Trojan horse might claim, and even appear, to be a game. When an unsuspecting user clicks on the Trojan horse to launch it, the program might erase the hard drive or steal any personal data stored on the computer.

Spyware is software that secretly gathers user information through the user's Internet connection without his or her knowledge, usually for advertising purposes. Spyware applications are typically bundled with other programs downloaded from the Internet. Once installed, the spyware monitors user activity on the Internet and transmits that information in the background to someone else.

Attacks by malware are not limited to computers and computer networks. Users of smart phones have reported a sharp increase in viruses, worms, and other forms of malware. A recent malware scare known as Backdoor AndroidOS.Obad.a is a Trojan horse that infects the Android handsets of unsuspecting users. It duplicates itself, installs additional malware, distributes malicious software to other phones via Bluetooth, and performs remote commands in the handset, while racking up enormous charges to premium-rate phone numbers.[9]

As viruses, worms, botnets, and Trojan horses become more complex, the technology to fight them must increase in sophistication as well. The simplest way to protect against computer viruses is to install one of the many available antivirus software programs, such as Norton AntiVirus and McAfee VirusScan. These programs, which also protect against worms and some Trojan horses, continuously monitor systems for viruses and automatically eliminate any they spot. Users should regularly update them by downloading the latest virus definitions. In addition, computer users should also install and regularly update antispyware programs because many Trojan horses are forms of spyware.

Information Systems and Ethics

Not surprisingly, the scope and power of today's information systems raise a number of ethical issues and concerns. These affect both employees and organizations. For instance, it is not uncommon for organizations to have specific ethical standards and policies regarding the use of information systems by employees and vendors. These standards include obligations to protect system security and the privacy and confidentiality of data. Policies also may cover the personal use of computers and related technologies, both hardware and software, by employees.

Ethical issues also involve organizational use of information systems. Organizations have an obligation to protect the privacy and confidentiality of data about employees and customers. Employment records contain sensitive personal information, such as bank account numbers, which, if not protected, could lead to identity theft. Another ethical issue is the use of computer technology to monitor employees while they are working.

Q | Answer the **Concept Check** questions.

Disaster Recovery and Backup

Natural disasters, power failures, equipment malfunctions, software glitches, human error, and terrorist attacks can disrupt even the most sophisticated computer information systems. While these problems can cost businesses and other organizations billions of dollars, even more serious consequences can occur. For example, one study found that 60 percent of companies that lose their data will shut down within six months of the disaster.[10]

Disaster recovery planning—deciding how to prevent system failures and continue operations if computer systems fail—is a critical function of all organizations. Disaster prevention programs can avoid some of these costly problems. The most basic precaution is routinely backing up software and data—at the organizational and individual levels. However, the organization's data center cannot be the sole repository of critical data because a single location is vulnerable to threats from both natural and human-caused disasters. Consequently, off-site data backup is a necessity, whether in a separate physical location or online. Companies that perform online backups store the encrypted data in secure facilities that in turn have their own backups. The initial backup may take a day or more, but subsequent ones take far less time because they involve only new or modified files.

Q | Answer the **Concept Check** questions.

Information System Trends

Computer information systems are constantly—and rapidly—evolving. To keep their information systems up to date, firms must continually keep abreast of changes in technology. Some of the most significant trends in information systems today include the changing face of the workforce, the increased use of application service providers, on-demand computing, and cloud and grid computing.

The Distributed Workforce

As discussed in earlier chapters, many companies rely more and more on a *distributed workforce*—employees who no longer work in traditional offices but rather in what are called *virtual offices*, including at home. Information technology makes a distributed workforce possible. Computers, networks, and other components of information systems allow workers to do their jobs effectively almost anywhere. For instance, none of JetBlue's reservations agents work in offices; they all work at home, connected to the airline's information system. Today, most employers have a policy regarding employees' remote access to their firm's network.

Application Service Providers

As with other business functions, many firms find it makes sense to outsource at least some of their information technology function. Because of the increasing cost and complexity of obtaining and maintaining information systems, many firms hire an **application service provider (ASP)**, an outside supplier that provides both the computers and the application support for managing an information system. An ASP can simplify complex software for its customers so that it is easier for them to manage and use. When an ASP relationship is successful, the buyer can then devote more time and resources to its core businesses instead of struggling to manage its information systems. Other benefits include stretching the firm's technology dollar farther and giving smaller companies more competitive information power. Even large companies turn to ASPs to manage some or all of their information systems. Microsoft outsourced much of its internal information technology services to Infosys Technology to save money and streamline, simplify, and support its services.[11]

A company that decides to use an ASP should check the background and references of a firm before hiring it to manage critical systems. In addition, customers should try to ensure that the service provider has strong security measures to block computer hackers or other unauthorized access to the data, that its data centers are running reliably, and that adequate data and applications backups are maintained.

On-Demand, Cloud, and Grid Computing

Another recent trend is **on-demand computing**, also called *utility computing*. Instead of purchasing and maintaining expensive software, firms essentially rent the software time from application providers and pay only for software usage, similar to purchasing electricity from a utility.

Cloud computing uses powerful servers to store applications software and databases. Users access the software and databases via the web using anything from a PC to a smart phone. The software as a service (SaaS) movement is an example of cloud computing.

Some small and medium-sized companies occasionally find themselves with jobs that require more computing power than their current systems offer. A cost-effective solution may be something called **grid computing**, which consists of a network of smaller computers running special software that creates a virtual mainframe or even a supercomputer.

> **Q** Answer the **Concept Check** questions.

> **WP LS** Go to your WileyPLUS Learning Space course for video episodes, examples, art, tables, Concept Checks, practice, and resources that will help you success in this course.

UNDERSTANDING ACCOUNTING AND FINANCIAL STATEMENTS

> **WP LS** Go to your WileyPLUS Learning Space course for video episodes, examples, art, tables, Concept Checks, practice, and resources that will help you success in this course.

Users of Accounting Information

Accounting is the process of measuring, interpreting, and communicating financial information to enable people both inside and outside the firm to make informed decisions. In many ways, accounting is the language of business. People both inside and outside an organization rely on accounting information to help them make business decisions. ■ **Figure 15.1** lists the users of accounting information and the applications they find for that information. Firms like Deloitte provide such information and help their customers make the best use of it.

Users	Applications
Owners, Stockholders, Potential Investors, Creditors	To Evaluate Operations of the Firm To Make Investment Decisions
Management	To Plan and Control
Employees, Union Officials	To Use in Contract Negotiations
Lenders, Suppliers	To Evaluate Credit Ratings
Government Agencies, Economic Planners, Consumer Groups	To Evaluate Tax Liabilities To Approve New Issues of Stocks and Bonds

See **FIGURE 15.1 Users of Accounting Information**

Managers with a business, government agency, or not-for-profit organization are the major users of accounting information because it helps them plan and control daily and long-range operations. Business owners and boards of directors of not-for-profit groups also rely on accounting data to determine how well managers are running the organizations. Union officials use accounting data in contract negotiations, and employees refer to it as they monitor their firms' productivity and profitability performance.

To help employees understand how their work affects the bottom line, many companies share sensitive financial information with their employees and teach them how to understand and use financial statements. Proponents of what is often referred to as *open book management* believe that allowing employees to view financial information helps them better understand how their work contributes to the company's success, which in turn benefits them.

Outside a firm, potential investors evaluate accounting information to help them decide whether to buy a firm's stock. As will be discussed in more detail later in the chapter, any company whose stock is traded publicly is required to report its financial results on a regular basis. So anyone can find out, for example, what Costco's sales were last year or how much money Intel made during the last quarter. Bankers and other lenders use accounting information to evaluate a potential borrower's financial soundness. The Internal Revenue Service (IRS) and state tax officials use it to determine a company's tax liability. Citizens' groups and government agencies use such information in assessing the efficiency of operations such as Massachusetts General Hospital; the Topeka, Kansas, school system; Community College of Denver; and the Art Institute of Chicago.

Accountants play fundamental roles not only in business but also in other aspects of society. Their work influences each of the business environments discussed earlier in this book. They clearly contribute important information to help managers deal with the competitive and economic environments.

Less obvious contributions help others understand, predict, and react to the technological, regulatory, and social and cultural environments. For instance, thousands of people volunteer each year to help people with their taxes. One of the largest organized programs is Tax-Aide, sponsored by AARP (formerly known as the American Association of Retired Persons). For more than 40 years this volunteer program has assisted about 50 million low- and middle-income Americans—especially people age 60 and older—with their income tax preparation.[3]

Business Activities Involving Accounting

The natural progression of a business begins with financing. Subsequent steps, including investing, lead to operating the business. All organizations, profit-oriented and not-for-profit, perform these three basic activities, and accounting plays a key role in each one:

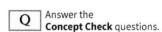
Answer the **Concept Check** questions.

- Financing activities provide necessary funds to start a business and expand it after it begins operating.
- Investing activities provide valuable assets required to run a business.
- Operating activities focus on selling goods and services, but they also consider expenses as important elements of sound financial management.

Accounting Professionals

Accounting professionals work in a variety of areas in and for business firms, government agencies, and not-for-profit organizations. They can be classified as public, management, government, and not-for-profit accountants.

Public Accountants

A **public accountant** provides accounting services to individuals or business firms for a fee. Most public accounting firms provide three basic services to clients: (1) auditing, or examining, financial records; (2) tax preparation, planning, and related services; and (3) management consulting. Because public accountants are not employees of a client firm, they can provide unbiased advice about the firm's financial condition.

Although there are hundreds of public accounting firms in the United States, a handful of firms dominate the industry. The four largest public accounting firms—Deloitte, PwC (PricewaterhouseCoopers), EY (Ernst & Young), and KPMG—referred to as the Big Four—earned more than $50 billion in the United States in a recent fiscal year. In contrast, McGladrey LLP, the nation's fifth-largest accounting firm, had annual revenues of almost $1.5 billion.[4]

Some years ago, public accounting firms came under sharp criticism for providing management consulting services to many of the same firms they audited. Critics argued that when a public accounting firm does both—auditing and management consulting—an inherent conflict of interest is created. In addition, this conflict of interest may undermine confidence in the quality of the financial statements that accounting firms audit. The bankruptcies of some high-profile firms increased pressure on public accounting firms to end this practice. Legislation also established strict limits on the types of consulting services auditors can provide.

A growing number of public accountants are also certified as *forensic accountants,* and some smaller public accounting firms actually specialize in forensic accounting. These professionals, and the firms that employ them, focus on uncovering potential fraud in a variety of organizations.

Certified public accountants (CPAs) demonstrate their accounting knowledge by meeting state requirements for education and experience and successfully completing a number of rigorous tests in accounting theory and practice, auditing, law, and taxes. Other accountants who meet specified educational and experience requirements and pass certification exams carry the title *certified management accountant, certified internal auditor,* or *certified fraud examiner.*

Management Accountants

An accountant employed by a business other than a public accounting firm is called a *management accountant.* Such a person collects and records financial transactions and prepares financial statements used by the firm's managers in decision making. Management accountants provide timely, relevant, accurate, and concise information that executives can use to run their firms more effectively and more profitably than they could without this input. In addition to preparing financial statements, a management accountant plays a major role in interpreting them. A management accountant should provide answers to many important questions:

- Where is the company going?
- What opportunities await it?

- Do certain situations expose the company to excessive risk?
- Does the firm's information system provide detailed and timely information to all levels of management?

Management accountants frequently specialize in different aspects of accounting. A cost accountant, for example, determines the cost of goods and services and helps set their prices. An internal auditor examines the firm's financial practices to ensure that its records include accurate data and that its operations comply with federal, state, and local laws and regulations. A tax accountant works to minimize a firm's tax bill and assumes responsibility for its federal, state, county, and city tax returns. Some management accountants achieve a *certified management accountant (CMA)* designation through experience and passing a comprehensive examination.

Government and Not-for-Profit Accountants

Federal, state, and local governments also require accounting services. Government accountants and those who work for not-for-profit organizations perform professional services similar to those of management accountants. Accountants in these sectors concern themselves primarily with determining how efficiently the organizations accomplish their objectives.

Not-for-profit organizations, such as churches, labor unions, charities, schools, hospitals, and universities, also hire accountants. In fact, the not-for-profit sector is one of the fastest growing segments of accounting practice. An increasing number of not-for-profits publish financial information because contributors want more accountability from these organizations and are interested in knowing how the groups spend the money that they raise.

Q | Answer the **Concept Check** questions.

The Foundation of the Accounting System

To provide reliable, consistent, and unbiased information to decision makers, accountants follow guidelines, or standards, known as **generally accepted accounting principles (GAAP)**. These principles encompass the conventions, rules, and procedures for determining acceptable accounting and financial reporting practices.

All GAAP standards are based on four basic principles: consistency, relevance, reliability, and comparability. Consistency means that all data should be collected and presented in the same manner across all periods. Any change in the way in which specific data are collected or presented must be noted and explained. Relevance states that all information being reported should be appropriate and assist users in evaluating that information. Reliability implies that the accounting data presented in financial statements are reliable and can be verified by an independent party such as an outside auditor. Comparability ensures that one firm's financial statements can be compared with the financial reporting of another firm.

In the United States, the **Financial Accounting Standards Board (FASB)** is primarily responsible for evaluating, setting, or modifying GAAP. The U.S. Securities and Exchange Commission (SEC), the chief federal regulator of the financial markets and accounting industry, actually has the statutory authority to establish financial accounting and reporting standards for publicly held companies.

The FASB carefully monitors changing business conditions, enacting new rules and modifying existing rules when necessary. It also considers input and requests from all segments of its diverse constituency, including corporations and the SEC. One major change in accounting rules recently dealt with executive and employee stock options. Stock options give the holder the right to buy stock at a fixed price. The FASB now requires firms that give employees stock options to calculate the cost of the options and treat the cost as an expense, similar to salaries.

In response to well-known cases of accounting fraud and questions about the independence of auditors, the Sarbanes-Oxley Act—commonly known as SOX—created the Public Accounting Oversight Board. The five-member board has the power to set audit standards and to investigate and sanction accounting firms that certify the books of publicly traded firms. Members of the Public Accounting Oversight Board are appointed by the SEC. No more than two of the five members of the board can be certified public accountants.

In addition to creating the Public Accounting Oversight Board, SOX also added to the reporting requirements for publicly traded companies. For example, senior executives including the CEO and chief financial officer (CFO) must personally certify that the financial information reported by the company is correct. As noted earlier, these requirements have increased the demand for accounting professionals, especially managerial accountants. One result of this increased demand has been higher salaries.

The **Foreign Corrupt Practices Act** is a federal law that prohibits U.S. citizens and companies from bribing foreign officials in order to win or continue business. This law was later extended to make foreign officials subject to penalties if they in any way cause similar corrupt practices to occur within the United States or its territories.

Q Answer the
Concept Check questions.

The Accounting Cycle

Accounting deals with financial transactions between a firm and its employees, customers, suppliers, and owners; bankers; and various government agencies. For example, payroll checks result in a cash outflow to compensate employees. A payment to a vendor results in receipt of needed materials for the production process. Cash, check, and credit purchases by customers generate funds to cover the costs of operations and to earn a profit. Prompt payment of bills preserves the firm's credit rating and its future ability to earn a profit. The procedure by which accountants convert data about individual transactions to financial statements is called the **accounting cycle**.

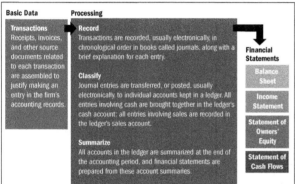

Figure 15.2 illustrates the activities involved in the accounting cycle: recording, classifying, and summarizing transactions. Initially, any transaction that has a financial impact on the business, such as wages or payments to suppliers, should be documented. All these transactions are recorded in journals, which list transactions in chronological order. Journal listings are then posted to ledgers. A ledger shows increases or decreases in specific accounts such as cash or wages. Ledgers are used to prepare the financial statements, which summarize financial transactions. Management and other interested parties use the resulting financial statements for a variety of purposes.

See **FIGURE 15.2 The Accounting Cycle**

The Accounting Equation

Three fundamental terms appear in the accounting equation: assets, liabilities, and owners' equity. An **asset** is anything of value owned or leased by a business. Assets include land, buildings, supplies, cash, accounts receivable (amounts owed to the business as payment for credit sales), and marketable securities.

Although most assets are tangible assets, such as equipment, buildings, and inventories, intangible possessions such as patents and trademarks are often some of a firm's most important assets. This kind of asset is especially essential for many companies, including computer software firms, biotechnology companies, and pharmaceutical companies.

Two groups have claims against the assets of a firm: creditors and owners. A **liability** of a business is anything owed to creditors—that is, the claims of a firm's creditors. When a firm borrows money to purchase inventory, land, or machinery, the claims of creditors are shown as accounts payable, notes payable, or long-term debt. Wages and salaries owed to employees also are liabilities (known as *wages payable* or *accrued wages*).

Owners' equity is the owners' initial investment in the business plus profits that were not paid out to owners over time in the form of cash dividends. A strong owners' equity position often is used as evidence of a firm's financial strength and stability.

The **accounting equation** (also referred to as the *accounting identity*) states that assets must equal liabilities plus owners' equity. This equation reflects the financial position of a firm at any point in time:

$$\text{Assets} = \text{Liabilities} + \text{Owners' Equity}$$

Because financing comes from either creditors or owners, the right side of the accounting equation also represents the business's financial structure.

The accounting equation also illustrates **double-entry bookkeeping**—the process by which accounting transactions are recorded. Because assets must always equal liabilities plus owners' equity, each transaction must have an offsetting transaction. For example, if a company increases an asset, either another asset must decrease, a liability must increase, or owners' equity must increase. So if a company uses cash to purchase inventory, one asset (inventory) is increased while another (cash) is decreased by the same amount. Similarly, a decrease in an asset must be offset by either an increase in another asset, a decrease in a liability, or a decrease in owners' equity. If a company uses cash to repay a bank loan, both an asset (cash) and a liability (bank loans) decrease, and by the same amount.

The relationship expressed by the accounting equation underlies the development of the firm's financial statements. Three statements form the foundation of the financial statements: the balance sheet, the income statement, and the statement of owners' equity. The information found in these statements is calculated using the double-entry bookkeeping system and reflects the basic accounting equation. A fourth statement, the statement of cash flows, is also prepared to focus specifically on the sources and uses of cash for a firm from its operating, investing, and financing activities.

The Impact of Computers and the Internet on the Accounting Process

For hundreds of years, bookkeepers recorded, or posted, accounting transactions as manual entries in journals. They then transferred the information, or posted it, to individual accounts listed in ledgers. Computers have streamlined the process, making it both faster and easier. For instance, point-of-sale terminals in retail stores perform a number of functions each time they record a sale. These terminals not only recall prices from computer system memory and maintain constant inventory counts of individual items in stock but also automatically perform accounting data entry functions.

Because the accounting needs of entrepreneurs and small businesses differ from those of larger firms, accounting software makers have designed programs that meet specific user needs. Some examples of accounting software programs designed for entrepreneurs and small businesses, and designed to run on personal computers, include QuickBooks and Sage 50 (formerly Peachtree). Software programs designed for larger firms, often requiring more sophisticated computer systems, include products from NetSuite, Oracle, and SAP.

For firms that conduct business worldwide, software producers have introduced new accounting programs that handle all of a company's accounting information for every country in which it operates. The software handles different languages and currencies as well as the financial, legal, and tax requirements of each nation in which the firm conducts business.

The Internet also influences the accounting process. Several software producers offer web-based accounting products designed for small and medium-sized businesses. Among other benefits, these products allow users to access their complete accounting systems from anywhere using a standard web browser.

[Q] Answer the **Concept Check** questions.

Financial Statements

Financial statements provide managers with essential information they need to evaluate the liquidity position of an organization—its ability to meet current obligations and needs by converting assets into cash; the firm's profitability; and its overall financial health. The balance sheet, income statement, statement of owners' equity, and statement of cash flows provide a foundation on which managers can base their decisions. By interpreting the data provided in these statements, managers can communicate the appropriate information to internal decision makers and to interested parties outside the organization.

Of the four financial statements, only the balance sheet is considered to be a permanent statement; its amounts are carried over from year to year. The income statement, statement of owners' equity, and statement of cash flows are considered temporary because they are closed out at the end of each fiscal year.

Public companies are required to report their financial statements at the end of each three-month period as well as at the end of each fiscal year. Annual statements must be examined and verified by the firm's outside auditors. These financial statements are public information available to anyone. A fiscal year need not coincide with the calendar year, and companies set different fiscal years. For instance, Starbucks' fiscal year runs from October 1 to September 30 of the following year. Nike's fiscal year consists of the 12 months between June 1 and May 31. By contrast, GE's fiscal year is the same as the calendar year, running from January 1 to December 31.

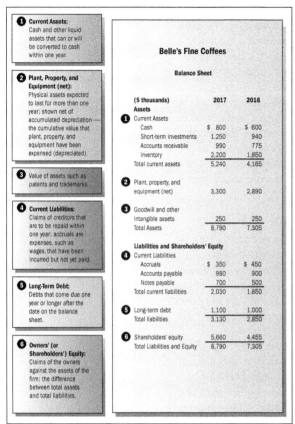

See **FIGURE 15.3** Belle's Fine Coffees Balance Sheet (Fiscal Year Ending December 31)

① Current Assets:
Cash and other liquid assets that can or will be converted to cash within one year.

② Plant, Property, and Equipment (net):
Physical assets expected to last for more than one year; shown net of accumulated depreciation—the cumulative value that plant, property, and equipment have been expensed (depreciated).

③ Value of assets such as patents and trademarks.

④ Current Liabilities:
Claims of creditors that are to be repaid within one year; accruals are expenses, such as wages, that have been incurred but not yet paid.

⑤ Long-Term Debt:
Debts that come due one year or longer after the date on the balance sheet.

⑥ Owners' (or Shareholders') Equity:
Claims of the owners against the assets of the firm; the difference between total assets and total liabilities.

Belle's Fine Coffees

Balance Sheet

($ thousands)	2017	2016
Assets		
① Current Assets		
Cash	$ 800	$ 600
Short-term investments	1,250	940
Accounts receivable	990	775
Inventory	2,200	1,850
Total current assets	5,240	4,165
② Plant, property, and equipment (net)	3,300	2,890
③ Goodwill and other intangible assets	250	250
Total Assets	8,790	7,305
Liabilities and Shareholders' Equity		
④ Current Liabilities		
Accruals	$ 350	$ 450
Accounts payable	980	900
Notes payable	700	500
Total current liabilities	2,030	1,850
⑤ Long-term debt	1,100	1,000
Total liabilities	3,130	2,850
⑥ Shareholders' equity	5,660	4,455
Total Liabilities and Equity	8,790	7,305

The Balance Sheet

A firm's **balance sheet** shows its financial position on a particular date. It is similar to a photograph of the firm's assets together with its liabilities and owners' equity at a specific moment in time. Balance sheets must be prepared at regular intervals because a firm's managers and other internal parties often request this information every day, every week, or at least every month. On the other hand, external users, such as stockholders or industry analysts, may use this information less frequently, perhaps every quarter or once a year.

The balance sheet follows the accounting equation. On the left side of the balance sheet are the firm's assets—what it owns. These assets, shown in descending order of liquidity (in other words, convertibility to cash), represent the uses that management has made of available funds. Cash is always listed first on the asset side of the balance sheet.

On the right side of the equation are the claims against the firm's assets. Liabilities and shareholders' equity indicate the sources of the firm's assets and are listed in the order in which they are due. Liabilities reflect the claims of creditors—financial institutions or bondholders that have loaned the firm money; suppliers that have provided goods and services on credit; and others to be paid, such as federal, state, and local tax authorities. Shareholders' equity represents the owners' claims (those of stockholders, in the case of a corporation) against the firm's assets. It also amounts to the excess of all assets over liabilities.

Figure 15.3 shows the balance sheet for Belle's Fine Coffees, a small coffee wholesaler. The accounting equation is illustrated by the three classifications of assets, liabilities, and shareholders' equity on the company's balance sheet. Remember, total assets must always equal the sum of liabilities and shareholders' equity. In other words, the balance sheet must always balance.

The Income Statement

Whereas the balance sheet reflects a firm's financial situation at a specific point in time, the **income statement** indicates the flow of resources that reveals the performance of the organization over a specific time period. Resembling a video rather than a photograph, the income statement is a financial record summarizing a firm's financial performance in terms of revenues, expenses, and profits over a given time period, say, a quarter or a year.

In addition to reporting the firm's profit or loss results, the income statement helps decision makers focus on overall revenues and the costs involved in generating these revenues. Managers of a not-for-profit organization use this statement to determine whether its revenues from contributions, grants, and investments will cover its operating costs. Finally, the income statement provides much of the basic data needed to calculate the financial ratios managers use in planning and controlling activities. **Figure 15.4** shows the income statement for Belle's Fine Coffees.

An income statement (sometimes called *a profit-and-loss,* or *P&L, statement*) begins with total sales or revenues generated during a month, a quarter, or a year. Subsequent lines then deduct all of the costs related to producing the revenues. Typical categories of costs include those involved in producing the firm's goods or services, operating expenses, interest, and taxes. After all of them have been subtracted, the remaining net income may be distributed to the firm's owners (stockholders, proprietors, or partners) or reinvested in the company as retained earnings. The final figure on the income statement—net income after taxes—is literally the *bottom line.*

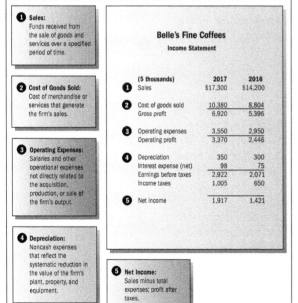

See **FIGURE 15.4** Belle's Fine Coffees Income Statement (Fiscal Year Ending December 31)

① Sales:
Funds received from the sale of goods and services over a specified period of time.

② Cost of Goods Sold:
Cost of merchandise or services that generate the firm's sales.

③ Operating Expenses:
Salaries and other operational expenses not directly related to the acquisition, production, or sale of the firm's output.

④ Depreciation:
Noncash expenses that reflect the systematic reduction in the value of the firm's plant, property, and equipment.

⑤ Net Income:
Sales minus total expenses; profit after taxes.

Belle's Fine Coffees

Income Statement

($ thousands)	2017	2016
① Sales	$17,300	$14,200
② Cost of goods sold	10,380	8,804
Gross profit	6,920	5,396
③ Operating expenses	3,550	2,950
Operating profit	3,370	2,446
④ Depreciation	350	300
Interest expense (net)	98	75
Earnings before taxes	2,922	2,071
Income taxes	1,005	650
⑤ Net income	1,917	1,421

Keeping costs under control is an important part of running a business. Too often, however, companies concentrate more on increasing revenue than on controlling costs. Regardless of how much money a company collects in revenues, it won't stay in business for long unless it eventually earns a profit.

Statement of Owners' Equity

The **statement of owners'**, or shareholders', **equity** is designed to show the components of the change in equity from the end of one fiscal year to the end of the next. It uses information from both the balance sheet and income statement. A somewhat simplified example is shown in ▣ **Figure 15.5** for Belle's Fine Coffees.

Note that the statement begins with the amount of equity shown on the balance sheet at the end of the prior year. Net income is added, and cash dividends paid to owners are subtracted (both are found on the income statement for the current year). If owners contributed any additional capital, say, through the sale of new shares, this amount is added to equity. On the other hand, if owners withdrew capital, for example, through the repurchase of existing shares, equity declines. All of the additions and subtractions, taken together, equal the change in owners' equity from the end of the last fiscal year to the end of the current one. The new amount of owners' equity is then reported on the balance sheet for the current year.

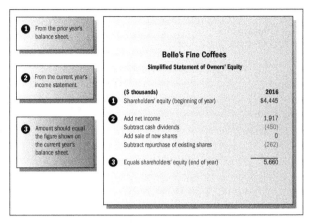

See **FIGURE 15.5 Belle's Fine Coffees Simplified Statement of Owners' Equity (Fiscal Year Ending December 31)**

The Statement of Cash Flows

In addition to the statement of owners' equity, the income statement, and the balance sheet, most firms prepare a fourth accounting statement—the **statement of cash flows**. Public companies are required to prepare and publish a statement of cash flows. In addition, commercial lenders often require a borrower to submit a statement of cash flows. The statement of cash flows provides investors and creditors with relevant information about a firm's cash receipts and cash payments for its operations, investments, and financing during an accounting period. ▣ **Figure 15.6** shows the statement of cash flows for Belle's Fine Coffees.

Companies prepare a statement of cash flows due to the widespread use of accrual accounting. **Accrual accounting** recognizes revenues and costs when they occur, not when actual cash changes hands. As a result, there can be differences between what is reported as sales, expenses, and profits, and the amount of cash that actually flows into and out of the business during a period of time. An example is depreciation. Companies depreciate fixed assets—such as machinery and buildings—over a specified period of time, meaning that they systematically reduce the value of the asset. Depreciation is reported as an expense on the firm's income statement (see Figure 15.4) but does not involve any actual cash. The fact that depreciation is a noncash expense means that what a firm reports as net income (profits after tax) for a particular period actually understates the amount of cash the firm took in, less expenses, during that period of time. Consequently, depreciation is added back to net income when calculating cash flow.

The fact that *cash flow* is the lifeblood of every organization is evidenced by the business failure rate. Many owners of failed firms blame inadequate cash flow for their company's demise. Those who value the statement of cash flow maintain that its preparation and scrutiny by various parties can prevent financial distress for otherwise profitable firms, too many of which are forced into bankruptcy due to a lack of cash needed to continue day-to-day operations.

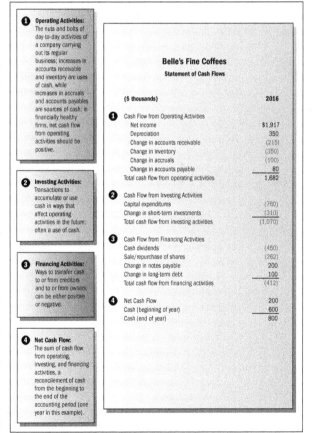

See **FIGURE 15.6 Belle's Fine Coffees Statement of Cash Flows (Fiscal Year Ending December 31)**

Even for firms for which bankruptcy is not an issue, the statement of cash flows can provide investors and other interested parties with vital information. For instance, assume that a firm's income statement reports rising earnings. At the same time, however, the statement

Q Answer the
Concept Check questions.

of cash flows shows that the firm's inventory is rising faster than sales—often a signal that demand for the firm's products is softening, which may in turn be a sign of impending financial trouble.

Financial Ratio Analysis

Accounting professionals fulfill important responsibilities beyond preparing financial statements. In a more critical role, they help managers interpret the statements by comparing data about the firm's current activities to those for previous periods and to results posted by other companies in the industry. *Ratio analysis* is one of the most commonly used tools for measuring a firm's liquidity, profitability, and reliance on debt financing, as well as the effectiveness of management's resource utilization. This analysis also allows comparisons with other firms and with the firm's own past performance.

Liquidity Ratios

A firm's ability to meet its short-term obligations when they must be paid is measured by *liquidity ratios*. Increasing liquidity reduces the likelihood that a firm will face emergencies caused by the need to raise funds to repay loans. On the other hand, firms with low liquidity may be forced to choose between default and borrowing from high-cost lending sources to meet their maturing obligations.

Two commonly used liquidity ratios are the current ratio and the acid-test, or quick, ratio. The current ratio compares current assets to current liabilities, giving executives information about the firm's ability to pay its current debts as they mature. The current ratio of Belle's Fine Coffees can be computed as follows (unless indicated, all amounts from the balance sheet or income statement are in thousands of dollars):

$$\text{Current Ratio} = \frac{\text{Current Assets}}{\text{Current Liabilities}} = \frac{5{,}240}{2{,}030} = 2.58$$

In other words, Belle's Fine Coffees has $2.58 of current assets for every $1.00 of current liabilities. In general, a current ratio of 2:1 is considered satisfactory liquidity. This rule of thumb must be considered along with other factors, such as the nature of the business, the season, and the quality of the company's management team. Belle's Fine Coffees' management and other interested parties are likely to evaluate this ratio of 2.58:1 by comparing it with ratios for previous operating periods and with industry averages.

The acid-test (or quick) ratio measures the ability of a firm to meet its debt payments on short notice. This ratio compares quick assets—the most liquid current assets—against current liabilities. Quick assets generally consist of cash and equivalents, short-term investments, and accounts receivable. So, generally quick assets equal total current assets minus inventory.

Belle's Fine Coffees' current balance sheet lists total current assets of $5.24 million and inventory of $2.2 million. Therefore, its quick ratio is as follows:

$$\text{Acid-Test Ratio} = \frac{\text{Current Assets} - \text{Inventory}}{\text{Current Liabilities}}$$

$$= \frac{(5{,}240 - 2{,}200)}{2{,}030} = 1.50$$

Because the traditional rule of thumb for an adequate acid-test ratio is around 1:1, Belle's Fine Coffees appears to have a strong level of liquidity. However, the same cautions apply here as for the current ratio. The ratio should be compared with industry averages and data from previous operating periods to determine whether it is adequate for the firm.

Activity Ratios

Activity ratios measure the effectiveness of management's use of the firm's resources. One of the most frequently used activity ratios, the inventory turnover ratio, indicates the number of times merchandise moves through a business:

$$\text{Inventory Turnover} = \frac{\text{Cost of Goods Sold}}{\text{Average Inventory}}$$

$$= \frac{10{,}380}{[(2{,}200 + 1{,}850)/2]} = 5.13$$

Average inventory for Belle's Fine Coffees is determined by adding the inventory as of December 31 of the current year ($2.2 million) with the inventory as of December 31 of the previous year ($1.85 million) and dividing it by 2. Comparing the 5.13 inventory turnover ratio with industry standards gives a measure of efficiency. It is important to note, however, that inventory turnover can vary substantially, depending on the products a company sells and the industry in which it operates.

If a company makes a substantial portion of its sales on credit, measuring receivables turnover can provide useful information. Receivables turnover can be calculated as follows:

$$\text{Receivables Turnover} = \frac{\text{Credit Sales}}{\text{Average Accounts Receivable}}$$

Because Belle's Fine Coffees is a wholesaler, let's assume that all of its sales are credit sales. Average receivables equals the simple average of current year's receivables and previous year's receivables. The ratio for the company is:

$$\text{Receivables Turnover} = \frac{17,300}{[(990 + 775)/2]} = 19.60$$

Dividing 365 by the figure for receivables turnover, 19.6, equals the average age of receivables, 18.62 days. Assume Belle's Fine Coffees expects its retail customers to pay outstanding bills within 30 days of the date of purchase. Given that the average age of its receivables is less than 30 days, Belle's Fine Coffees appears to be doing a good job collecting its credit sales.

Another measure of efficiency is total asset turnover. It measures how much in sales each dollar invested in assets generates:

$$\text{Total Asset Turnover} = \frac{\text{Sales}}{\text{Average Total Assets}}$$

$$= \frac{17,300}{[(8,790 + 7,305)/2]} = 2.15$$

Average total assets for Belle's Fine Coffees equals total assets as of December 31 of the current year ($8.79 million) plus total assets as of December 31 of the previous year ($7.305 million) divided by 2.

Belle's Fine Coffees generates about $2.15 in sales for each dollar invested in assets. Although a higher ratio generally indicates that a firm is operating more efficiently, care must be taken when comparing firms that operate in different industries. Some industries simply require higher investment in assets than do other industries.

Profitability Ratios

Some ratios measure the organization's overall financial performance by evaluating its ability to generate revenues in excess of operating costs and other expenses. These measures are called *profitability ratios*. To compute these ratios, accountants compare the firm's earnings with total sales or investments. Over a period of time, profitability ratios may reveal the effectiveness of management in operating the business. Three important profitability ratios are gross profit margin, net profit margin, and return on equity:

$$\text{Gross Profit Margin} = \frac{\text{Gross Profit}}{\text{Sales}} = \frac{6,920}{17,300} = 40.0\%$$

$$\text{Net Profit Margin} = \frac{\text{Net Income}}{\text{Sales}} = \frac{1,917}{17,300} = 11.1\%$$

$$\text{Return on Equity} = \frac{\text{Net Income}}{\text{Average Equity}}$$

$$= \frac{1,917}{[(5,660 + 4,455)/2]} = 37.9\%$$

All of these ratios indicate positive evaluations of the current operations of Belle's Fine Coffees. For example, the net profit margin indicates that the firm realizes a profit of slightly more than 11 cents on each dollar of merchandise it sells. Although this ratio varies widely among business firms, Belle's Fine Coffees compares favorably with wholesalers in general, which have an average net profit margin of around 5 percent. However, like other profitability ratios, this ratio should be evaluated in relation to profit forecasts, past performance, or more specific industry averages to enhance the interpretation of results. Similarly, although the firm's return on equity of almost 38 percent appears outstanding, the degree of risk in the industry also must be considered.

Leverage Ratios

Leverage ratios measure the extent to which a firm relies on debt financing. They provide particularly interesting information to potential investors and lenders. If management has assumed too much debt in financing the firm's operations, problems may arise in meeting future interest payments and repaying outstanding loans. As Chapter 17 points out, borrowing money does have advantages. However, relying too heavily on debt financing may lead to bankruptcy. More generally, both investors and lenders may prefer to deal with firms whose owners have invested enough of their own money to avoid overreliance on borrowing. The debt ratio and long-term debt to equity ratio help interested parties evaluate a firm's leverage:

$$\text{Debt Ratio} = \frac{\text{Total Liabilities}}{\text{Total Assets}} = \frac{3,130}{8,790} = 35.6\%$$

$$\text{Long-Term Debt to Equity} = \frac{\text{Long-Term Debt}}{\text{Owners' Equity}} = \frac{1,100}{5,660} = 19.43\%$$

A total liabilities to total assets ratio greater than 50 percent indicates that a firm is relying more on borrowed money than on owners' equity. Because Belle's Fine Coffees' total liabilities to total assets ratio is 35.6 percent, the firm's owners have invested considerably more than the total amount of liabilities shown on the firm's balance sheet. Moreover, the firm's long-term debt to equity ratio is only 19.43 percent, indicating that Belle's Fine Coffees has only about 19.4 cents in long-term debt to every dollar in equity. The long-term debt to equity ratio also indicates that Belle's Fine Coffees hasn't relied very heavily on borrowed money.

The four categories of financial ratios relate balance sheet and income statement data to one another, help management pinpoint a firm's strengths and weaknesses, and indicate areas in need of further investigation. Large multiproduct firms that operate in diverse markets use their information systems to update their financial ratios every day or even every hour. Each company's management must decide on an appropriate review schedule to avoid the costly and time-consuming mistake of overmonitoring.

In addition to calculating financial ratios, managers, investors, and lenders should pay close attention to how accountants apply a number of accounting rules when preparing financial statements. GAAP gives accountants leeway in reporting certain revenues and expenses. Public companies are required to disclose, in footnotes to the financial statements, how the various accounting rules were applied.

Q | Answer the **Concept Check** questions.

Budgeting

Although the financial statements discussed in this chapter focus on past business activities, they also provide the basis for planning in the future. A **budget** is a planning and controlling tool that reflects the firm's expected sales revenues, operating expenses, and cash receipts and outlays. It quantifies the firm's plans for a specified future period. Because it reflects management estimates of expected sales, cash inflows and outflows, and costs, the budget is a financial blueprint and can be thought of as a short-term financial plan. It becomes the standard for comparison against actual performance.

Budget preparation is frequently a time-consuming task that involves many people from various departments within the organization. The complexity of the budgeting process varies with the size and complexity of the organization. Large corporations such as United Technologies, Paramount Pictures, and Verizon maintain complex and sophisticated budgeting systems. Besides being planning and controlling tools, their budgets help managers integrate their numerous divisions. But budgeting in both large and small firms is similar to household budgeting in its purpose: to match income and expenses in a way that accomplishes objectives and correctly times cash inflows and outflows.

Because the accounting department is an organization's financial nerve center, it provides many of the data for budget development. The overall master, or operating, budget is actually a composite of many individual budgets for separate units of the firm. These individual budgets typically include the production budget, the cash budget, the capital expenditures budget, the advertising budget, the sales budget, and the travel budget. When you travel for business, you are responsible for keeping track of and recording your own financial transactions for the purpose of preparing your expense report.

Technology has improved the efficiency of the budgeting process. The accounting software products discussed earlier—such as QuickBooks—all include budgeting features. Moreover, modules designed for specific businesses are often available from third parties. Many banks now offer their customers personal financial management tools (PFMs) developed by software companies. Whether or not your bank offers PFMs, there are many providers offering low or no cost software to help individuals and businesses keep track of their finances. Many of these software solutions integrate with smart phones and tablets allowing consumers to manage their finances remotely.[5]

One of the most important budgets prepared by firms is the *cash budget*. The cash budget, usually prepared monthly, tracks the firm's cash inflows and outflows. ▣ **Figure 15.7** illustrates a sample cash budget for Birchwood Paper, a small paper products company. The company has set a $150,000 target cash balance. The cash budget indicates months in which the firm will need temporary loans—May, June, and July—and how much it will need (close to $3 million). The document also indicates that Birchwood will generate a cash surplus in August and can begin repaying the short-term loan. Finally, the cash budget produces a tangible standard against which to compare actual cash inflows and outflows.

Birchwood Paper Company
Four-Month Cash Budget

($ thousands)	May	June	July	August
Gross sales	$1,200.0	$3,200.0	$5,500.0	$4,500.0
Cash sales	300.0	800.0	1,375.0	1,125.0
One month prior	600.0	600.0	1,600.0	2,750.0
Two months prior	300.0	300.0	300.0	800.0
Total cash inflows	1,200.0	1,700.0	3,275.0	4,675.0
Purchases				
Cash purchases	1,040.0	1,787.5	1,462.5	390.0
One month prior	390.0	1,040.0	1,787.5	1,462.5
Wages and salaries	250.0	250.0	250.0	250.0
Office rent	75.0	75.0	75.0	75.0
Marketing and other expenses	150.0	150.0	150.0	150.0
Taxes		300.0		
Total cash outflows	1,905.0	3,602.5	3,725.0	2,327.5
Net cash flow				
(Inflows − Outflows)	(705.0)	(1,902.5)	(450.0)	2,347.5
Beginnning cash balance	250.0	150.0	150.0	150.0
Net cash flow	(705.0)	(1,902.5)	(450.0)	2,347.5
Ending cash balance	(455.0)	(1,752.5)	(300.0)	2,497.5
Target cash balance	150.0	150.0	150.0	150.0
Surplus (deficit)	(605.0)	(1,902.5)	(450.0)	2,347.5
Cumulative surplus (deficit)	(605.0)	(2,507.5)	(2,957.5)	610.0

 See **FIGURE 15.7 Four-Month Cash Budget for Birchwood Paper Company**

Q Answer the **Concept Check** questions.

International Accounting

Today, accounting procedures and practices must be adapted to accommodate an international business environment. The Coca-Cola Company and McDonald's both generate more than half their annual revenues from sales outside the United States. Nestlé, the giant chocolate and food products firm, operates throughout the world. It derives the majority of its revenues from outside Switzerland, its home country. International accounting practices for global firms must reliably translate the financial statements of the firm's international affiliates, branches, and subsidiaries and convert data about foreign currency transactions to dollars. Also, foreign currencies and exchange rates influence the accounting and financial reporting processes of firms operating internationally.

International Accounting Standards

The International Accounting Standards Committee (IASC) was established in 1973 to promote worldwide consistency in financial reporting practices and soon developed its first set of accounting standards and interpretations. In 2001, the IASC became the **International Accounting Standards Board (IASB). International Financial Reporting Standards (IFRS)** are the standards and interpretations adopted by the IASB. The IASB operates in much the same manner as the FASB does in the United States, interpreting and modifying IFRS.

Because of increased global trade, there is a real need for comparability of and uniformity in international accounting rules. Trade agreements such as NAFTA and the expansion of the European Union have only heightened interest in creating a uniform set of global accounting rules. In addition, an increasing number of investors are buying shares in foreign multinational corporations, and they need a practical way to evaluate firms in other countries. To assist global investors, more and more firms are beginning to report their financial information according to international accounting standards. This practice helps investors make informed decisions.

How does IFRS differ from GAAP? Although many similarities exist, they have some important differences. For example, under GAAP, plant, property, and equipment are reported on the balance sheet at the historical cost minus depreciation. Under IFRS, on the other hand, plant, property, and equipment are shown on the balance sheet at current market value. This gives a better picture of the real value of a firm's assets. Many accounting experts believe IFRS is less complicated than GAAP overall and more transparent.[6]

Q Answer the **Concept Check** questions.

WP LS Go to your WileyPLUS Learning Space course for video episodes, examples, art, tables, Concept Checks, practice, and resources that will help you success in this course.

THE FINANCIAL SYSTEM

> **WP LS** Go to your WileyPLUS Learning Space course for video episodes, examples, art, tables, Concept Checks, practice, and resources that will help you success in this course.

Understanding the Financial System

Households, businesses, government, financial institutions, and financial markets together form what is known as the **financial system**. A simple diagram of the financial system is shown in **Figure 16.1**.

On the left are savers—those with excess funds. For a variety of reasons, savers choose not to spend all of their current income, so they have a surplus of funds. Users are the opposite of savers; their spending needs exceed their current income, so they have a deficit. They need to obtain additional funds to make up the difference. Savings are provided by some households, businesses, and the government, but other households, businesses, and the government are also borrowers. Households may need money to buy automobiles or homes. Businesses may need money to purchase inventory or build new production facilities. Governments may need money to build highways and courthouses.

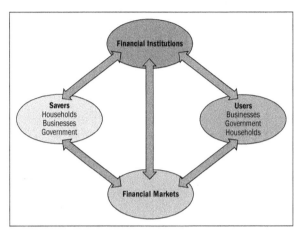

See **FIGURE 16.1 Overview of the Financial System and Its Components**

Generally, in the United States, households are net savers—meaning that as a whole they save more funds than they use—whereas businesses and governments are net users—meaning that they use more funds than they save. The fact that most of the net savings in the U.S. financial system are provided by households may be a bit of a surprise initially because Americans do not have a reputation for being thrifty. Yet even though the savings rate of American households is low compared with those of other countries, American households still save hundreds of billions of dollars each year.

Funds can be transferred between savers and users in two ways: directly and indirectly. A direct transfer means that the user raises the needed funds directly from savers. While direct transfers occur, the vast majority of funds flow through either financial markets or financial institutions. For example, assume a local school district needs to build a new high school. The district doesn't have enough cash on hand to pay for the school construction costs, so it sells bonds to investors (savers) in the financial market. The district uses the proceeds from the sale to pay for the new school and in return pays bond investors interest each year for the use of their money.

The other way in which funds can be transferred indirectly is through financial institutions—for example, commercial banks like Fifth Third Bank or Regions Bank. The bank pools customer deposits and uses the funds to make loans to businesses and households. These borrowers pay the bank interest, and it in turn pays depositors interest for the use of their money.

> **Q** Answer the **Concept Check** questions.

Types of Securities

For the funds they borrow from savers, businesses and governments provide different types of guarantees for repayment. **Securities**, also called *financial instruments*, represent obligations on the part of the issuers—businesses and governments—to provide the purchasers with expected or stated returns on the funds invested or loaned. Securities can be grouped into three categories: money market instruments, bonds, and stock. Money market instruments and bonds are both debt securities. Stocks are units of ownership in corporations like General Electric, McDonald's, Apple, and PepsiCo.

Money Market Instruments

Money market instruments are short-term debt securities issued by governments, financial institutions, and corporations. Money market instruments are generally low-risk securities and are purchased by investors when they have surplus cash. Examples of money market instruments include U.S. Treasury bills, commercial paper, and bank certificates of deposit.

Treasury bills are short-term securities issued by the U.S. Treasury and backed by the full faith and credit of the U.S. government. Treasury bills are sold with a maturity of 30, 90, 180, or 360 days and have a minimum denomination of $1,000. They are considered virtually risk-free and easy to resell. *Commercial paper* is securities sold by corporations, such as Raytheon, that mature in from 1 to 270 days from the date of issue. Although slightly riskier than Treasury bills, commercial paper is still generally considered a very low risk security.

A *certificate of deposit (CD)* is a time deposit at a financial institution, such as a commercial bank, savings bank, or credit union. The sizes and maturity dates of CDs vary considerably and can often be tailored to meet the needs of purchasers. CDs in denominations of $250,000 or less per depositor are federally insured.

Bonds

Bondholders are creditors of a corporation or government body. Bonds are issued in various denominations, or face values, usually between $1,000 and $25,000. Each issue indicates a rate of interest to be paid to the bondholder—stated as a percentage of the bond's face value—as well as a maturity date on which the bondholder is paid the bond's full face value. Because bondholders are creditors, they have a claim on the firm's assets that must be satisfied before any claims of stockholders in the event of the firm's bankruptcy, reorganization, or liquidation.

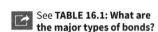
See **TABLE 16.1: What are the major types of bonds?**

A prospective bond investor can choose among a variety of bonds. The major types of bonds are summarized in **Table 16.1**. *Government bonds* are bonds sold by the U.S. Department of the Treasury. Because government bonds are backed by the full faith and credit of the U.S. government, they are considered the least risky of all bonds. The Treasury sells bonds that mature in 2, 5, 10, and 30 years from the date of issue.

Municipal bonds are bonds issued by state or local governments. Two types of municipal bonds are available. A *revenue bond* is a bond issue whose proceeds will be used to pay for a project that will produce revenue, such as a toll road or bridge. The proceeds of a *general obligation bond* are to be used to pay for a project that will not produce any revenue.

Corporate bonds are a diverse group and often vary based on the collateral—the property pledged by the borrower—that backs the bond. For example, a *secured bond* is backed by a specific pledge of company assets. These assets are collateral, just like a home is collateral for a mortgage. However, many firms also issue unsecured bonds, called *debentures*. These bonds are backed only by the financial reputation of the issuing corporation.

See **TABLE 16.2: Can you list the Standard & Poor's bond ratings?**

Two factors determine the price of a bond: its risk and its interest rate. Bonds vary considerably in terms of risk. One tool that bond investors use to assess the risk of a bond is its *bond rating.* Several investment firms rate corporate and municipal bonds, the best known of which are Standard & Poor's (S&P), Moody's, and Fitch. **Table 16.2** lists the S&P bond ratings. Moody's and Fitch use similar rating systems. Bonds with the lowest level of risk are rated AAA. As ratings descend, risk increases. Bonds with ratings of BBB and above are classified as *investment-grade bonds.* By contrast, bonds with ratings of BB and below are classified as *speculative* or *junk bonds.* Junk bonds attract investors by offering high interest rates in exchange for greater risk.

Another important influence on bond prices is the *market interest rate.* Because bonds pay fixed rates of interest, as market interest rates rise, bond prices fall, and vice versa. For instance, the price of a ten-year bond, paying 5 percent per year, would fall by about 8 percent if market interest rates rose from 5 percent to 6 percent.

Stock

The basic form of corporate ownership is embodied in **common stock**. Purchasers of common stock are the true owners of a corporation. Holders of common stock vote on major company decisions, such as purchasing another company or electing a board of directors. In return for the money they invest, they expect to receive some sort of return. This return can come in the form of dividend payments, expected price appreciation, or both. Dividends vary widely from firm to firm. As a general rule, faster-growing companies pay less in dividends because they need more funds to finance their growth. Consequently, investors expect stocks paying little or no cash dividends to show greater price appreciation compared with stocks paying more generous cash dividends.

Common stockholders benefit from company success, and they risk the loss of their investments if the company fails. If a firm dissolves, claims of creditors must be satisfied before stockholders receive anything. Because creditors have the first (or senior) claim to assets, holders of common stock are said to have a residual claim on company assets.

The market value of a stock is the price at which the stock is currently selling. For example, Facebook's stock price fluctuated between $68 and $90 per share during a recent year. What determines this market value is complicated; many variables cause stock prices to move up or down. However, in the long run, stock prices tend to follow a company's profits.

In addition to common stock, a few companies also issue *preferred stock*—stock whose holders receive preference in the payment of dividends. General Motors and Ford are examples of firms with preferred stock outstanding. Also, if a company is dissolved, holders of preferred stock have claims on the firm's assets that are ahead of the claims of common stockholders. On the other hand, preferred stockholders rarely have any voting rights, and the dividend they are paid is fixed, regardless of how profitable the firm becomes. Therefore, although preferred stock is legally classified as equity, many investors consider it to be more like a bond than common stock.

Q Answer the **Concept Check** questions.

Financial Markets

Securities are issued and traded in **financial markets**. Although there are many different types of financial markets, one of the most important distinctions is between primary and secondary markets. In the **primary markets**, firms and governments issue securities and sell them initially to the general public. When a company needs capital to purchase inventory, expand a plant, make major investments, acquire another firm, or pursue other business goals, it may sell a bond or stock issue to the investing public.

A stock offering gives investors the opportunity to purchase ownership shares in a firm and to participate in its future growth in exchange for providing current capital. When a company offers stock for sale to the general public for the first time, it is called an *initial public offering (IPO)*. Analysts predict IPOs from a number of American companies, notably Uber and Airbnb.[1]

Both profit-seeking corporations and government agencies also rely on primary markets to raise funds by issuing bonds. For example, the federal government sells Treasury bonds through an open auction to finance part of federal outlays such as interest on outstanding federal debt. State and local governments sell bonds to finance capital projects such as the construction of sewer systems, streets, and fire stations. Sales of most corporate and municipal securities are made via financial institutions such as Morgan Stanley. These institutions purchase the issue from the firm or government and then resell the issue to investors. This process is known as *underwriting*.

While the primary market is the way corporations and governments raise finds, most of the stock and bond trading that happens on a daily basis happens in the **secondary market**, a collection of financial markets in which previously issued securities are traded among investors. The corporations or governments that originally issued the securities being traded are not directly involved in the secondary market. They make no payments when securities are sold nor receive any of the proceeds when securities are purchased. The New York Stock Exchange (NYSE), for example, is a secondary market. In terms of the dollar value of securities bought and sold, the secondary market is four to five times as large as the primary market. Each day, more than 1.2 billion shares worth about $49 billion are traded on the NYSE.[2] The characteristics of the world's major stock exchanges are discussed in the next section.

Q Answer the **Concept Check** questions.

Understanding Stock Markets

Stock markets, or **exchanges**, are probably the best known of the world's financial markets. In these markets, shares of stock are bought and sold by investors. The two largest stock markets in the world, the New York Stock Exchange (NYSE) and the NASDAQ stock market, are located in the United States. The Dow Jones Industrial Average (often referred to as the Dow) is a price-weighted average of the 30 most significant stocks traded on the NYSE and the NASDAQ.

The New York Stock Exchange

The New York Stock Exchange—sometimes referred to as the Big Board—is the most famous and one of the oldest stock markets in the world, having been founded in 1792. Today, the stocks of more than 1,800 companies are listed on the NYSE. These stocks represent most of the largest, best-known companies in the United States and have a total market value exceeding $16 trillion. In terms of the total value of stock traded, the NYSE is the world's largest stock market.

The NASDAQ Stock Market

The world's second-largest stock market, NASDAQ, is very different from the NYSE. NASDAQ—which stands for National Association of Securities Dealers Automated Quotation—is actually a computerized communications network that links member investment firms. It is the world's largest intranet. All trading on NASDAQ takes place through its intranet rather than on a trading floor. Approximately 3,100 companies have their stocks listed on NASDAQ. While NASDAQ-listed corporations tend to be smaller firms and less well known than NYSE-listed ones, NASDAQ is also home to some of the largest U.S. companies and iconic brands—for example, Starbucks, Costco, Google, Intel, and Microsoft.

Foreign Stock Markets

Stock markets exist throughout the world. Virtually all developed countries and many developing countries have stock exchanges. Examples include Mumbai, Helsinki, Hong Kong, Mexico City, Paris, and Toronto. One of the largest stock exchanges outside the United States is the London Stock Exchange. Founded in the early 19th century, the London Stock Exchange lists approximately 3,000 stock and bond issues by companies from more than 70 countries around the world. Trading on the London Stock Exchange takes place using a NASDAQ-type computerized communications network.

Investor Participation in the Stock Markets

Because most investors aren't members of the NYSE or any other stock market, they need to use the services of a brokerage firm to buy or sell stocks. Examples of brokerage firms include Edward Jones and TD Ameritrade. Investors establish an account with the brokerage firm and then enter orders to trade stocks. The most common type of order is called a *market order*. It instructs the broker to obtain the best possible price—the highest price when selling and the lowest price when buying. If the stock market is open, market orders are filled within seconds. Another popular type of order is called a *limit order*. It sets a price ceiling when buying or a price floor when selling. If the order cannot be executed when it is placed, the order is left with the exchange's market maker. It may be filed later if the price limits are met.

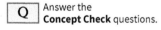
Q Answer the **Concept Check** questions.

Financial Institutions

One of the most important components of the financial system is **financial institutions**. They are an intermediary between savers and borrowers, collecting funds from savers and then lending the funds to individuals, businesses, and governments. Financial institutions greatly increase the efficiency and effectiveness of the transfer of funds from savers to users. Because of financial institutions, savers earn more and users pay less than they would without them. In fact, it is difficult to imagine how any modern economy could function without well-developed financial institutions. Think about how difficult it would be for a businessperson to obtain inventory financing or an individual to purchase a new home without financial institutions. Prospective borrowers would have to identify and negotiate terms with each saver individually.

Traditionally, financial institutions have been classified into depository institutions—institutions that accept deposits that customers can withdraw on demand—and nondepository institutions. Examples of depository institutions include commercial banks, such as US Bancorp and Sun Trust; savings banks, such as New York Community Bank and Ohio Savings Bank; and credit unions, such as the State Employees' Credit Union of North Carolina. Nondepository institutions include life insurance companies, such as Northwestern Mutual; pension funds, such as the Florida state employee pension fund; and mutual funds. In total, financial institutions have trillions of dollars in assets. ▣ **Figure 16.2** illustrates the size of the most prominent financial institutions.

Commercial Banks

Commercial banks are the largest and probably most important financial institution in the United States, and in most other countries as well. In the United States, the approximately 5,571 commercial banks hold total assets of more than $12.7 trillion.[3] Commercial banks offer the most services of any financial institution. These services include a wide range of checking and savings deposit accounts, consumer loans, credit cards, home mortgage loans, business loans, and trust services. Commercial banks also sell other financial products, including securities and insurance.

How Banks Operate

Banks raise funds by offering a variety of checking and savings deposits to customers. The banks then pool these deposits and lend most of them out in the form of consumer and business loans. Recently, banks held over $10.3 trillion in domestic deposits and had more than $7.4 trillion in outstanding loans.[4] The distribution of outstanding loans is shown in ▣ **Figure 16.3**. As the figure shows, banks lend a great deal of money to both households and businesses for a variety of purposes. Commercial banks are an especially important source of funds for small businesses. When evaluating loan applications, banks consider the borrower's ability and willingness to repay the loan.

Banks make money primarily because the interest rate they charge borrowers is higher than the rate of interest they pay depositors. Banks also make money from other sources, such as fees they charge customers for checking accounts and using automated teller machines.

Electronic Banking

More and more funds each year move through electronic funds transfer (EFT) systems, computerized systems for conducting financial transactions over electronic links. Millions of businesses and consumers now pay bills and receive payments electronically. Most employers, for example, directly deposit employee paychecks in their bank accounts rather than issue paper checks to employees. Today nearly all Social Security checks and other federal payments made each year arrive as electronic data rather than paper documents.

Online Banking

Today, many consumers do some or all of their banking on the Internet. Two types of online banks exist: Internet-only banks (*direct banks*), such as Ally Bank, and traditional brick-and-mortar banks with Web sites,

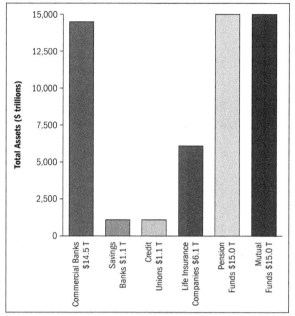

See **FIGURE 16.2 Assets of Major Financial Institutions**

Sources: American Council of Life Insurers, "2014 Fact Book," www.acli.com, accessed April 9, 2015; Federal Deposit Insurance Corporation, "Statistics at a Glance: Year-End 2014," www.fdic.gov, accessed April 9, 2015; Investment Company Institute, "2014 Investment Company Fact Book: Mutual Fund Trends," www.icifactbook.org, accessed April 9, 2015; company website, "Top Pension Fund Assets Hit $15 Trillion," www.towerswatson.com, accessed April 9, 2015; Michael Muckian, "Credit Unions Cash in on Improving Economy," *Credit Union Times,* accessed April 9, 2015, www.cutimes.com.

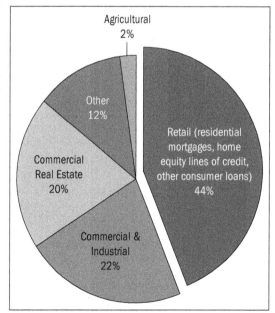

See **FIGURE 16.3 Distribution of Outstanding Commercial Bank Loans**

Source: St. Louis Federal Reserve, "An Overview of Bank Credit Expansion Since the Financial Crisis," *Banking Insights,* accessed April 9, 2015, https://www.stlouisfed.org.

such as Chase and PNC. It appears that direct banks are gaining in popularity. with a recent study showing market share gains for these types of banks compared with all other approaches.[5] Convenience is the primary reason people are attracted to online banking. Customers can transfer money, check account balances, and pay bills at any time. Plus with no branch offices to support, direct banks should be able to offer lower fees and better rates than their brick-and-mortar counterparts.

Federal Deposit Insurance

Most commercial bank deposits are insured by the **Federal Deposit Insurance Corporation (FDIC)**, a federal agency. Deposit insurance means that, in the event the bank fails, insured depositors are paid in full by the FDIC, up to $250,000. Federal deposit insurance was enacted by the Banking Act of 1933 as one of the measures designed to restore public confidence in the banking system. Before deposit insurance, so-called *runs* were common as people rushed to withdraw their money from a bank, often just on a rumor that the bank was in precarious financial condition. With more and more withdrawals in a short period, the bank was eventually unable to meet customer demands and closed its doors. Remaining depositors often lost most of the money they had in the bank. Deposit insurance shifts the risk of bank failures from individual depositors to the FDIC. Although banks still fail today, no insured depositor has ever lost any money on deposit up to the FDIC limit.

Savings Banks and Credit Unions

Commercial banks are by far the largest depository financial institution in the United States, but savings banks and credit unions also serve a significant segment of the financial community. Today, savings banks and credit unions offer many of the same services as commercial banks.

Previously, savings banks were called *savings and loan associations* or *thrift institutions.* They were originally established in the early 1800s to make home mortgage loans. Savings and loans raised funds by accepting only savings deposits and then lent these funds to consumers to buy homes. Today, around 867 savings banks operate in the United States, with total assets of about $1.069 trillion.[6] Although savings banks offer many of the same services as commercial banks, including checking accounts, they are not major lenders to businesses.

Credit unions are cooperative financial institutions that are owned by their depositors, all of whom are members. Approximately 99 million Americans belong to one of the nation's 6,273 credit unions. Combined, credit unions have more than $1.12 trillion in assets. By law, credit union members must share similar occupations, employers, or membership in certain organizations. This law effectively caps the size of credit unions. In fact, the nation's largest bank—JPMorgan Chase—holds more deposits than all the country's credit unions combined.[7]

Nondepository Financial Institutions

Nondepository financial institutions accept funds from businesses and households and invest it. Generally, these institutions do not offer checking accounts (demand deposits). Three examples of nondepository financial institutions are insurance companies, pension funds, and finance companies.

- **Insurance companies are organizations that** accept the risk from households and businesses in return for a series of payments, called *premiums. Underwriting* is the process insurance companies use to determine whom to insure and what to charge. During a typical year, insurance companies collect more in premiums than they pay in claims. After they pay operating expenses, they invest this difference. Life insurance companies alone have total assets of more than $6.1 trillion invested in everything from bonds and stocks to real estate.[8] Examples of life insurers include Prudential and New York Life.

- **Pension funds provide** retirement benefits to workers and their families. They are set up by employers and are funded by regular contributions made by employers and employees. Because pension funds have predictable long-term cash inflows and very predictable cash outflows, they invest heavily in assets, such as common stocks and real estate. U.S. pension funds have more than $15 trillion in assets.[9]

- **Finance companies** offer short-term loans to borrowers. Commercial finance companies, such as Ford Credit, John Deere Capital Corporation, and Loan Star, offer short-term funds to businesses that pledge tangible assets such as inventory, accounts receivable, machinery, or property as collateral for the loan. A consumer finance company plays a similar role for consumers.

Mutual Funds

One of the most significant types of financial institutions today is the mutual fund. *Mutual funds* are financial intermediaries that raise money from investors by selling shares. They then use the money to invest in securities that are consistent with the mutual fund's objectives, often hiring a professional manager to oversee the investments. Mutual funds have become extremely popular over the last few decades and currently have about $15 trillion in assets.[10]

Q Answer the **Concept Check** questions.

The Role of the Federal Reserve System

Created in 1913, the **Federal Reserve System**, or the **Fed**, is the central bank of the United States and an important part of the nation's financial system. The Fed has four basic responsibilities: regulating commercial banks, performing banking-related activities for the U.S. Department of the Treasury, providing services for banks, and setting monetary policy.

Monetary Policy

The Fed's most important function is monetary policy—that is, controlling the supply of money and credit. The Fed's job is to make sure the money supply grows at an appropriate rate, allowing the economy to expand and keeping inflation in check. If the money supply grows too slowly, economic growth will slow, unemployment will rise, and the risk of a recession will increase. If the money supply grows too rapidly, inflationary pressures will build. The Fed uses its policy to push interest rates up or down. By pushing the interest rates up, the growth rate of the money supply slows. By pushing the interest rates down, the growth rate of the money supply tends to rise.

The two common measures of the money supply are called M1 and M2. M1 consists of money in circulation and balances in bank checking accounts. M2 equals M1 plus balances in some savings accounts and money market mutual funds. The Fed has three major policy tools for controlling the growth in the supply of money and credit: reserve requirements, the discount rate, and open market operations.

The Fed requires banks to maintain reserves—defined as cash in their vaults plus deposits at district Federal Reserve banks or other banks—equal to a certain percentage of what the banks hold in deposits. For example, if the Fed sets the reserve requirement at 5 percent, a bank that receives a $500 deposit must reserve $25, so it has only $475 to invest or lend to individuals or businesses. By changing the reserve requirement, the Fed can affect the amount of money available for making loans. The higher the reserve requirement, the less banks can lend out to consumers and businesses. The lower the reserve requirement, the more banks can lend out. Because any change in the reserve requirement can have a sudden and dramatic impact on the money supply, the Fed rarely uses this tool.

Another policy tool is the so-called *discount rate,* the interest rate at which Federal Reserve banks make short-term loans to member banks. A bank may need a short-term loan if transactions leave it short of reserves. If the Fed wants to slow the growth rate in the money supply, it increases the discount rate. When this increase makes it more expensive for banks to borrow money, they in turn raise the interest rate they charge on loans to consumers and businesses. The end result is a slowdown in economic activity. Lowering the discount rate has the opposite effect.

The third policy tool, and the one most often used, is *open market operations,* the technique of controlling the money supply growth rate by buying or selling U.S. Treasury securities. If the Fed buys Treasury securities, the money it pays enters circulation, increasing the money supply and lowering interest rates. When the Fed sells Treasury securities, money is taken out of circulation and interest rates rise. When the Fed uses open market operations, it employs the so-called *federal funds rate*—the rate at which banks lend money to each other overnight—as its benchmark. **Table 16.3** illustrates how the Federal Reserve uses tools to regulate the economy.

See **TABLE 16.3: What three tools does the Fed use to regulate economic growth?**

Q Answer the **Concept Check** questions.

Regulation of the Financial System

Given the importance of the financial system, it is probably not surprising that many components are subject to government regulation and oversight. In addition, industry self-regulation is commonplace.

Bank Regulation

Banks are among the nation's most heavily regulated businesses—primarily to ensure public confidence in the safety and security of the banking system. Banks are critical to the overall functioning of the economy, and a collapse of the banking system can have disastrous results. Many believe one of the major causes of the Great Depression was the collapse of the banking system that started in the late 1920s.

Banks and credit unions are subject to periodic examination by state or federal regulators. Examinations ensure that the institution is following sound banking practices and is complying with all applicable regulations. These examinations include the review of detailed reports on the bank's operating and financial condition as well as on-site inspections. Regulators can impose penalties on institutions deemed not in compliance with sound banking practices, including forcing the delinquent financial institution into a merger with a healthier one.

Government Regulation of the Financial Markets

Regulation of U.S. financial markets is primarily a function of the federal government, although states also regulate them. Federal regulation grew out of various trading abuses during the 1920s. To restore confidence and stability in the financial markets after the 1929 stock market crash, Congress passed a series of landmark legislative acts that have formed the basis of federal securities regulation ever since. Many other regulations have followed, including the Dodd-Frank Wall Street Reform and Consumer Protection Act, signed into law in 2010.

The U.S. Securities and Exchange Commission (SEC), created in 1934, is the principal federal regulatory overseer of the securities markets. The SEC's mission is to administer securities laws and protect investors in public securities transactions. The SEC has broad enforcement power. It can pursue civil actions against individuals and corporations, but actions requiring criminal proceedings are referred to the U.S. Justice Department.

The SEC requires virtually all new public issues of corporate securities to be registered. As part of the registration process for a new security issue, the issuer must prepare a *prospectus*. The typical prospectus gives a detailed description of the company issuing the securities, including financial data, products, research and development projects, and pending litigation. It also describes the stock or bond issue and underwriting agreement in detail. The registration process seeks to guarantee full and fair disclosure. The SEC does not rule on the investment merits of a registered security. It is concerned only that an issuer gives investors enough information to make their own informed decisions.

One area to which the SEC pays particular attention is insider trading. **Insider trading** is defined as the use of material nonpublic information about a company to make investment profits. Examples of material nonpublic information include a pending merger or a major oil discovery, which could affect the firm's stock price.

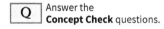

Q Answer the
Concept Check questions.

The Financial System: A Global Perspective

Not surprisingly, the global financial system is becoming more and more integrated each year. With financial markets in existence throughout the world, shares of U.S. firms trade in other countries and shares of international companies trade in the United States. In fact, investors in China and Japan own more U.S. Treasury securities than do domestic investors.

Financial institutions have also become a global industry. Major U.S. banks—such as JPMorgan Chase and Bank of America—have extensive international operations where they maintain offices, lend money, and accept deposits from customers.

Although most Americans recognize large U.S. banks such as Citibank among the global financial giants, three of the world's 20 largest banks (measured by total assets) are U.S.

institutions—JPMorgan Chase (ranked 6th), Bank of America (ranked 12th), and Citigroup (ranked 14th). The other 17 are based in Asia, Europe, and Great Britain. The world's largest bank is Industrial & Commercial Bank of China, with more than $3 trillion in assets. These international banks operate worldwide, including locations in the United States.[11]

Like the United States, virtually all nations have some sort of a central bank. These banks play roles much like that of the Federal Reserve, controlling the money supply and regulating the banks. Policymakers at those banks often respond to changes in the U.S. financial system by making changes in their own system. For example, if the Fed lowers interest rates, the central bank in Japan may do the same. Such changes can influence events around the world.

Q Answer the **Concept Check** questions.

WP LS Go to your WileyPLUS Learning Space course for video episodes, examples, art, tables, Concept Checks, practice, and resources that will help you success in this course.

Reading for
FINANCIAL MANAGEMENT

WP LS Go to your WileyPLUS Learning Space course for video episodes, examples, art, tables, Concept Checks, practice, and resources that will help you success in this course.

The Role of the Financial Manager

Because of the intense pressures they face today, organizations are increasingly measuring and reducing the costs of business operations as well as maximizing revenues and profits. This business function is called **finance.** As a result, **financial managers**—executives who develop and implement their firm's financial plan and determine the most appropriate sources and uses of funds—are among the most vital people on the corporate payroll.

See **FIGURE 17.1 A Typical Finance Organization**

■ **Figure 17.1** shows what the finance function of a typical company might look like. At the top is the chief financial officer (CFO). The CFO usually reports directly to the company's chief executive officer (CEO) or chief operating officer (COO). In some companies, the CFO is also a member of the board of directors. In the case of the software maker Oracle, both the current CFO and the former CFO serve on that company's board. Moreover, it's not uncommon for CFOs to serve as independent directors on other firms' boards, such as HP, Microsoft, and Target. As noted in Chapter 15, the CFO, along with the firm's CEO, must certify the accuracy of the firm's financial statements.

Reporting directly to the CFO are often three senior managers. Although titles can vary, these three executives are commonly called the *vice president for financial management* (or *planning*), the *treasurer,* and the *controller.* The vice president for financial management or planning is responsible for preparing financial forecasts and analyzing major investment decisions, such as new products, new production facilities, and acquisitions. The treasurer is responsible for all of the company's financing activities, including cash management, tax planning and preparation, and shareholder relations. The treasurer also works on the sale of new security issues to investors. The controller is the chief accounting manager. The controller's functions include keeping the company's books, preparing financial statements, and conducting internal audits.

In performing their jobs, financial professionals continually seek to balance risks with expected financial returns. Risk is the uncertainty of gain or loss; return is the gain or loss that results from an investment over a specified period of time. Financial managers strive to maximize the wealth of their firm's shareholders by striking the optimal balance between risk and return. This balance is called the **risk-return trade-off**. For example, relying heavily on borrowed funds may increase the return (in the form of cash) to shareholders, but the more money a firm borrows, the greater the risks to shareholders. An increase in a firm's cash on hand reduces the risk of being unable to meet unexpected cash needs. However, because cash in and of itself does not earn much, if any, return, failure to invest surplus funds in an income-earning asset—such as in securities—reduces a firm's potential return or profitability.

Financial managers must also learn to adapt to changes in the financial system. The recent credit crisis has made it more difficult for some companies to borrow money from traditional lenders such as banks. This, in turn, has forced firms to scale back expansion plans or seek funding from other sources such as commercial financing companies. In addition, financial managers must adapt to internal changes as well.

Q Answer the **Concept Check** questions.

Financial Planning

Financial managers develop their organization's **financial plan**, a document that specifies the funds needed by a firm for a given period of time, the timing of inflows and outflows, and the most appropriate sources and uses of funds. Some financial plans, often called *operating plans,* are short term in nature, focusing on projections no more than a year or two in the future. Other financial plans, sometimes referred to as *strategic plans,* have a much longer time horizon, perhaps up to five or ten years.

Regardless of the time period, a financial plan is based on forecasts of production costs, purchasing needs, plant and equipment expenditures, and expected sales activities for the period covered. Financial managers use forecasts to determine the specific amounts and timing of expenditures and receipts. They build a financial plan based on the answers to three questions:

- What funds will the firm require during the planning period?
- When will it need additional funds?
- Where will it obtain the necessary funds?

Some funds flow into the firm when it sells its goods or services, but funding needs vary. The financial plan must reflect both the amounts and timing of inflows and outflows of funds. Even a profitable firm may face a financial squeeze as a result of its need for funds when sales lag, when the volume of its credit sales increases, or when customers are slow in making payments.

In general, preparing a financial plan consists of three steps:

1. Forecasting sales.
2. Determining longer-term profits.
3. Estimating what the firm will need to support projected sales.

The sales forecast is the key variable in any financial plan because without an accurate sales forecast, the firm will have difficulty accurately estimating other variables, such as production costs and purchasing needs. The best method of forecasting sales depends on the nature of the business. For instance, a retailer's CFO might begin with the current sales-per-store figure. Then he or she would look toward the near future, factoring in expected same-store sales growth, along with any planned store openings or closings, to come up with a forecast of sales for the next period. If the company sells merchandise through other channels, such as online, the forecast is adjusted to reflect those additional channels.

Next, the CFO uses the sales forecast to determine the expected level of profits for future periods. This longer-term projection involves estimating expenses such as purchases, employee compensation, and taxes. Many expenses are themselves functions of sales. For instance, the more a firm sells, generally the greater its purchases. Along with estimating future profits, the CFO would also determine what portion of these profits will likely be paid to shareholders in the form of cash dividends.

Next, the CFO estimates how many additional assets the firm will need to support projected sales. Increased sales, for example, might mean the company needs additional inventory, stepped-up collections for accounts receivable, or even new plants and equipment. Depending on the nature of the industry, some businesses need more assets than do other companies to support the same amount of sales. The technical term for this requirement is *asset intensity.* For instance, DuPont has approximately $1.93 in assets for every dollar in sales. So for every $100 increase in sales, the firm would need about $193 of additional assets. Costco, by contrast, has roughly $0.27 in assets for every dollar in sales. It would require an additional $ 27 of assets for every $100 of additional sales. This difference is not surprising; manufacturing is a more asset-intensive business than retailing.[1]

A simplified financial plan illustrates these steps. Assume a growing company forecasts that next year's sales will increase by $40 million to $140 million. After estimating expenses, the CFO believes that after-tax profits next year will be $12 million and the firm will pay nothing in dividends. The projected increase in sales next year will require the firm to invest another $20 million in assets, and because increases in assets are uses of funds, the company will need an additional $20 million in funds. The company's after-tax earnings will contribute $12 million, meaning that the other $8 million must come from outside sources. So the financial plan tells the CFO how much money will be needed and when it will be needed. Armed with this knowledge, and given that the firm has decided to borrow the needed funds, the CFO can then begin negotiations with banks and other lenders.

The cash inflows and outflows of a business are similar to those of a household. The members of a household depend on weekly or monthly paychecks for funds, but their expenditures vary greatly from one pay period to the next. The financial plan should indicate when the flows of funds entering and leaving the organization will occur and in what amounts. One of the most significant business expenses is employee compensation.

A good financial plan also includes financial control, a process of comparing actual revenues, costs, and expenses with forecasts. This comparison may reveal significant differences between projected and actual figures, so it is important to discover them early to take quick action.

Q Answer the **Concept Check** questions.

Managing Assets

As we noted in Chapter 15, assets consist of what a firm owns. But assets also represent uses of funds. To grow and prosper, companies need to obtain additional assets. Sound financial management requires assets to be acquired and managed as effectively and efficiently as possible.

Short-Term Assets

Short-term, or current, assets consist of cash and assets that can be (or are expected to be) converted into cash within a year. The major current assets are cash, marketable securities, accounts receivable, and inventory.

- **Cash and marketable securities** are used mainly to pay day-to-day expenses, much as when individuals maintain a balance in a checking account to pay bills or buy food and clothing. Most organizations also strive to maintain a minimum cash balance in order to have funds available in the event of unexpected expenses. As noted earlier, because cash earns little, if any, return, most firms invest excess cash in so-called *marketable securities*—low-risk securities that either have short maturities or can be easily sold in secondary markets. Money market instruments are popular choices for firms with excess cash.

- **Accounts receivable** are uncollected credit sales and can be a significant asset. The financial manager's job is to collect the funds owed the firm as quickly as possible while still offering sufficient credit to customers to generate increased sales. In general, a more liberal credit policy means higher sales but also increased collection expenses, higher levels of bad debt, and a higher investment in accounts receivable.

  Management of accounts receivable is composed of two functions: determining an overall credit policy and deciding which customers will be offered credit. Formulating a credit policy involves deciding whether the firm will offer credit and, if so, on what terms. Will a discount be offered to customers who pay in cash? Often, the overall credit policy is dictated by competitive pressures or general industry practices. If all your competitors offer customers credit, your firm will likely have to as well. The other aspect of a credit policy is deciding which customers will be offered credit. Managers must consider the importance of the customer as well as its financial health and repayment history.

- **Inventory management** can be complicated because the cost of inventory includes more than just the acquisition cost. It also includes the cost of ordering, storing, insuring, and financing inventory as well as the cost of stockouts, or lost sales due to insufficient inventory. Financial managers try to minimize the cost of inventory, but production, marketing, and logistics also play important roles in determining proper inventory levels. Also, trends in the inventory turnover ratio can be early warning signs of impending trouble. For instance, if inventory turnover has been slowing for several consecutive quarters, it indicates that inventory is rising faster than sales. This may suggest that customer demand is softening and the firm needs to take action, such as reducing production or increasing promotional efforts.

Capital Investment Analysis

In addition to current assets, firms also invest in long-lived assets. Unlike current assets, long-lived assets are expected to produce economic benefits for more than one year. These investments often involve substantial amounts of money. For example, auto manufacturer BMW recently announced it would spend an additional $1 billion over the next several years to expand its production facility in Spartanburg, South Carolina, bringing the company's total investment in the state to more than $7 billion.[2]

The process by which decisions are made regarding investments in long-lived assets is called *capital investment analysis.* Firms make two basic types of capital investment decisions: expansion and replacement. The BMW South Carolina plant investment is an example of expansion decisions. Replacement decisions involve upgrading assets by substituting new ones. A retailer might decide to replace an old store with a new Supercenter, as Walmart did in Oxford, Ohio.

Financial managers must estimate all of the costs and benefits of a proposed investment, which can be quite difficult, especially for very long-lived investments. Only those investments that offer an acceptable return—measured by the difference between benefits and costs—should be undertaken. BMW's financial managers believe that the benefits of continuing to expand the South Carolina production facility outweigh the costs. Through a series of expansions, BMW has outpaced its rivals, Audi and Mercedes, as the world's top-selling brand. More than half of the vehicles built at the South Carolina facility are exported across the globe. The expected profits from the sales of these autos have certainly been considered in the company's expansion decisions. Some other expansion benefits cited by BMW include lower production costs, improved logistics, and expanded use of renewable energy. The Spartanburg facility has produced more than 2.5 million vehicles.[3]

Q Answer the **Concept Check** questions.

Sources of Funds and Capital Structure

The use of debt for financing can increase the potential for return as well as increase loss potential. Recall the accounting equation introduced in Chapter 15:

$$\text{Assets} = \text{Liabilities} + \text{Owners' Equity}$$

If you view this equation from a financial management perspective, it reveals that there are only two types of funding: debt and equity. *Debt capital* consists of funds obtained through borrowing. *Equity capital* consists of funds provided by the firm's owners when they reinvest earnings, make additional contributions, liquidate assets, issue stock to the general public, or raise capital from outside investors. The mix of a firm's debt and equity capital is known as its **capital structure**.

Companies often take very different approaches to choosing a capital structure. As more debt is used, the risk to the company increases since the firm is now obligated to make the interest payments on the money borrowed, regardless of the cash flows coming into the company. Choosing more debt increases the fixed costs a company must pay, which in turn makes a company more sensitive to changing sales revenues. Debt is frequently the least costly method of raising additional financing dollars, one of the reasons it is so frequently used.

Differing industries choose varying amounts of debt and equity to use when financing. For example, we find that the automotive industry has debt ratios (the ratio of liabilities to assets) of close to 60 percent for both Toyota and Honda in a recent year. These companies are primarily using debt to finance their asset expenditures. Food service companies such as Burger King and Starbucks use 50 percent and 33 percent, respectively. The mixture of debt and equity a company uses is a major management decision.[4]

Leverage and Capital Structure Decisions

Raising needed cash by borrowing allows a firm to benefit from the principle of **leverage**, increasing the rate of return on funds invested by borrowing funds. The key to managing leverage is to ensure that a company's earnings remain larger than its interest payments, which increases the leverage on the rate of return on shareholders' investment. Of course, if the company earns less than its interest payments, shareholders lose money on their original investment.

■ **Figure 17.2** shows the relationship between earnings and shareholder returns for two identical hypothetical firms that

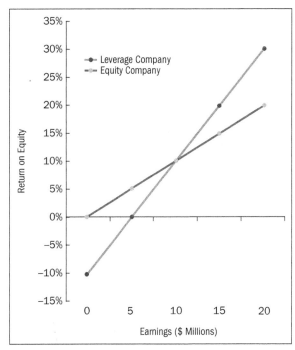

See **FIGURE 17.2 How Leverage Works**

Note: The example assumes that both companies have $100 million in capital. Leverage Company consists of $50 million in equity and $50 million in bonds (with an interest rate of 10 percent). Equity Company consists of $100 million in equity and no bonds. This example also assumes no corporate taxes.

choose to raise funds in different ways. Leverage Company obtains 50 percent of its funds from lenders who purchase company bonds. Leverage Company pays 10 percent interest on its bonds. Equity Company raises all of its funds through sales of company stock.

Notice that if earnings double—from, say, $10 million to $20 million—returns to shareholders of Equity Company also double, from 10 percent to 20 percent. But returns to shareholders of Leverage Company more than double, from 10 percent to 30 percent. However, leverage works in the opposite direction as well. If earnings fall from $10 million to $5 million—a decline of 50 percent—returns to shareholders of Equity Company also fall by 50 percent, from 10 percent to 5 percent. By contrast, returns to shareholders of Leverage Company fall from 10 percent to zero. Thus, leverage increases potential returns to shareholders but also increases risk.

A key component of the financial manager's job is to weigh the advantages and disadvantages of debt capital and equity capital, creating the most appropriate capital structure for the firm.

See **FIGURE 17.3 Johnson & Johnson's Mix of Short- and Long-Term Funds**

Source: Johnson & Johnson balance sheet, Yahoo! Finance, http://finance.yahoo.com, accessed April 12, 2015.

Mixing Short-Term and Long-Term Funds

Another decision financial managers face is determining the appropriate mix of short- and long-term funds. Short-term funds consist of current liabilities, and long-term funds consist of long-term debt and equity. Short-term funds are generally less expensive than long-term funds, but they also expose the firm to more risk. This is because short-term funds have to be renewed, or rolled over, frequently. Short-term interest rates can be volatile. During a recent 12-month period, for example, rates on commercial paper, a popular short-term financing option, ranged from a high of 10 percent (for 90-day loans) to a low of 6 percent (for 1-day loans).[5]

Because short-term rates move up and down frequently, interest expense on short-term funds can change substantially from year to year. For instance, if a firm borrows $50 million for ten years at 5 percent interest, its annual interest expense is fixed at $2.5 million for the entire ten years. On the other hand, if it borrows $50 million for one year at a rate of 4 percent, its annual interest expense of $2 million is only fixed for that year. If interest rates increase the following year to 6 percent, $1 million will be added to the interest expense bill. Another potential risk of relying on short-term funds is availability. Even financially healthy firms can occasionally find it difficult to borrow money.

Because of the added risk of short-term funding, most firms choose to finance all of their long-term assets, and even a portion of their short-term assets, with long-term funds. Johnson & Johnson is typical of this choice. ◾ **Figure 17.3** shows a recent balance sheet broken down between short- and long-term assets and short- and long-term funds.

Dividend Policy

Along with decisions regarding capital structure and the mix of short- and long-term funds, financial managers also make decisions regarding a firm's dividend policy. *Dividends* are periodic cash payments to shareholders. The most common type of dividend is paid quarterly and is often labeled as a *regular dividend*. Occasionally, firms make one-time special or extra dividend payments, as Microsoft did some years ago. Earnings that are paid in dividends are not reinvested in the firm and don't contribute additional equity capital.

Firms are under no legal obligation to pay dividends to shareholders of common stock. Although some companies pay generous dividends, others pay nothing. Until 2010, Starbucks never paid a dividend to its shareholders, and Apple recently started paying dividends for the first time in more than 20 years. In contrast, 3M has paid dividends for 30-plus consecutive years, during which time the amount has more than quadrupled.

Many factors determine a company's dividend policy, one of which is its investment opportunities. If a firm has numerous investment opportunities and wishes to finance some or all of them with equity funding, it will likely pay little, if any, of its earnings in dividends. Shareholders may actually want the company to retain earnings, because if they are reinvested, the firm's future profits, and the value of its shares, will increase faster. By contrast, a firm with more limited investment opportunities generally pays more of its earnings in dividends.

Q Answer the **Concept Check** questions.

Short-Term Funding Options

Many times throughout a year, an organization may discover that its cash needs exceed its available funds. Retailers generate surplus cash for most of the year, but they need to build up inventory during the late summer and fall to get ready for the holiday shopping season. Consequently, they often need funds to pay for merchandise until holiday sales generate revenue. Then they use the incoming funds to repay the amount they borrowed. In these instances, financial managers evaluate short-term sources of funds. By definition, short-term sources of funds are repaid within one year. Three major sources of short-term funds exist: trade credit, short-term loans, and commercial paper. Large firms often rely on a combination of all three sources of short-term financing.

Trade Credit

Trade credit is extended by suppliers when a firm receives goods or services, agreeing to pay for them at a later date. Trade credit is common in many industries such as retailing and manufacturing. Suppliers routinely ship billions of dollars of merchandise to retailers each day and are paid at a later date. Without trade credit, the retailing sector would probably look much different—with fewer selections. Under this system, the supplier records the transactions as an account receivable, and the retailer records it as an account payable. The main advantage of trade credit is its easy availability because credit sales are common in many industries. The main drawback to trade credit is that the amount a company can borrow is limited to the amount it purchases.

Short-Term Loans

Loans from commercial banks are a significant source of short-term financing for businesses. Often businesses use these loans to finance inventory and accounts receivable. For example, late fall and early winter is the period of highest sales for a small manufacturer of ski equipment. To meet this demand, it has to begin building inventory during the summer. The manufacturer also has to finance accounts receivable (credit sales to customers) during the fall and winter. So it takes out a bank loan during the summer. As the inventory is sold and accounts receivable collected, the firm repays the loan.

There are two types of short-term bank loans: lines of credit and revolving credit agreements. A line of credit specifies the maximum amount the firm can borrow over a period of time, usually a year. The bank is under no obligation actually to lend the money, however. It does so only if funds are available. Most lines of credit require the borrower to repay the original amount, plus interest, within one year. By contrast, a revolving credit agreement is essentially a guaranteed line of credit—the bank guarantees that the funds will be available when needed. Banks typically charge a fee, on top of interest, for revolving credit agreements.

Another form of short-term financing backed by accounts receivable is called *factoring*. The business sells its accounts receivable to either a bank or finance company—called a *factor*—at a discount. The size of the discount determines the cost of the transaction. Factoring allows the firm to convert its receivables into cash quickly without worrying about collections.

Commercial Paper

Commercial paper is a short-term IOU sold by a company (this concept was briefly described in Chapter 16). Commercial paper is typically sold in multiples of $100,000 to $1 million and has a maturity that ranges from 1 to 270 days. Most commercial paper is unsecured. It is an attractive source of financing because large amounts of money can be raised at rates that are typically 1 to 2 percent less that those charged by banks. Recently, almost $1.09 trillion in commercial paper was outstanding.[6] Although commercial paper is an attractive short-term financing alternative, only a small percentage of businesses can issue it. That is because access to the commercial paper market has traditionally been restricted to large, financially strong corporations.

> [Q] Answer the **Concept Check** questions.

Sources of Long-Term Financing

Funds from short-term sources can help a firm meet current needs for cash or inventory. However, a larger project or plan, such as acquiring another company or making a major investment in real estate or equipment, usually requires funds for a much longer period of time. Unlike short-term sources, long-term sources are repaid over many years.

Organizations acquire long-term funds from three sources. One is long-term loans obtained from financial institutions such as commercial banks, life insurance companies, and pension funds. A second source is bonds—certificates of indebtedness—sold to investors. A third source is equity financing that is acquired by selling stock in the firm or reinvesting company profits.

Public Sale of Stocks and Bonds

Public sales of securities such as stocks and bonds are a major source of funds for corporations. Such sales provide cash inflows for the issuing firm and either a share in its ownership (for a stock purchaser) or a specified rate of interest and repayment at a stated time (for a bond purchaser). Because stock and bond issues of many corporations are traded in the secondary markets, stockholders and bondholders can easily sell these securities. Public sales of securities, however, can vary substantially from year to year, depending on conditions in the financial markets. Bond sales, for instance, tend to be higher when interest rates are lower.

Chapter 16 discussed the process by which most companies sell securities publicly—through investment bankers via a process called *underwriting.* Investment bankers purchase the securities from the issuer and then resell them to investors. The issuer pays a fee to the investment banker, called an *underwriting discount.*

Private Placements

Some new stock or bond issues are not sold publicly but instead to a small group of major investors such as pension funds and insurance companies. Such a sale is referred to as a *private placement.* Companies will often raise funds with private placements because they are generally less expensive and quicker to complete than a public offering. Institutional investors such as insurance companies and pension funds buy private placements because they typically carry slightly higher interest rates than publicly issued bonds. In addition, the terms of the issue can be tailored to meet the specific needs of both the issuer and the institutional investors. Of course, the institutional investor gives up liquidity because privately placed securities do not trade in secondary markets.

Private Equity Funds

A *private equity fund* is an investment company that raises funds from wealthy individuals and institutional investors and uses those funds to make large investments in both public and privately held companies. Private equity funds invest in all types of businesses, including mature ones. For example, 3G Capital, a Brazilian private equity firm, teamed up with Warren Buffett's Berkshire Hathaway to purchase ketchup maker H.J. Heinz for $28 billion a few years ago. The two companies recently acquired the Kraft Foods Group for about $49 billion, merging it with Heinz to form one of the world's largest food and beverage companies.[7] Often, private equity funds invest in a leveraged buyout—a transaction that takes a public company private. In such transactions, discussed in more detail in the next section, a public company reverts to private status.

A variation of the private equity fund is the so-called *sovereign wealth fund.* This type of company is owned by a government and invests in a variety of financial and real assets, such as real estate. Although sovereign wealth funds generally make investments based on the best risk-return trade-off, political, social, and strategic considerations also play a role in their investment decisions. The assets of the ten largest sovereign wealth funds are shown in 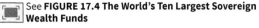 **Figure 17.4**. Together, these ten funds have more than $7 trillion in assets.

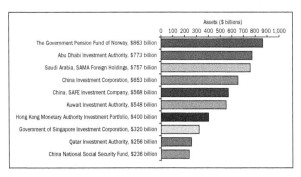

See **FIGURE 17.4 The World's Ten Largest Sovereign Wealth Funds**

Source: Sovereign Wealth Fund Institute, "Sovereign Wealth Fund Rankings," http://www.swfinstitute.org, accessed April 13, 2015.

Hedge Funds

A *hedge fund* is a private investment company open only to qualified large investors. Operating much like a mutual fund, hedge funds raise capital from investors and then hire a manager to oversee investments matching the fund's stated goals. In recent years, hedge funds have become a significant presence in U.S. financial markets. Before the recent recession, some analysts estimated that hedge funds accounted for about 60 percent of all secondary bond market trading and around one-third of all activity on stock exchanges.

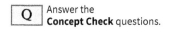
Answer the **Concept Check** questions.

Mergers, Acquisitions, Buyouts, and Divestitures

Chapter 5 briefly described mergers and acquisitions. A merger is a transaction in which two or more firms combine into one company. In an acquisition, one firm buys the assets and assumes the obligations of another firm, such as Facebook's recent acquisition of WhatsApp, a mobile messaging app, for $19 billion. Transactions like mergers, acquisitions, buyouts, and divestitures have financial implications.

Even in a merger, there is a buyer and seller (called the *target*). Financial managers evaluate a proposed merger or acquisition in much the same way they would evaluate any large investment—by comparing the costs and benefits. Mergers are generally a transaction between two firms of roughly the same size. The merger between American Airlines Inc. and U.S. Airways Inc. is a good example of this type of merger. Unlike acquisitions, where the acquiring firm most often determines how the transaction will proceed, in mergers both firms have a significant stake in how the deal is structured. Who will be on the management team? Which corporate office will be the merged company headquarters? How much of the staff will be retained, doing what jobs, and in which locations? These and thousands of other questions must be discussed and resolved. To complete the American Airlines and U.S. Airways merger, the companies established 29 different committees, dealing with everything from in-flight service (will each customer receive a whole can of soda?) to who will be the new CEO (Doug Parker, formerly the CEO of U.S. Airways, is the CEO of the new American Airlines Group).[8] Whatever the reason for the merger, the term often used to describe the benefits produced by a merger or acquisition is *synergy*—the notion that the combined firm is worth more than the companies are individually. The American Airlines and U.S. Airways merger will result in a combined company that is better able to compete with other U.S. carriers.

In a **leveraged buyout**, or **LBO**, the shareholders of a public company are bought out and the firm reverts to private status. The term *leverage* comes from the fact that many of these transactions are financed with high degrees of debt—often in excess of 75 percent. Private equity companies and hedge funds provide equity and debt financing for many LBOs. The firm's incumbent senior management is often part of the buyout group. LBO activity decreased sharply with the recent economic downturn, but as the economy began to recover, LBO activity increased again.

In a sense, a **divestiture** is the reverse of a merger—that is, a company sells an asset, such as a subsidiary, a product line, or a production facility. Two types of divestitures exist: sell-offs and spin-offs. In a *sell-off,* a firm sells an asset to another firm.

The other type of divestiture is a *spin-off.* In this transaction, a new firm is formed by the sale of the assets. Shareholders of the divesting firm become shareholders of the new firm as well. For example, online auction site eBay recently spun off its PayPal business into a separate company in an effort to increase shareholder value. In a recent year, PayPal accounted for more than 40 percent of eBay's total revenues, and the mobile online payment system facilitates one in every six dollars spent online. Mobile payments are expected to grow to more than $118 billion over the next several years. As a separate company, PayPal will face increased competition in the mobile payment sector, with Apple's introduction of Apple Pay as a way for consumers to make mobile payments.[9]

Answer the **Concept Check** questions.

Go to your WileyPLUS Learning Space course for video episodes, examples, art, tables, Concept Checks, practice, and resources that will help you success in this course.

Notes

Chapter 1

[1] National Center for Charitable Statistics, "Quick Facts About Nonprofits," http://nccs.urban.org, accessed February 2, 2015.

[2] Kathryn Dill, "The Best Places to Work in 2015," *Forbes*, accessed February 2, 2015, www.forbes.com.

[3] Eugene Kim, "This 24-Year-Old High School Dropout Is Tackling a Problem Every Startup Hates to Deal With," *Business Insider,* accessed February 2, 2015, www.businessinsider.com.

[4] Government website, "About the Bureau of Competition," www.ftc.gov, accessed February 2, 2015.

[5] "Best Global Brands: 2014," *Interbrand,* accessed February 2, 2015, http://bestglobalbrands.com.

[6] Andreas Kaplan and Michael Haenlein, "Users of the World, Unite! The Challenges and Opportunities of Social Media," *Business Horizons* 53:59–68, 2010.

[7] "Census: More Diversity, Slower Growth in U.S.A. 2050," press release, *IM Diversity*, accessed February 2, 2015, www.imdiversity.com.

[8] Organization website, "The DiversityInc Top 50 List," www.diversityinc.com, accessed February 2, 2015.

[9] "World's Most Admired Companies 2015," *Fortune,* accessed May 14, 2015, http://fortune.com.

Chapter 2

[1] Steve Strunsky, "Port Authority Manager Fired for Misrepresenting Academic Credentials," *Star-Ledger,* accessed February 17, 2015, www.nj.com.

[2] "Office Productivity Loss," *Staff Monitoring,* accessed February 17, 2015, www.staffmonitoring.com.

[3] Saul McLeod, "Kohlberg Stages of Moral Development," *Simply Psychology,* accessed February 17, 2015, www.simplypsychology.org.

[4] Company website, www.jnj.com, accessed February 17, 2015; "Making a Difference: J&J's Credo," *Leaders Online,* accessed February 17, 2015, www.leadersmag.com.

[5] "Walt Pavlo," *The Summit,* accessed February 17, 2015, www.nwasummit.com.

[6] Associated Press, "Indiana Hospital Fires 8 Workers Who Refused Flu Shot," *Fox News,* accessed February 17, 2015, www.foxnews.com.

[7] "LBGT Equality at the Fortune 500," *Human Rights Campaign,* accessed February 17, 2015, www.hrc.org.

[8] Craig Malloy, "Managing Millennials and Boomers in the Workplace," *Forbes,* accessed February 17, 2015, www.forbes.com.

[9] Government website, "Charges Alleging Sexual Harassment FY 2010–FY 2014," www.eeoc.gov, accessed February 17, 2015.

[10] Organization website, "Wage Gap Narrows Slightly But Statistically Unchanged," www.pay-equity.org, accessed February 17, 2015.

[11] Michael Calia, "CVS Revenue Rises on Strength at Pharmacy," *The Wall Street Journal,* accessed February 17, 2015, www.wsj.com; Rachel Abrams, "CVS Stores Stop Selling All Tobacco Products," *The New York Times,* accessed February 17, 2015, www.nytimes.com; Elizabeth Landau, "CVS Stores to Stop Selling Tobacco," *CNN,* accessed February 17, 2015, www.cnn.com.

[12] Company website, www.subway.com, accessed February 17, 2015; Jared Foundation, www.jaredfoundation.org, accessed February 17, 2015.

[13] "Supplier Environmental Sustainability Scorecard," www.pgscorecard.com, accessed February 19, 2015; Heather Clancy, "Kaiser Permanente Joins Apple, Walmart in Clean Energy Buying Spree," *Green Biz,* accessed February 19, 2015, www.greenbiz.com.

[14] Company website, www.teslamotors.com, accessed February 19, 2015.

[15] Campbell Robertson and Clifford Krauss, "BP May Be Fined Up to $18 Billion for Spill in Gulf," *The New York Times,* accessed February 19, 2015, www.nytimes.com.

[16] Company website, www.biodiesel.com, accessed February 19, 2015.

[17] Government website, "Tuffy's Pet Foods, Inc. Issues Voluntary Recall of a Limited Quantity of Nutrisca Dry Dog Food Because of Possible Health Risk," www.fda.gov, accessed February 19, 2015.

[18] Company website, "Rules & Policies," http://pages.ebay.com, accessed February 19, 2015.

Chapter 3

[1] Larissa MacFarquhar, "When Giants Fail," *The New Yorker,* accessed February 20, 2015, www.newyorker.com.

[2] Marguerite Reardon, "13 Things You Need to Know About the FCC's net Neutrality Regulation," *CNET*, accessed May 17, 2015, www.cnet.com.

[3] Company website, "Who We Are," https://www.salliemae.com, accessed February 19, 2015.

[4] *World Factbook,* Central Intelligence Agency, https://www.cia.gov, accessed February 20, 2015.

[5] Susan Abrams, "Where the Jobs Will (and Won't) Be in 2015," *Forbes,* accessed February 20, 2015, www.forbes.com; Josh Mitchell, "Job Growth Rebounds, But Wages Lag," *The Wall Street Journal,* accessed February 20, 2015, www.wsj.com.

[6] Company website, "The Veterans Welcome Home Commitment," http://walmartcareer swithamission.com, accessed February 20, 2015.

[7] U.S. National Debt Clock, www.brillig.com, accessed February 20, 2015.

Chapter 4

[1] Organization website, http://data.worldbank.org, accessed February 21, 2015.

[2] Company website, "Walmart International," http://corporate.walmart.com, accessed February 21, 2015.

[3] U.S. Census, "Top Trading Partners—December 2014," www.census.gov, accessed February 21, 2015.

[4] U.S. Census, "U. S. International Trade in Goods and Services, Exhibit 2: Origin of Movement of U.S. Exports of Goods by State by NAICS-Based Product Code Groupings, Not Seasonally Adjusted: 2014," www.census.gov, accessed February 21, 2015.

[5] Bureau of Economic Analysis, "U.S. International Trade in Goods and Services: December 2014," press release, www.bea.gov, accessed February 21, 2015.

[6] Ben Fritz and James T. Areddy, "Shanghai Disneyland Opening Pushed to First Half of 2016," *The Wall Street Journal,* accessed February 21, 2015.

[7] "Daily Foreign Exchange Volumes Hit $5.3 Trillion in January after SNB Removes Franc Cap," *Reuters,* accessed February 21, 2015, www.reuters.com.

[8] U.S. Department of Agriculture, Foreign Agricultural Services, "Sugar Import Program," www.fas.usda.gov, accessed February 21, 2015.

[9] Office of the United States Trade Representative, "CAFTA-DR," https://ustr.gov, accessed February 21, 2015.

[10] Organization website, "Countries," http://europa.eu, accessed February 21, 2015.

Chapter 5

[1] U.S. Small Business Administration, "Advocacy Small Business Statistics and Research," http://web.sba.gov/faqs, accessed February 24, 2015.

[2] Ibid.

[3] U.S. Small Business Administration, "Guide to SBA's Definitions of Small Business," http://archive.sba.gov; "Table of Small Business Size Standards Matched to North American Industry Classification System Codes, www.sba.gov, accessed February 24, 2015.

⁴ U.S. Small Business Administration," Frequently Asked Questions," http://archive.sba.gov/advo/stats/sbfaq.pdf, accessed February 24, 2015.

⁵ U.S. Small Business Administration, "SBA Hits Another Lending Record in FY 2014; "SBA Lending Activity in FY 2013 Shows SBA Continuing to Help Small Businesses Grow and Create Jobs," press releases, www.sba.gov, accessed February 24, 2015.

⁶ U.S. Small Business Administration, "Frequently Asked Questions"; BOC Network Facts," www.bocnet.org, accessed February 24, 2015.

⁷ "Leading Social Networks as of January 2015, Ranked by Number of Active Users," *Statista,* accessed February 24, 2015, www.statista.com; company website, http://newsroom.fb.com, accessed February 24, 2015.

⁸ U.S. Small Business Administration, "Frequently Asked Questions."

⁹ Patricia Schaefer, "The Seven Pitfalls of Business Failure and How to Avoid Them," *Business Know-How,* accessed February 24, 2015, www.businessknowhow.com.

¹⁰ W. Mark Crain, "The Impact of Regulatory Costs on Small Firms," Office of Advocacy, U.S. Small Business Administration, accessed February 24, 2015, http://archive.sba.gov/advo/research/rs264tot.pdf.

¹¹ U.S. Small Business Administration, "What We Do," and "Mission Statement," www.sba.gov, accessed February 24, 2015.

¹² U.S. Small Business Administration, "Local Resources," www.sba.gov, accessed February 24, 2015.

¹³ U.S. Small Business Administration, "Microloans," www.sba.gov, accessed February 24, 2015.

¹⁴ Randy Maniloff, "Class Action Lawyers Hope Target Is a Bulls-Eye," *The Wall Street Journal,* accessed February 24, 2015, www.wsj.com.

¹⁵ Internal Revenue Service, "IRS Launches Study of S Corporation Reporting Compliance," www.irs.gov, accessed February 24, 2015.

¹⁶ Organization website, "About City Year," www.cityyear.org, accessed February 24, 2015.

¹⁷ Organization website, "Co-operative Facts & Figures," http://ica.coop, accessed February 24, 2015.

¹⁸ Susan Carey and Jack Nicas, "American Airlines and US Airways Complete Merger," *The Wall Street Journal,* accessed February 24, 2015, www.wsj.com.

¹⁹ "Renault Agrees to Build China Plant with Dongfeng Motors," *Bloomberg Businessweek,* accessed February 24, 2015, www.businessweek.com.

Chapter 6

¹ Diane Stafford, "Entrepreneurship Gets Attention, Kauffman Foundation says, But Funding and Success Rates Are Lacking," *The Kansas City Star,* accessed February 12, 2015, www.kansascity.com; Patricia Clark, "Entrepreneurship Education Is Hot. Too Many Get It Wrong," *Bloomberg Business,* accessed February 12, 2015, www.bloomberg.com.

² Company website, www.dell.com, accessed February 12, 2015; "Examples of Businesses Started by College Entrepreneurs," *Quintessential Careers,* accessed February 12, 2015, www.quintcareers.com.

³ Company website, www.lollywollydoodle.com, accessed February 12, 2015; Tom Foster, "The Startup That Conquered Facebook Sales," *Inc.,* accessed February 12, 2015, www.inc.com.

⁴ Organization website, www.keiretsuforum.com, accessed February 13, 2015.

⁵ Chance Barnett, "Crowdfunding Sites in 2014," *Forbes,* accessed February 13, 2015, www.forbes.com.

⁶ Association website, www.nbia.org, accessed February 13, 2015.

⁷ Government website, "About Commerce Business Daily," www.gpo.gov, accessed February 13, 2015.

⁸ Company website, "Russell Simmons," www.rushcommunications.com, accessed February 13, 2015.

⁹ Dr. Howard Markel, "The Real Story Behind Penicillin," *PBS News Hour,* accessed February 13, 2015, www.pbs.com.

¹⁰ Company website, www.planetfitness.com, accessed February 13, 2015.

[11] Company website, www.fortheloveofdog.com, accessed February 13, 2015; organization website, "U.S. Pet Industry Spending Figures & Future Outlook," www.americanpetproducts.org, accessed February 13, 2015.

[12] Company website, http://consciousco.co, accessed February 16, 2015; Randy Miller, "We Want Everything in Olivia Wilde's Birchbox," *Self,* accessed February 16, 2015, www.self.com; Caroline Howard, "30-under-30 Who Are Changing the World," *Forbes,* accessed February 16, 2015, www.forbes.com.

[13] "A Day in the Life of an Entrepreneur," *Princeton Review,* accessed February 16, 2015, www.princetonreview.com.

[14] "Startup Business Failure Rate by Industry," *Statistic Brain,* accessed February 16, 2015, www.statisticbrain.com.

[15] Organization website, "About IFA," www.franchise.org, accessed February 16, 2015.

[16] Company website, "About Us," www.baskinrobbins.com, accessed February 16, 2015.

[17] Company website, "Own a Franchise," www.subway.com, accessed February 16, 2015.

[18] Randall S. Hansen, "Franchising Pros and Cons: Is Franchising Right for You?" *Quintessential Careers,* accessed February 16, 2015, www.quintcareers.com.

[19] John Webb, "How Dreamworks, LinkedIn and Google Build Intrapreneurial Cultures," *Innovation Excellence,* accessed February 16, 2015, www.innovationexcellence.com.

Chapter 7

[1] Company website, "2014 Temkin Customer Service Rankings," http://temkinratings.com, accessed March 11, 2015.

[2] Scott D. Anthony, "Google's Management Style Grows Up," *Bloomberg Businessweek,* accessed March 11, 2015, www.businessweek.com.

[3] Dylan Stableford, "Sully: 5 Years after the Miracle on the Hudson," *Yahoo News,* accessed March 11, 2015, http://news.yahoo.com; Dean Foust, "US Airways: After the Miracle on the Hudson," *Bloomberg Businessweek,* accessed March 11, 2015, www.businessweek.com.

[4] Craig Chappelow, "5 Rules for Making Your Vision Stick," *Fast Company,* accessed March 11, 2015, www.fastcompany.com.

[5] Bruce I. Jones, "People Management Lessons from Disney," *Training Industry,* accessed March 11, 2015, www.trainingindustry.com.

[6] Company website, "Wild-Caught Seafood Sustainability Ratings," www.wholefoodsmarket.com, accessed March 11, 2015.

[7] Company website, "Our Story," http://speech4good.com, accessed March 11, 2015; Issie Lapowsky, "Balbus Speech: Speech Therapy in Your Pocket: 2013 America's Coolest College Start-ups," *Inc.,* accessed March 11, 2015, www.inc.com.

[8] Barry Glassman, "What Zappos Taught Us About Creating the Ultimate Client Experience," *Forbes,* accessed March 11, 2015, www.forbes.com.

[9] Company website, http://investors.activision.com, accessed March 11, 2015.

[10] Company website, www.petswelcome.com, accessed March 11, 2015.

[11] Company website, "Brands and Innovation," www.pg.com, accessed March 11, 2015.

[12] "10 Leadership Tips from Eileen Fisher," *Inc.,* accessed March 11, 2015, www.inc.com.

Chapter 8

[1] Government website, "Fact Sheet on Employment Tests and Selection Procedures," http://eeoc.gov, accessed March 15, 2015.

[2] "100 Best Companies to Work For: 2015," *Fortune,* accessed March 15, 2015, http://fortune.com.

[3] Bill Poovey, "S.C. Training Programs a Global Model," *GSA Business,* accessed March 15, 2015, http://gsabusiness.com.

[4] "Turn Your Performance Review System into One That Works," *Quality Digest Magazine,* accessed March 15, 2015.

[5] Bureau of Labor Statistics, "Employer Costs for Employee Compensation—December 2014," press release, www.bls.gov, released March 11, 2015.

[6] Company website, "Benefits," www.qualcomm.com, accessed March 15, 2015.

[7] Margaret Collins and Carol Hymowitz, "The Best 401(k)s: Retire at 60 from Conoco with $3.8 Million; Facebook Last," *Bloomberg Business,* accessed March 15, 2105, www.bloomberg.com.

[8] Saul McLeod, "Maslow's Hierarchy of Needs," *Simply Psychology,* accessed March 15, 2015, www.simplypsychology.org.

[9] Bureau of Labor Statistics, "Union Members—2014 press release," www.bls.gov, accessed March 15, 2015.

[10] Organization websites: www.nea.org; www.seiu.org; www.afscme.org, www.teamster.org, www.ufcw.org; www.uaw.org, accessed March 15, 2015.

[11] Bureau of Labor Statistics, "Major Work Stoppages in 2014," www.bls.gov, accessed March 15, 2015.

[12] "Twinkies-maker Hostess Brands Going Up for Sale," *Fortune,* accessed March 15, 2015, http://fortune.com.

[13] "Union Members—2014 press release."

Chapter 9

[1] Company website, "About KIND," www.kindsnacks.com, accessed March 18, 2015; Jacquelyn Smith, "How to Create an Authentic and Transparent Work Environment," *Forbes,* accessed March 18, 2015, www.forbes.com.

[2] National Center for Employee Ownership, "A Brief Overview of Employee Ownership in the U.S.," www.nceo.org, accessed March 18, 2015.

[3] Organization website, "ESOP Companies Report Economic Growth in 2014," www.esopassociation.org, accessed March 18, 2015.

[4] National Center for Employee Ownership, "A Statistical Profile of Employee Ownership," updated June 2014, www.nceo.org, accessed March 18, 2015.

[5] National Center for Employee Ownership, "Employee Ownership as a Retirement Plan," www.nceo.org, accessed March 18, 2015.

[6] National Center for Employee Ownership, "Employee Stock Options Fact Sheet," www.nceo.org, accessed March 18, 2015.

[7] Ibid.

[8] Katie Thomas, "New Recalls by Johnson & Johnson Raise Concern About Quality Control Improvements," *The New York Times,* accessed March 18, 2015, www.nytimes.com; Natasha Singer and Reed Abelson, "Will Johnson & Johnson Get Its Act Together?" *The New York Times*, accessed March 18, 2015, www.nytimes.com.

[9] Company website, "Whole Foods Market's Core Values," www.wholefoodsmarket.com, accessed March 18, 2015.

[10] Michiel Kruyt, Judy Malan, and Rachel Tuffield, "Three Steps to Building a Better Top Team," *Forbes,* accessed March 18, 2015, www.forbes.com; Tara Duggan, "Leadership vs. Conflict Resolution," *Chron,* accessed March 18, 2015, http://smallbusiness.chron.com.

[11] Stephanie Clifford, "U.S. Textile Plants Return, with Floors Largely Empty of People," *The New York Times,* accessed March 18, 2015, www.nytimes.com; Sarah Lybrand, "World's Best Hoodie Is Proud to Be American Made," *Yahoo Finance,* accessed March 18, 2015, http://finance.yahoo.com.

[12] Company website, www.sanebox.com, accessed March 18, 2015.

[13] Company website, "How to Foster a Culture of Open Communication," www.peterstark.com, accessed March 18, 2015.

[14] John Boe, "How to Read Your Prospect Like a Book!" www.johnboe.com, accessed March 18, 2015.

Chapter 10

[1] Company website, "About," www.custommade.com, accessed March 19, 2015.

[2] Company website, "Mondelez International to Invest in $190 Million in Largest Plant in Asia Pacific," http://ir.mondelezinternational.com, accessed March 19, 2015.

[3] Company website, www.ariba.com, accessed March 19, 2015; "More Than Two Thirds of Global 2000 Connect to Ariba Network to Simplify Commerce," *IT Business Net*, accessed March 19, 2015, www.itbusinessnet.com.

[4] Company website, "About 3D Systems," www.3dsystems.com, accessed March 19, 2015.

[5] Gail Sullivan, "Lululemon Still Suffering from Sheer Pants Debacle. Founder in Warrior Pose," *Washington Post*, accessed March 19, 2015, www.washingtonpost.com; Hayley Peterson, "The Sheer Yoga Pants that Lululemon Recalled Are Back in Stores and Selling for $92," *Business Insider*, accessed March 19, 2015, www.businessinsider.com.

[6] Organization website, "About ISO," www.iso.org, accessed March 19, 2015.

Chapter 11

[1] Association website, "Definition of marketing," https://www.ama.com, accessed March 24, 2015.

[2] American Heart Association, "Heart Attack Tools and Resources," www.heart.org, accessed March 24, 2015.

[3] Company website, www.netjets.com, accessed March 24, 2015; company website, "About Us," www.airbnb.com, accessed March 24, 2015.

[4] Resources for Entrepreneurs staff, "Consumer Habits Could Be Permanently Changed by Recession," *Resources for Entrepreneurs*, accessed March 24, 2015, www.gaebler.com; Joshua Brustein, "Walgreen's Beth Stiller on Customer Behavior Since the Recession," *Bloomberg Business*, accessed March 24, 2015, www.bloomberg.com.

[5] Company website, "What Is Big Data?" www-01.ibm.com, accessed March 24, 2015; Kimberly A. Whitler, "The Big Data Challenge: Generating Actionable Insight," *Forbes*, accessed March 24, 2015, www.forbes.com.

[6] Andrew McMains, "CEO Pushes Soup Giant to Move Faster, 'Think Outside the Can,'" *AdWeek*, accessed March 24, 2014, www.adweek.com.

[7] U.S. Census Bureau, "Resident Population Projections by Sex and Age: 2010 to 2050," www.censusbureau.gov, accessed March 24, 2015.

[8] Micah Solomon, "2015 Is the Year of the Millennial Customer: 5 Key Traits These 80 Million Consumers Share," *Forbes*, accessed March 24, 2015, www.forbes.com.

[9] Melanie Hicken, "Average Cost of Raising a Child Hits "$245,000," *CNN Money*, accessed March 24, 2015, http://money.cnn.com.

[10] Company website, "People & Planet," www.ikea.com, accessed March 24, 2015.

[11] Company website, "17th Annual Serv-a-palooza Kicks Off!" http://responsibility.timberland.com, accessed March 24, 2015.

[12] Company website, www.netcall.com, accessed March 24, 2015.

Chapter 12

[1] Dave Smith, "Apple Is Losing the Tablet Market It Created with the iPad," *Business Insider*, accessed March 26, 2015, www.businessinsider.com

[2] Company website, "About Future Motion," http://rideonewheel.com, accessed March 26, 2015; Ryan Lawler, "How Self-Balancing Electric Skateboard Onewheel Goes from Assembly Line to Users' Homes," *Tech Crunch*, accessed March 26, 2015, http://techcrunch.com.

[3] James K. Sanborn, "Tropical Uniform Prototypes Fail to Deliver," *Navy Times*, accessed March 26, 2015, http://archive.navytimes.com.

[4] "What Daimler's Mercedes Is Doing to Close In on BMW Before This Decade Ends," *Forbes*, accessed March 26, 2015, www.forbes.com; Jeremy Korzeniewski, Mercedes S600 Takes Its Place As Brand's Halo Sedan," *Auto Blog*, accessed March 26, 2015, www.autoblog.com.

[5] U.S. Census Bureau, "Monthly Wholesale Trade: Sales and Inventories, January 2015," and "County Business Patterns," www.census.gov, accessed March 26, 2015.

[6] Company website, "About Ace Hardware," www.acehardware.com, accessed March 26, 2015.

[7] U.S. Census Bureau, "Quarterly Retail E-Commerce Sales: 4th Quarter 2014," https://www.census.gov, accessed March 26, 2015.

[8] Judy Keen, "As Enclosed Malls Decline, 'Lifestyle Centers' Proliferate," *MinnPost,* accessed March 26, 2015, www.minnpost.com.

[9] Organization website, "Reports, Trends & Statistics," www.trucking.org, accessed March 26, 2015.

[10] Organization website "Railroad 101," www.aar.org, accessed March 26, 2015.

Chapter 13

[1] Alexandra Sifferlin, "Why We're Spending $1 Trillion on Health Medications," *Time,* accessed March 27, 2015, http://heartland.time.com; Persuading the Prescribers: Pharmaceutical Industry Marketing and Its Influence on Physicians and Patients," *Pew Health Research,* accessed March 27, 2015, www.pewtrusts.org.

[2] Chris Woodyard, "Hot, Small Luxury Cars Target Younger Buyers," *USA Today,* accessed March 27, 2015.

[3] David Lamoureux, "How Many Marketing Messages Do We See in a Day?" *Fluid Drive Media,* accessed March 27, 2015, www.fluiddrivemedia.com.

[4] Nathalie Tadena, "Ad Companies Slightly Lower 2015 Global Ad Forecasts," *The Wall Street Journal,* accessed March 27, 2015, www.wsj.com.

[5] "Distribution of Global Advertising Spending in 1st Quarter 2013 and 1st Quarter 2014 by Industry Sector," *Statista,* accessed March 27, 2015, www.statista.com.

[6] Interactive Advertising Bureau, "Digital Ad Revenues Hit Landmark High in First Half High of 2014, Surging to $23.1 Billion, According to IAB Internet Advertising Revenue Report," www.iab.net, accessed March 27, 2015.

[7] Ken Doctor, "Newsonomics: How Deep Is the Newspaper Industry's Money Hole?"*Nieman Lab,* accessed March 27, 2015, www.niemanlab.org.

[8] Erik Sass, "Half of U.S. Listeners Tune into Online Radio," *Media Post,* accessed March 27, 2015, www.mediapost.com.

[9] Organization website, "OOH Ad Spend 2009–2014," www.oaaa.org, accessed March 27, 2015.

[10] Chris Smith, "Nascar's Most Valuable Teams 2015," *Forbes,* accessed March 27, 2015, www.forbes.com

[11] Bureau of Labor Statistics, "Employment by Major Occupational Group," www.bls.gov, accessed March 27, 2015.

[12] Nick Jaynes, "Porsche 918 Spyder Looks Like a Million Bucks—Because It Is," *Digital Trends,* accessed March 27, 2015, www.digitaltrends.com; "1,200,000 Piano: The Kuhn Bösendorfer," *YouTube,* accessed March 27, 2015, www.youtube.com; Bailey S. Barnard, "Best of the Best 2014 Home Entertainment: Prima Cinema," *Robb Report,* accessed March 27, 2015, http://robbreport.com.

[13] Olsy Sorokina, "9 B2B Social Media Marketing Tips for Social Media Managers," *Hootsuite*, accessed March 27, 2015, http://blog.hootsuite.com.

[14] Liza Hughes, "Chef Big Shake: Didn't Get 'Shark' Deal But Still Made $5M," *CNBC,* accessed March 27, 2015, www.cnbc.com; Carol Tice, "How One Entrepreneur Used the Law of Publicity to Get Investors," *Entrepreneur,* accessed March 27, 2015, www.entrepreneur.com.

Chapter 14

[1] Museum website, "Timeline of Computer History," www.computerhistory.org, accessed March 29, 2015.

[2] Steven J. Vaughan-Nichols, "Six Clicks: The Six Fastest Computers in the World," *ZDNet,* accessed March 29, 2015, www.zdnet.com.

[3] Louis Columbus, "Gartner Forecasts Tablet Shipments Will Overtake PCs in 2015," *Forbes*, accessed March 29, 2015, www.forbes.com.

[4] Kathryn Zickuhr and Lee Rainie, "Tablet and E-Reader Ownership," *Pew Research Center,* accessed March 29, 2015, www.pewinternet.org.

[5] Company website, www.virtual.com, accessed March 29, 2015.

[6] Leena Rao, "Google Voice Founder Sets His Sights on VoIP Once Again," *Tech Crunch,* accessed March 29, 2015, http://techcrunch.com; Bryan M. Wolfe, "AT&T Offering VoIP

International Calls for Anyone with a Smartphone," *App Advice,* accessed March 29, 2015, http://appadvice.com.

[7] Shelly Banjo, "Home Depot Hackers Exposed 53 Million Email Addresses," *The Wall Street Journal,* accessed March 29, 2015, www.wsj.com.

[8] Teri Robinson, "Breaches, Malware to Cost $491 Billion in 2014, Study Says," *SC Magazine,* accessed March 29, 2015, www.scmagazine.com.

[9] Joshua Levinson, "Watchout—There's a New Android Trojan Horse About," *Cult of Android*, accessed March 29, 2015, http://cultofandroid.com.

[10] Company website, "Data Loss Statistics," www.bostoncomputing.net, accessed March 29, 2015.

[11] Company website, http://infosys.com, accessed March 29, 2015.

Chapter 15

[1] Association website, "About AARP Foundation Tax-Aide," www.aarp.org, accessed April 6, 2015.

[2] "Leading Accounting Firms in the United States in 2014, by U.S. Revenue," *Statista,* accessed April 6, 2015, www.statista.com.

[3] "2015 Best Personal Finance Software Review," *Top 10 Reviews,* accessed April 6, 2015, http://personal-finance-software-review.toptenreviews.com.

[4] Association website, "Busting Some Myths about IFRS and GAAP," www.ifrs.org, accessed April 6, 2015; company website, "IFRS and US GAAP: Similarities and Differences," www.pwc.com, accessed April 6, 2015.

Chapter 16

[1] Nathaniel Popper, "An Uber I.P.O. Looms, and Suddenly Bankers Are Using Uber. Coincidence?" *The New York Times*, accessed July 13, 2015, www.nytimes.com; "The IPO Class of 2015," *Forbes*, accessed April 9, 2015, www.forbes.com.

[2] Organization website, "Daily NYSE Group Volume in NYSE Listed, 2015," www.nyxdata.com, accessed April 9, 2015.

[3] Government website, "Commercial Banks in US: 2014," https://research.stlouisfed.org, accessed April 9, 2015; Board of Governors of the Federal Reserve System, "Assets and Liabilities of Commercial Banks in the United States (weekly)," www.federalreserve.gov, accessed April 9, 2015.

[4] "Deposit Data: All U.S. Banks" www.bankregdata.com, accessed April 9, 2015; government website, "Commercial Banks in US: 2014," https://research.stlouisfed.org, accessed April 9, 2015.

[5] American Bankers Association, "More Consumers Embracing Mobile Banking," www.aba.com, accessed April 9, 2015.

[6] Federal Deposit Insurance Corporation, "Statistics on Depository Institutions Report: Savings Institutions, 2014," https://www2.fdic.gov, accessed April 9, 2015.

[7] Government website, "Industry at a Glance," www.ncua.gov, accessed April 9, 2015; "America's Biggest Banks," *Forbes,* accessed April 9, 2015, www.forbes.com.

[8] American Council of Life Insurers, "2014 Fact Book," www.acli.com, accessed April 9, 2015.

[9] Company website, "Top Pension Fund Assets Hit $15 Trillion," www.towerswatson.com, accessed April 9, 2015.

[10] Investment Company Institute, "2014 Investment Company Fact Book: Mutual Fund Trends," www.icifactbook.org, accessed April 9, 2015.

[11] Maria Tor and Saad Sarfraz, "Largest 100 Banks in the World," *SNL Financial,* accessed April 9, 2015, https://www.snl.com.

Chapter 17

[1] "DuPont de Nemours: Financials," and "Costco Wholesale Corporation: Capital Intensity," www.4-traders.com, accessed April 12, 2015.

[2] Neal E. Boudette and William Boston, "BMW Readies U.S. Factory Expansion," *The Wall Street Journal,* accessed April 12, 2015, www.wsj.com.

[3] Joann Muller, "BMW to Spend $1B to Expand Output at South Carolina Factory by 50%," *Forbes,* accessed April 12, 2015, www.forbes.com.

[4] "Debt Ratios: Toyota, Honda, Starbucks, and Burger King," www.barchart.com, accessed April 12, 2015.

[5] Federal Reserve, "Commercial Paper Rates," www.federalreserve.gov, accessed April 12, 2015.

[6] Federal Reserve, "Year-End Commercial Paper Outstanding," www.federalreserve.gov, accessed April 12, 2015.

[7] Dana Cimilluca, Dana Mattioli, and Chelsey Dulaney, "Kraft, Heinz to Merge, Forming Food Giant," *The Wall Street Journal*, accessed April 13, 2015, www.wsj.com.

[8] Jack Nicas, "Challenges Await Year Two of American Airlines–US Airways Merger," *The Wall Street Journal,* accessed April 13, 2015, www.wsj.com; Terry Maxon, "As American Airlines Merger Date Nears, Questions Abound," *Dallas Morning News,* accessed April 13, 2015, www.dallasnews.com.

[9] Sue Chang, "EBay Board Approves PayPal Spinoff," *Market Watch*, accessed July 15, 2015, www.marketwatch.com; Chris Isidore, "EBay Spinning Off PayPal as Separate Company," *CNN Money*, accessed April 13, 2015, http://money.cnn.com.

Printed in the USA
K068205SCI102617   01S29053000000002351